THE
COLLECTING
MAN

ALSO BY JOHN BEDFORD

More Looking in Junk Shops
Looking in Junk Shops
Talking About Teapots

THE COLLECTING MAN

John Bedford

DAVID McKAY COMPANY, INC.

NEW YORK

ACKNOWLEDGEMENTS

For permission to use photographs of pieces in their possession, thanks are due to the following persons and institutions:

Associazione Amatori Armi Antiche, Milan. p. 10   Lady Bangor, London. pp. 16, 54   Bernard Black Gallery, New York. p. 21   The Bodleian Library, Oxford. pp. 173, 175   British Museum, London. pp. 19, 38, 46, 68, 98, 172, 182   Delieb Antiques Ltd., London. pp. 192, 193, 211   Farmers Weekly, London. pp. 52, 53, 88, 89   'Frank', The Chequers Inn, Lamberhurst, Kent. p. 159   W. Greenwood & Sons Ltd, Harrogate, Yorks. p. 102   George Hartfield Esq. Sussex. pp. 122, 126   A. E. Henson Esq., Barnet, Herts. p. 42   The Imperial Tobacco Co. Ltd. (Ingham Foster Collection). p. 173   Musée Royal d'Art et d'Histoire, Brussels. p. 189   Museo Nazionale Scienza e Technica, Milan. pp. 40, 41   National Army Museum, Aldershot, Surrey. pp. 148, 149, 150, 151   National Gallery, London. p. 58   New York Public Library. p. 174   Presidential Art Models, Inc. Englewood, Ohio. pp. 66, 71   Princeton University Library. p. 87   P. J. Radford, Denmead, Portsmouth, Hants. p. 140   Gerry Richards Esq., London. p. 157   Charles J. Sawyer, London. pp. 47, 101, 107   Miss Elisabeth Scott, Manchester. p. 162   B. A. Seaby Ltd., London. p. 215   Sotheby & Co., London. pp. 44, 60, 64, 88, 89, 91, 184, 227   Spinks & Sons Ltd., London. p. 78   Sunderland Museum and Art Gallery, Sunderland-on-Tyne. p. 75 (bottom)   Victoria & Albert Museum, London. pp. 32, 33, 48, 51, 56, 75 (top centre) 94, 96, 120, 132, 134, 137, 138, 154, 159, 160, 207, 222, 225, 228   Wallace Collection, London. pp. 27, 81 (left group) 105, 110, 118, 119 (*except* top left) 167, 201, 202, 206   Wallis and Wallis, Lewes, Sussex. pp. 30, 57, 62, 63, 71 (right group) 99, 100, 104, 113, 119 (top left) 142, 144, 145, 146, 147, 152, 153, 164, 165, 166, 169, 170, 178, 189, 190, 195, 197, 209.

First American Edition 1968

LIBRARY OF CONGRESS CATALOG CARD NUMBER: 68-54167

MANUFACTURED IN THE UNITED STATES OF AMERICA

CONTENTS

WHY COLLECT?

Books flow steadily from the presses for such characters as the Golfing Man, the Motoring Man, the Drinking Man. What of the Collecting Man—as distinct, for example, from the Collecting Woman? There are, obviously, items which interest and delight both; but because of the well-known difference between them, these things will usually appeal in a different way. A woman, for instance, may be interested in china, a man in COMMEMORATIVE POTTERY.

Beyond these bridging items, however, there is a vast field of collecting which is much more likely to interest a man than a woman. Man is usually more interested than woman in history, in technical matters, in expertise, in the odd and the curious; and when he sets out to collect he generally wants to make a real job of it. It may well develop into a kind of madness; and men, perhaps because they are born romantics, are usually much better at being crazy than women.

This book, then, selects about eighty items of the subjects most likely to be of interest to a man who has heard about the Collecting Man and is open to ideas about becoming one. Perhaps he was a collector in his glorious youth and would like to know what there is to garner besides butterflies, fossils, coins and stamps: perhaps he is a serious collector already but—like my friend mentioned under TIN BOXES—happens to have everything there is in his own field and wants to make a corner in something else.

But, first of all, what *is* collecting, and anyway why do it? It may be helpful to try and work out the last question first, to discover what collecting is by looking at motives of collectors.

One of the first discoveries we make is that there have been men collectors ever since there was anything to collect—land, houses, supporters, women, slaves—just plain hoarding, like a squirrel with his nuts. Then there is hoarding for pleasure, like a magpie with its jewels.

Men also collect to build value, to dodge inflation or the tax-

7

gatherer, even to preserve themselves in difficult times. In our own generation people hounded out of their homes and their countries have been able, by thoughtful collecting of well-chosen valuables, to carry in a small suitcase the key to a new life.

Other collectors like to match their wits against the whirligig of time and the roundabout of taste. They buy when an object is undesired, and therefore cheap, and sell when interest in it reawakens, perhaps increasing its value several times. Many an old family, not extraordinarily wealthy, can be seen buying things which you would have thought far beyond their means: perhaps they have just sold some items which they have been holding—and using and enjoying—for many years but which have now become fashionable and are therefore too valuable for them to hold. So they are selling out and reinvesting: in this way they have parted successively with Carolean silver, Georgian furniture, French Impressionists, Victorian Academy pictures: now, perhaps, they are carefully unloading their *Art Nouveau*. It would be fascinating to know what they are taking on board—perhaps Renaissance furniture, perhaps Pop Art?

By now we have arrived at connoisseurship but hardly at collecting. So let us look at another kind of buyer of things, a much more ordinary sort of Joe.

He has probably started to collect by accident. His Uncle Zedekiah left him an album of stamps and, as a boy, he filled in the gaps with pretty, unused stamps from those small states which seem to live entirely on such issues. He has come across the album in the attic on a wet Saturday afternoon and finds himself wondering about all those nineteenth-century German states old Uncle Zed collected: how many more of them were there: could you go on and complete the collection? Or he buys a bag of old golfclubs in a junk store for a song because he has seen a useful putter among them; but in with them too is a bundle of rusty old oriental SWORDS. He gets them home and cleans them, and they look fine, but what's this? An inscription on one of them, in Arabic or something. So he wants to know who made them, and do the different shapes have any special names, and so on?

Curiosity and interest drive him on. Perhaps he gets a book

on the subject and finds himself more curious than ever. He goes to museums and looks at the things he has read about in the books; transported on a magic carpet to realms beyond his commuter's train, he becomes absorbed in a new world.

Perhaps there *isn't* a book on this particular subject, for not enough people have yet thought of collecting the item: so this Joe of ours starts looking harder at the things in the museums— or if they aren't even there yet he haunts dealers' shops and scrapyards, hunts out old tradesmen's catalogues, pores over old volumes of illustrated magazines. He builds up his own store of knowledge about the subject and when he sees a specimen which he knows is rare, but the dealer doesn't, he learns to hold his tongue.

Then, to his surprise, he finds there are other people about who are collecting exactly the same thing. They get friendly and find it pays them to pool their knowledge, to compare pieces, swop them, share notes about them. A certain amount of gloating rivalry goes on at these sessions, but everybody gets a turn, and one good gloat deserves—and usually gets— another.

So they start a club or a society, perhaps found a mutual collection which they can show to the public and all gloat over together. They may build themselves a set-up like the one enjoyed by that friendly band of collectors, the Associazione Amatori Armi Antiche, of Milan, who have a mediaeval tower in the middle of that industrial city—once a great centre of the craft—where they keep a fine collection of ARMOUR and WEAPONS; and—as if that isn't enough—at the first sign of summer the genial curator, Signor Giorgetti, hares off to another castle tower they have in the tiny Republic of San Marino, where the Society collects money from tourists—to spend on adding items to their collection.

A number of things have happened to Joe by now. First, he has accumulated a great deal of expertise—not only facts, but feeling, touch, instinct, smell—about a particular thing or field of collecting. In doing so, he will inevitably have extended his range of general knowledge. He will have become a bit of an historian, a bit of an archaeologist, a bit of a connoisseur of art. In the case of arms and armour he will have learnt not only to

9

In the Museo della Pusterla, Milan, where the Associazione Amatori Armi Antiche (Association of Amateurs of Antique Arms) house their collection of arms and armour.

distinguish between the productions of one centre and another, but the reason these differences developed. He will have noted the effect historical events had upon the development of arms and armour and also the way these things affected history. He will not only *know* that they were simple and austere in one age and elaborately decorative in another, but understand *why* they were, because he can see the relationship between them and the other things made at the time—chalices and clothing, books and buildings. Therefore, in learning about these things, and using his knowledge of styles and workmanship to help him in his collecting, he will also, almost without realising it, have acquired an æsthetic instinct. He will have sprouted antennae for distinguishing between good design and bad, between a shoddy, botched-up piece of work and a master-piece, between originality and imitation, between vigour and decadence. By becoming a collector he has, in the true sense of the word, become an *amateur*—like our friends the *Amatori* of Milan.

As all this develops, of course, Joe will have been changing his method of collecting. In his early days, he grabbed every-thing he could lay his hands on, sometimes straying way out beyond the main channel—at that stage he was not too sure where the main channel of his subject lay. He bought good and bad, not yet knowing the difference, picking up on the way all the FAKES AND FORGERIES there were around. This was no bad thing really, as one has noted under that heading, for there is nothing so educative as a good shelf of bogus items, especially if they've cost you dear.

But as Joe's eye gets keener, his knowledge wider, his nose for the trail sharper, he no longer accepts everything that comes his way. He becomes highly selective; he discards his mistakes, swops or sells his duplicates, exchanges inferior specimens for better ones.

At about this time he also makes another important discovery. He finds that even if he lives to be as old as Methuselah he will not have time to gather everything in his field; also that even if he moves into a castle he won't have room to house it all. So he becomes selective in another way. He narrows down his field of operations, takes some particular aspect of his subject and

11

specialises in it. He may limit himself to a particular period of time, he may set himself a standard of quality, he may aim at completeness within a very narrow range—like the AUTOGRAPH collector who is interested only in 'Signers', the autographs of all the persons who signed the Declaration of Independence. In doing so, of course, he makes his collection more valuable, quite apart from any intrinsic value in the items which make it up.

Now, astonishingly, something else has happened to Joe: he has become an authority. People get to hear about his collection and ask him to write articles or give lectures on it. He finds himself drawn into correspondence with people from all over the world, asking his opinion on this or that. He is courted by curators of museums begging him to lend them specimens for a special exhibition; and on further acquaintance tactfully suggesting that it would be all right with the museum if he donated a few pieces to it.

Joe may even find himself making a career of his collection, like Farran Zerbe of Philadelphia. As an eleven-year-old boy— we are told by the Rigbys in their fascinating book on the whole subject of collecting [RL 245]—Zerbe came across an unusual coin stamped '50 cents', and on taking it to the bank to exchange it for a more ordinary and therefore more spendable specimen, he found that it was really a piece for 50 centimes —a 'foreigner' worth nothing. With the true collector's instinct, young Zerbe decided that the only thing really wrong with his coin was that there was only one of it; and he started to collect all those coins nobody else seemed to want. This led him on a long, long trail, in the course of which he became a world-renowned collector, writer and authority on coins, eventually, when the Chase National Bank took over his collection, being appointed its curator.

Many a collecting man has become a dealer or auctioneer in his subject—like one of the partners in the establishment at Lewes, in Sussex, which we shall meet when discussing the CURRENT PRICES of MILITARIA and other such collectables. Dealers, in fact, are often collectors, or think of themselves as such; for in the course of their lifetime the same pieces will be passing and re-passing through their hands on the way from one private collector to another and they get a very personal feeling about them. Such men are the salt of the collecting earth, and Joe, in his present state of grace, no longer tries to outwit them but trusts them, realising that the more a dealer is regarded as an authority on a subject the less likely he is to want to lose his reputation by misleading serious collectors.

At various stages in his collecting career, Joe will have been faced with the problem of housing and, especially, preserving his collection. The honourable and respected Mi Fei, an eleventh-century Chinese amateur, had two collections, one for display to all and sundry, the other for inspection by genuine connoisseurs. He reasoned that the ignorant would want to touch the precious paintings and manuscripts, which would leave upon them a minute spot of grease, which there-upon had to be cleaned off; and every time this was done it inevitably shortened the life of something which was expected to last for a thousand years.

The collector will therefore find his own way of keeping his pieces, according to whether they can or cannot be safely handled, using cabinets, walls, drawers, even outhouses. Some-times there are special problems, as with a man who collected spiders' webs, but they can be solved with a little thought—this collector, of course, put his finds between sheets of glass.

But if Joe is to pursue the course we have laid out for him, he must by no means confine himself to hoarding up his pieces. In becoming a collector at all, he has made a corner in some-thing which interests us all, and he has a responsibility to the rest of us. What we want, during and after his lifetime, is descriptive chapter and verse, not only about the collection itself, but on the way he collected it and what he learnt in the process.

We want him to document his finds, telling us where and in what circumstances he found them. In the fields of ETHNOGRAPHICA and archaeology, devastating harm has been done to the cause of scientific and social history by thoughtless and indiscriminate looting and excavating, destroying forever much data and robbing posterity of vital knowledge. When Joe finds a thing lying in a place where it has been undisturbed for centuries, it is his duty to his fellow man to record the place

13

and the date and the circumstances of the find. This applies even to the humblest of all collecting items: we want to know beside what fireplace Joe found his HORSE BRASSES, in what village he came across that Victorian squash, American whiskey or Georgian wine BOTTLE: it may yield a critical piece of information. In other words, Joe, like Farran Zerbe, must become the responsible curator of his own museum.

So far, then, Joe has built up a fine and possibly unique gathering, which may have cost him anything from one million pounds sterling to fifty-seven dollars U.S.—or any other sum in any currency you can think of. Generally speaking, the less he has spent the more fun he has had, not because he has been able to save money, but because his collecting will have been the result of using his wits, discrimination and enterprise, something we are all the better for doing. He has extended his knowledge and taste, perhaps achieved some distinction and fame. Now, as his time draws near, as old friends in the saloon or club cluck their tongues sadly over his tottering step and his rheumy eye, he has a problem. What—since he so obviously cannot take it in the hearse with him—is going to happen to that collection? After he has ridden in state down to the cemetery, heading a procession for the first time in his life, what is to become of all those pieces which he has so much enjoyed introducing to each other and showing to other men like himself? Broken up, thrown away, sold?

Having achieved distinction, fame and even perhaps the respect of his family, Joe now has an opportunity of achieving immortality. If he is in the million-dollar class he can endow an entire foundation, as Henry Clay Folger the oil magnate did for his unique collection of Shakespeariana at Washington, D.C., or he can found a wing of an existing establishment. More modestly, he may fill a few cases for that local curator.

If Joe does feel as magnanimous as this, there are one or two points he should bear in mind. The late Andrew Mellon, when he left his wonderful collection of paintings and sculpture to the American people, deliberately refrained from insisting that it should bear his name, for fear that this would deter other collectors from adding to it. This hope, to the great benefit of the collection itself, has been realised in the munificent bequests

14

made since by other magnates. If Joe's collection still has a long way to go before it is complete, he may like to brood upon this.

Similarly, he should remember that if he insists on his collection being kept intact, this may present problems for his beneficiaries. Much valuable material may be banished forever to the darkness of cellars and cupboards, which could either be sold to fill gaps or handed over to less fortunate establishments. Andrew Mellon was enlightened enough to allow the trustees to dispose of any items which they might, at a later date, in the light of new knowledge or more subtle appreciation, consider to be below par. Moreover, to stipulate that a collection must be kept together in one place may seriously hamper its logical arrangement for the instruction of new generations of collectors. Even in the Victoria and Albert Museum one must often dodge from one gallery to another to compare and appraise items of the same class. Pepys was a fine and generous man, but generations of keepers at the Bodleian must have wished he had not insisted that his books should for all eternity be shelved by their binding sizes rather than their subjects or their authors' names.

But Joe, as he happily breathes his last—for all successful collectors are happy men—may well find more pleasure in having his collection dispersed. He may rock with celestial laughter at the thought of having willed away to rival collectors pieces he has seized from under their very noses; or he may decide that it will give them more fun if he makes them compete for these prizes. Many collectors have directed their treasures to be sold so that they can bequeath the pleasure they have had in making acquisitions to some inheritor of their own tastes and interests.

Joe, however, is not dead yet: in fact, as a collector, he is waiting to be born. So perhaps—at last—one owes him a word about the scope and arrangement of this book.

It will be realised, of course, that no single volume could possibly contain everything there is to say about everything a man can collect. Similarly, nobody will expect a single author to hold forth with equal and profound authority on all these different subjects. The best he can do is to give a taste of them, and then offer guidelines. The last ten years have seen a wonder-

Collectors' Klondyke: 'Trad' in the Portobello Road, London, where Lady Bangor sells—as you can see—many of the items mentioned in this book.

ful proliferation of specialist books on many of these aspects of collecting: the READING LIST at the end mentions some of these and also earlier authorities who may be found through a good library service. Rather than spatter the main text with figures, I have reserved comments on prices to the section CURRENT PRICES.

It will be noticed that several quite large collecting subjects are missing, for example, postage stamps, fossils and items of natural history; but these are such large matters that it was thought better to omit reference to them altogether rather than try to summarise. In certain cases very wide subjects have been represented by sections of them, for example, the world of numismatics has COMMEMORATIVE MEDALS and TOKENS, while pottery offers APOTHECARIES' JARS, COMMEMORATIVE POTTERY, HISPANO-MORESQUE WARES, SALTGLAZED STONEWARES and TOBY

16

JUGS; from the vast family of scientific instruments I have singled out pocket DIALS AND NOCTURNALS, while the collector of glass may here specialise in BOTTLES AND FLASKS or DRINKING GLASSES.

It may be objected that I would have made life easier for the reader if instead of writing short specialised pieces and arranging them alphabetically I had neatly grouped everything in chapters and sections—for example, MILITARIA, ETHNOGRAPHICA —terms which are here used mainly for cross reference.

But I have jumbled them in this way quite unashamedly because I wanted to catch the reluctant reader unawares, to entrap him into taking new paths. It may thereupon be objected that there is no man alive who can pass from ANCESTOR FIGURES to ANIMALIER BRONZES, that there are no correspondences between the collector of BOOK BINDINGS and BICYCLES, of POST-CARDS and PRAYER WHEELS, of SAND-GLASSES and SWORDS. This may be so, but just as there are many different kinds of men in the world, so there are many different kinds of men inside one single man.

I believe, too, that not only is the age of serendipity by no means dead, but it is more alive now than ever, that even more people nowadays have the time and the disposition to enjoy coming across one interesting thing while in search of another. In this way, one hopes, Joe's work need never be done. 'Enlightenment,' as another great Chinese collector remarked as he gave away his treasures to people who liked them, 'is the real art of living.'

ANCESTOR FIGURES If it seems to you, as it certainly does to me, that these carved wooden figures have some kind of mysterious life, not usually found in sculpture, it is worth considering for a moment the purpose they served. In the African villages where they were made, Mr. Wingert tells us [RL 251], they are the most important members of the community. They know all that goes on among their living descendants, and they are in touch not only with even more powerful and numerous village ancestors who pre-deceased them, but with the spirits, malignant and benign, who influence the prosperity or misfortune of the people. Humanity is always in need of security, of reassurance that it will pass safely through the successive stages of this life, and others to come; and in primitive societies, where the forces of nature generally seem bent upon the destruction of one's person, village or tribe, aid from one's ancestors was invoked through these figures in prescribed ritual and ceremony.

It was not, then, as works of art that they were created, though that may be our interest in them today. But it is significant that where a primitive society has continued to make them after long contact with what we call civilization they tend to lose some of their æsthetic appeal to us as works of art. This is true, for example, of the exquisitely formed and finished figures made by the Baulé people of the Ivory Coast, where the subtle irregularities which gave so much vitality to the older work have often given way to a characterless perfection of symmetry.

These sculptors, therefore, were not trying to make a pleasing object or to copy the external features of man or woman but to express what they saw and felt about the life around them. So far as the dead person was concerned, the family who commissioned him would be satisfied if the figure was given a particular style of head-dress or the scarification of the skin used in that particular community. But they would expect the sculptor to work inside the local tradition in his basic forms and treatment; and it is interesting that artists in the West, for example, Picasso and Braque, found in this most traditional of arts a means of breaking away from what seemed to be a vitiated tradition of their own.

18

Bushongo (Bakuba) Royal Commemorative portrait figure of the Nyimi (or King) Shamba Bololongo, who reigned circa 1600– 1620.

Sometimes these figures were considered to be the permanent resting places of the ancestor's spirit, passing into it at the time of death; in other cases the spirit had to be persuaded by ritual to take up temporary habitation there. Often it was necessary to give effect to this by painting in a special way, or by adding attachments of, for example, beads, feathers, ivory, raffia, shells.

Another class of figures—for example, the royal 'portrait' statues of the Bushongo (Bakuba) peoples—were in the nature of memorials commemmorating an especially important king or chief, and making his spirit available to subsequent generations of the tribe when they fell in need of counsel or aid.

Most of these figures were made in wood, usually painted black or red, but sometimes in polychrome—for instance, among the Yoruba—and they can range in size from four inches up, though few are larger than two feet high. They are difficult to date: except for those in bronze or ivory, not many could have survived tropical conditions for more than half a century. There are, of course, some fakes in circulation, and according to Dr. Leonhard Adam [RL 249] the European makers of them did not always even take the trouble to use native woods. Careful treatment is applied by various methods to give the proper surface impression, but they are usually betrayed to the connoisseur's eye by the style of carving. Exceptions are where professional European sculptors have made pieces 'for experimental purposes' in the same kind of way that painters made copies of works of older masters for their own instruction. If these are made of proper materials they are among the most difficult to detect.

ANIMALIER BRONZES Something like the bronze animals opposite may be familiar to you: you have perhaps seen them in smaller versions, mounted on inkwells, clocks, book-rests and other such objects. Perhaps you've sometimes wondered how such fine modelling found its way on to everyday articles of this kind.

These little bronzes—they are mostly between four and eight inches high—are the work of an interesting group of sculptors who flourished in France in the nineteenth century and later.

Because many of the subjects were birds and animals, these artists became known as the *Animaliers*. A few years ago an exhibition of over a hundred of these pieces appeared in an exhibition put on by Mallet at Bourdon House, London [RL 245]; and in a public already looking out the best in nineteenth-century art they immediately aroused wide interest. As bronzes go—especially the kind which isn't a mere hack piece from the foundry, but has been worked on by the sculptor himself after being cast from the clay model—they weren't expensive, say, twenty to forty pounds apiece: but of course they have appreciated somewhat in value since then.

Anyone with an eye for an animal's ways will find good collecting here, for although nineteenth-century sculptors often tended to become mawkish and sentimental in the representation of human beings, they could give plenty of life and character to animals.

'Animalier' bronze group of 'Horse surprised by Lion', by Antoine Louis Barye (1795–1875).

In the exhibition I mentioned above, for example, there was a setter loping along with one eye cocked up at his master; a magnificently male bull, and a very lively racehorse and jockey, among many other fine things by Pierre Jules Mêne (1810–1879), who usually did portraits of actual animals rather than generalisations. Some of his models are to be found in the white stoneware known as Parian: they were put out by Copelands about 1860, and bear that famous Staffordshire firm's mark. From Jules Moigniez (1835–1894)—he specialised in birds—there was a plover which was Startled Rage itself ('You keep away from my damn nest!'); also a fine trotting horse—again an actual horse rather than an idealised one. Moigniez also did portrait plaquettes and medallions.

Another fine figure was of a 'Dog Stretching'—he is closing his eyes in enormous ecstasy—by Emanuel Fremiet (1824–1910). He is well known throughout France for his equestrian statues, but his small cats and dogs, which he considered only his 'off duty' work, have life and character, even humour.

The only lady *animalier* represented was the famous Rosa Bonheur, who started her career as a sculptor, but later in life went over to painting and won world-wide fame: she died in 1899, aged 77, having carried off honours never before awarded to a woman.

Perhaps the most famous of the *animaliers,* however, was Antoine Barye (1795–1875), who worked in a highly romantic style which tended to depersonalise his animals; but he did render very profoundly the ferocity, strength and fears of wild beasts—there was a 'Jaguar Devouring a Hare', and a 'Running Elephant' in this show which brought out these qualities admirably.

Other names you may find on these little bronzes are those of Auguste Nicolas Cain (1821–1894), whose work was very popular in his lifetime but who has been criticised as being derivative, as has Paul Delabrière (1829–1912). But Christophe Fratin (1800–1864) was an originator, carrying the same romantic spirit into the quieter field of farm and domestic animals as did Barye with wild ones—there was a touching 'Mare and Foal' in the show. An often-encountered TOBACCO JAR has a bear on it by Fratin.

The craftsmanship of the *animaliers* was excellent, and in many ways as good as that of the bronzes of the Renaissance. Most of them show excellent patination—by which one means they have the fine bloom which comes, first from skilled finishing, then from years of loving caresses by the silk cloth (or tweed, as some prefer) of the collector.

APOTHECARIES' JARS   They stood in rows upon the shelves of the apothecaries' shops, holding drugs, unguents, elixirs and other remedies for the deadly plagues, the agues and the fluxes which afflicted mankind in days gone by.

They may still be seen thus in such re-creations of these establishments as the Squibb Ancient Pharmacy [RL 247], fruit of forty years' collecting in Europe and now housed in the Smithsonian Institute, Washington, D.C. There are not only the jars, but pharmaceutical antiques of all kinds, also the inner study or workshop equipped exactly as the one which Romeo remembered when he mournfully resolved to follow his Juliet to the grave:

> *And in his needy shop a tortoise hung,*
> *An alligator stuff'd, and other skins*
> *Of ill-shaped fishes.*

These jars may also be seen in many an old-fashioned 'chemist's shop' or *Apotheke* in Europe, as well as in the council chambers of learned societies; there are also many private collectors who meet in battle with such societies on the floors of auction rooms. In fact, the jars are not in short supply, and at the moment, if one avoids great rarities, a gathering of them can be put together for a fairly modest sum.

They came into existence with the pharmacies established in monasteries and noblemen's palaces and castles in mediaeval times. The collector of them therefore looks back farthest at the versions in glazed mediaeval earthenware, then at the magnificent *albarelli* in Persian and Syrian pottery, and HISPANO-MORESQUE lustre wares. These are vessels of a slightly waisted form (though with many delicate variations of it as Mr. Honey has shown [RL 254]—with a flanged neck around which its original owner tied a parchment cover to protect its

23

contents. The waist is there so that one jar may be easily grasped when it stands in a tightly packed row; and while some hold that on that account its name derives from the bamboo, others prefer to derive it from the Persian *el barani,* a drug jar.

The form moved from Spain across to Italy, and in being shipped through Majorca, these and other Hispano-Moresque wares gave a name to *maiolica,* the earliest and perhaps finest of the tin-glazed earthenwares—which had as one of its descendants Lambeth and Bristol delft. Upon them the Italian maiolica potters (of, for example, Faenza, Deruta, Castel Durante, etc.) painted the magnificent colours of the Renaissance—here, incidentally, preserved more vividly than upon dirty (or over-cleaned) canvas.

Such splendour might seem surprising on pieces designed for the dusty shelves of apothecaries' shops; but in fact in those alchemical times such establishments were the intellectual clubs of the day, the resort and rendezvous of its leading scientific and literary spirits.

Collectors look next to drug jars in the *majolica* of the Netherlands, the *faience* or *fayence* (after Faenza) made in France and Germany, and the delftware (after Delft, though pre-dating it in some respects) of England. By now those intended for wet drugs had taken on almost a globular shape and were mounted upon a spreading foot: the English ones are usually painted in blue upon the white opaque tin-glaze with legends describing the contents, accompanied first by angels (which sometimes surprisingly acquire wigs in the contemporary fashion) and later by birds and cherubs (these also appear on the Dutch jars): collectors classify them by these decorative styles [RL 247].

By studying their legends, you could make a fine collection of remedies covering most human ailments: for example, *S.E.SUCC.ROS.* is claimed to 'strengthen the heart, comfort the spirit, build the body, help fluxes and corrosion and gnawing of the guts, and stay vomiting'.

Professional bodies tend to grab a great many apothecaries' jars when they come upon the market, but they are not in short supply.

ARMOUR   A full suit of *Maximilian* or *Gothic* armour, as you may see by reference to CURRENT PRICES, could cost you a great deal of money, and you would scarcely have an opportunity of buying one every day. But suits of armour are often offered at sales as 'composed', and separate pieces become available quite frequently. It should therefore be no very difficult task for the collector to do his own 'composing'. In doing so he may find more than a little assistance from miniatures, which are often contemporaries of the full-size suits of armour they represent.

No finer method could be found for instructing oneself in the art and mystery of the armourer, and also in that knife-edge balance between attack and defence, referred to under WEAPONS, which is of perpetual interest to the student of MILITARIA AND NAVALIA. If causes have usually been won by men with weapons in their hands, they have also been saved by those who have learned to protect themselves from such weapons.

As is to be seen in HELMETS, the age of steel has by no means ended: while the era of that modern form of armour, chemically protective clothing, has just begun. This seems to have taken us full circle, for Sir James Mann [RL 248] has well described *Mail,* the earliest of armours, as a 'protective textile'; no doubt he was also thinking of the padded hide and coat of scales which preceded it, but which we shall hardly expect to be able to find today.

In European mail, still occasionally to be found, the links are nearly always rivetted or forged solid; and its strength, worn over a padded coat, astonished the Saracens at Tiberias in the year 1187 when, alone in the Christian army, the mailclad knights stood fast for two days against heavy arrow showers. By the fourteenth century the fire power of weapons like the BOW had so far advanced that plates of steel were added to the mail, and eventually took over from it.

Much nonsense has been talked about having to lift fully-armed knights into their saddles by cranes. A full suit weighed on the average about 60 lbs—a lighter burden than many a soldier carried in the First World War—and combatants wearing it could jump in and out of a saddle whenever they wished. It was tiring to march a long way in full armour, but well-advised commanders avoided this: if King John of France had done so at Poitiers the Black Prince might never have taken him prisoner.

As fighting gear, armour will not come to life for you until it is realised that both body and head covering had to fit well and be worn over appropriate clothes, all equipped with 'points' for close and comfortable attachment. In the Tower of London Armoury there is a suit marvellously articulated which covers every square inch of the body.

The men who made plate armour of this kind were craftsmen, and in fact engineers of a high order—as one may see by looking closely at the ingenious mechanism of the separate plates in a gauntlet, and the way it allows the wearer to clench and unclench his hands in grasping his weapons.

Connoisseurs of both artistry and technical skill distinguish between the work of the various centres—in south Germany, around Nuremburg and Augsberg, and in Northern Italy, especially Milan and Brescia, as well as in other places—all of which developed their own methods and styles. There is a classic age of armour when it was used (apart from in the tilt-yard, which had its own variety), for the serious business of military action: and this is the era perhaps which interests the devotee of MILITARIA. On the other hand the admirer of high craftsmanship in the cause of splendid display may prefer the work of that later age when, having been tested by firearms, armour was used for its magnificence and for the show of rank and authority. This called on the resources of some of the greatest artists of the Renaissance, realising in this as in other media the great revival in classical styles during the fifteenth and sixteenth centuries.

This matter of style is, in fact, as fascinating as any side of armour connoisseurship. The pointed arch and fan vaulting of *Gothic* architecture has its expression in armour, and the term is used by arms collectors for styles showing rippled fluting, pointed edges and shell-like ridges—all well seen in the equestrian suit from the Wallace Collection, London.

After a brief spell of plainer and more rounded armour, when the 'glancing surface' was the main consideration, this decoration was developed into the so-called *Maximilian*

thic war harness for man and horse, the only complete example surviving.
was made about 1475–85 for a Freiherr von Freyburg, of Schloss
henaschau in the Bavarian Alps, close to the Tyrolese border.

armour, channelled with parallel fluting; so that the *Gothic* was the armour of the Wars of the Roses, of the great Italian *condottieri,* of the fall of Constantinople, of Dürer's knights; whereas the *Maximilian* was that of King Henry VIII's meeting with Francis I at the Field of the Cloth of Gold. The armour of this time even took on the puffing and slashing of the clothes of the day, especially when worn by the swaggering braves called *Landsknechts,* whose SWORDS we shall presently be examining.

This was also the era of the great engravers and etchers— Albrecht Dürer, Hans Holbein, Martin van Heemskerk, Daniel Hopfer and other men turned aside from their copper plates for the PRINTS of the day to work here in steel.

With the coming of firearms, heavy suits of protective armour gave way to lighter half-armour, making the wearer more active and mobile, but still affording him some protection from the envious cut and thrust. In fact it seems from the researches of practical men like Dr. Bashford Dean [RL 246] that it was this need for mobility rather than the penetrating power of the firearm which led to the fairly rapid shedding, little by little, of all armour by, say, the English Civil War— although it seems to have lingered on in America until the French and the Indian Wars and, of course, much later in the East. In the end, so far as body armour is concerned, we were left with only the ceremonial cuirass for cavalry and, finally, the vestigial GORGET.

The great national collections throughout the world— which must be the study of the would-be collector—mostly originated in the outbreak of antiquarian interest in the eighteenth and early nineteenth centuries, when the wealthy everywhere hung their walls with arms and filled their halls with armour. A French ambassador appeared at a Court Ball at Buckingham Palace in armour which he claimed had been worn by Joan of Arc: the rich American, Edwin Brett, sent an Englishman, Samuel Whawell, to hunt the length and breadth of Europe for rare pieces; one of his gatherings, it is said, was removed only after pursuit by the traditional pack of ravenous wolves.

In Britain the national collections at the Tower of London

and at Windsor Castle, comprehensively technical, are complemented æsthetically by the fine gathering at London's Wallace Collection, mainly from the earlier collections of Sir Samuel Meyrick and the Comte de Nieuwerkerke (*Surintendant des Beaux-Arts* under Napoleon III), aided by that astute and resourceful dealer Frederic Spitzer—and here is as good a place as any to recommend embryo collectors never to under-rate the rôle of a dealer in collecting. There are important collections in America at the Metropolitan Museum in New York, and in continental Europe there is the *Real Ameria* at Madrid, which would have been even more comprehensive than it is had it not been raided by a desperate population when the French invaded their land in the Peninsular Wars—also the Musée de L'Armée at the Invalides in Paris, the armouries at Dresden, and the Deutches Museum at Munich.

ASSOCIATION ITEMS   Here is a field of collecting which may take you into most of the sections of this book—although your motif is actually very single-minded. What you are gathering is anything and everything not *about* a particular person, theme or event—this is subject collecting—but *associated* with them in some way. A relic is perhaps the best example of an associated item.

Naturally, an object you collect may, in fact, tell you something about the object of your interest or veneration—for example, a lock of hair may indicate her colouring, a pair of shoes the fact that their owner was flatfooted. The AUTOGRAPH collector—who is also association collecting—often learns a great deal from his A.L.s. as we see in that place.

But knowledge is not the only object of the exercise. In this field the collector does not find so much interest in the edition of a book as in a name scribbled on its flyleaf. A library that I know has a copy of an obscure soldier's diary which bears some green pencil marks made by Sir Winston Churchill when he was writing the life of his famous ancestor, the Duke of Marlborough: I wonder no association man—and there must be many on the lookout for such Churchilliana—has not purloined it.

29

Items collected associated with murder cases of the famous English advocate, Sir Edward Marshall Hall.

Illustrated here is a double association item, for not only is it a collection of items made by one of the greatest advocates of his day—the late Sir Edward Marshall Hall—but each item in it is associated in some way with one of his cases. There is a water colour of Sir Edward by Robert Wood, the talented little glass painter whose vanity so nearly lost him his life when he was accused of the savage murder of a London prostitute; there is the Smith and Wesson double-action five-shot .38 with which a violent and drunken Wolverhamptonian is said to have killed his wife; the .32 FN automatic, bearing the label of Bow Street Police Court, with which a cruelly tortured young

30

French woman shot her brutal husband 'Prince' Fahmey Bey in the Savoy Hotel, London, during a violent thunderstorm; a Bowie-type KNIFE with which a young Doncaster man killed a 'Peeping Tom'. There are also the bullets (for the weapon was never found) which passed through the jaw of a girl as she cycled along a country lane, and which could also have killed a raven sitting on a fence nearby: in destroying the suggestion that the raven had died from gorging on the girl's blood this proved a key point in saving a man's life. Association collecting can lead us into some strange and interesting paths.

Provenance, of course, is the great problem. It is all very well to find a snuffbox at an auction sale which bears a label 'attesting' that it once belonged to George Washington, but who put the label there, how honest was he? Can one establish a clear line of descent in ownership—as, for example, the glassmaking Chance family of Birmingham could with some Nailsea glass which they thereupon proved to have been actually made at Nailsea.

Many so-called association items accuse themselves in some way; for example, the piece could not possibly have been owned by the person claimed, for it wasn't made at the time he lived. Here it will be necessary for the collector to study the subjects of other collectors. A good general knowledge is also serviceable; otherwise he may fall for the wiles of someone like the forger mentioned by Mr. Savage [RL 256] who successfully sold letters signed by Plato and Mary Magdalene which were written in French.

AUTOGRAPHS

Life is a leaf of paper white
Whereon each one of us may write
His word or two—then comes the night.

Some collectors of autographs are literally concerned only with a word or two—the bare signature of some famous or notorious person. These are they—usually youngsters—who clamber over the heads of others to thrust a book under the nose of someone who has ventured into the seas of fame or infamy.

31

But solo signatures are poor stuff—unless they are on cheques, or perhaps on presentation copies of books, especially first editions. What interests one most is the full autograph letter or document: as the catalogues have it, the A.L.s. (autograph letter signed). Other designations are the L.s. (letter, with the signature only in the hand of the writer); the A.Doc.s. (autograph document signed); and Doc.s. (document, again signed only); or, in modern times, the T.L.s. (typewritten letter signed).

The fascination of the autograph letter or document is that it comes to us straight from the past and from the person, persons or group in which we are interested: there is no editor, no censor, no interpreter. There before us is the man or woman, writing without any idea that one day strangers will read his

From a picture-framer's account book, showing an entry of July 11, 1814, covering the framing of two prints for Lord Byron.

Dean Swift's holograph resolutions on how he proposes to behave 'When I come to be old'.

words written on the actual paper he handled, showing the unblurred strokes made by his pen, swift and bold, faltering and weak.

If the autograph is newly discovered, or if the collector who newly comes into possession of it happens to have special knowledge of his subject whereby he can read a new significance into the words, then something has been added to our store of knowledge. For this reason the more informative the letter, the more interest and, of course, the greater value it has. A note from a great celebrity acknowledging a cheque is probably of

Portrait of Elizabeth I on a silver medal commemorating the Spanish Armada, 1588, together with her autograph.

less account than a revealing exchange between two comparatively lesser-known figures. With knowledge of an author's work you may come across the germ of an idea for a work or a character; or in the case of an historical figure you may suddenly perceive that the reference books have missed a vital point in the chain of evidence.

If it occurs to you to start writing to famous people of your own day, in the hope of getting an autograph letter out of them, you will have to be more subtle than your predecessors, for not everyone nowadays would show the courtesy and charm of Robert Louis Stevenson in a reply to such an applicant, quoted by Mr. Broadley [RL 248]:

Vailima, Upolu, Samoa

You have sent me a slip to write on; you have sent me an addressed envelope; you have sent me it stamped; many have done as much before. You have spelt my name right, and some have done that. In one point you stand alone: you have sent me the stamps for my post office, not the stamps of yours. What is asked for with so much consideration I take a pleasure to grant. Here, since you value it, and have been at pains to earn it by such unusual attention—here is the signature,

Robert Louis Stevenson

For the one civil autograph collector, Charles R.

You may, on the other hand, be lucky enough to come across someone like the irritated Archbishop of York who, in reply to a request, sent a full A.L.s. reading: 'Sir, I never give my autograph and never will.'

Portrait medal and auto-graph of Henry VIII.

BELLARMINES

Thou thing,
Thy belly looks like to some strutting hill,
O'ershadowed by thy rough beard like a wood
Or like a larger jug that some men call
A Bellarmine, *but we a* Conscience . . .

An old antique dealer once pointed out to me a man of middle age who was passing along the street in front of his window. 'I always knew that man would be a collector, from the time he was a little boy,' he said. 'When he came in here one day with his daddy I asked the lad what he would like to have out of all the stuff in the shop; and he picked out one of them damn old ugly things'—he pointed to a bellarmine jug—'and nobody *but* a collector would want one of them, would they?'

These stoneware jugs or bottles—which are also called *Greybeards* or *Longbeards*—have in fact collected a good many collectors in their days, which also have been many.

They seem first to have appeared in the mottled 'tiger ware' of the sixteenth and seventeenth centuries, but as they were sent to England from Cologne and Frechen in the Rhineland,

36

they became known there as 'Cologne Ware'—although all the potteries had been removed to Frechen by about 1600 (according to Mr. Honey as the result of a feud between the potters and the Cologne municipal authorities). In England, apparently, a *gallonier* contained a gallon, a *pottle pot* two quarts, a *pot* a quart and a *little pot* a pint.

Don't be put off by the duller kinds of imitations which were turned out in the later years, and also in the nineteenth century. The earliest of them are tremendous pieces of pottery, although to find any you will perhaps have to go to Germany, where they call this kind of ware *Rheinischer Steinzeug*—taking with you as authority the works of Herr Otto von Falke [RL 248], and asking not for Bellarmines, but *Bartmannkruge*. In French-speaking countries this ware is *Grès* and the pieces will answer to the name *Barbmans*. They often have very fine additional decoration in the form of oak leaves on scrolled stems in applied relief: this kind are quite globular, something over a foot high, and with a very short neck. Another type is pear-shaped with a longer neck, having the mottled grey and brown glaze already mentioned and perhaps just a single medallion, sometimes heraldic: one said by Joseph Marryat to have been dug up in the gardens of Westminster about 1850 bore the arms of Amsterdam.

John Dwight of Fulham (*c*.1637–1703) took out a patent for making 'stoneware, vulgarly called Cologne ware' in 1671, and Mr. Honey [RL 254] believes that much of his work—or that of the rivals against whom he took legal action in 1693—exists today catalogued as Rhenish wares. Doultons of Lambeth, across the river from Fulham, made a great many finely potted versions in the nineteenth century in blue and grey.

Why Bellarmines? Ben Jonson, as quoted above, hints at some kind of moral or religious significance—although characters in one of his plays simply and naturally say let's 'have one Bellarmine' before bidding '*bonus nocius*'. He also explains their origin rather ribaldly, in telling a story of 'Justice Jug's daughter, then sheriff of the county, who, running away with a kinsman of our captain's, and her father persuing her to the Marches, he great with justice, she great with jugling, they were both for the time turned into stone

37

Cardinal Bellarmino (1542–1621), after whom the famous Bellarmine mask jugs are said to have been named.

upon sight of each other here in Chester: till at last (see the wonder!) a jug of the town ale reconciling them the memorial of both their gravities—his in beard and hers in belly—hath remained ever since preserved in picture upon the most stone jugs of the kingdom.'

The name seems to be that of Cardinal Roberto Bellarmino, held to have been responsible for persecution of the Netherlanders during the Spanish occupation of the Low Countries. Perhaps he earned it in derision, as Joseph Marryat suggests, because of his celebrated letter—which called forth a tart rejoinder from James I—seeking to detach the English Roman Catholics from their allegiance to the Crown. At all events, here are the features of the prelate in question, from an engraving published in Rome about 1640, so you may judge for yourself whether the later jugs—though obviously not the earlier ones—were modelled in his likeness.

One odd thing about them, however, is that they have often been found buried with fetish objects in them—such as hearts pierced with pins, or fingernail parings and hair: perhaps this had something to do with the Bellarmino attribution as well. Maybe this race of pots will magic you into taking an interest in the family of SALTGLAZED STONEWARE.

38

BICYCLES AND TRICYCLES Even *Dicycles* and *Quadricycles*.

The true cycle, one takes it, however many wheels it has, is not that 'manumotive vehicle propelled by hand cranks or pulling an endless rope connected through gearing to the road wheels' which was designed in 1418 or 1419 by Giovanni Fontana, Rector of the Faculty of Arts at the University of Padua; examples of which, it appears, were constructed by Johann Hautsch, the Nuremberg mechanic, about the middle of the seventeenth century.

Neither, presumably, is it a *Draisienne*; nor even that version of it called the *Celifère* or *Velocifère,* which the Comte de Sivrac demonstrated in the garden of the Palais Royal in Paris in 1791. This was, in fact, a small wooden horse with two wheels, propelled by pushing away the ground with each foot alternatively. Its chief disadvantage was that it had no means of steering except by leaning or banking, so that successful progress depended upon there being a long straight road in the direction in which one wanted to go—something not easily found in the eighteenth century. The charmingly named Nicéphore Nièpce of Chalons, known to collectors of cameras as the father of photography, added an animal's head to this machine in 1816 but did little to help in the matter of steering.

The pedal-operated machine seems first to have arrived with the Reverend Edmund Cartwright's *Quadricycle* of 1819; but the invention of the *Bicycle* is attributed by Mr. Caunter [RL 248] to Kirkpatric Macmillan (1810–1878), a blacksmith of Courthill in Dumfriesshire, whose still-existing forge bears a plaque which celebrates his discovery 'that one could ride free upon a machine equipped with two wheels placed in line and propelled by treadles and cranks fitted to one of the axles'—in other words: 'Look, no feet!'

The *Bone-shaker* bicycle, apart from incunabula produced in the intervening decades by village blacksmiths and private persons, appeared commercially in the 1860s, first in France, then in England. The reputed *'inventeurs et propagateurs'* of this *Velocipède,* Pierre and Ernest Michaux, have a memorial at Bar-le-Duc. The vélocipède was patented in America by Pierre Lallement, a mechanic employed by the Michaux *père et fils,*

39

Draisienne of 1820; a development of the hobby-horse, by the Baron von Drais de Sauerbrun (1785–1851), a novel and useful feature of which was that it could be steered.

who had apparently made a substantial contribution to the design of the machine and felt he had not been getting sufficient credit for it. His associate was James Carrel, of Ausonia, Conn., and another American patent was taken out by F. G. Hoppner in 1867.

The *Ordinary* or *Penny-farthing*, with hugely enlarged front wheels and equally diminished rear wheels—so designed, of course, to provide increased speed for the same pedalling rate —appeared about 1870, while the *Kangaroo* cycle of 1878 offered a chain drive, though still working from the front wheels.

Persons who preferred a machine which did not, on braking, tip you over the front wheel on to your head, made an enthusiastic public for the *Safety Bicycle*, such as that made in 1873/4 by Harry Lawson and produced from 1879 as the *Bicyclette*.

Ordinary, or penny-farthing, bicycle of 1874—about four years after its invention.

Variable speed gears made hill climbing more tolerable from about 1889, while the free-wheel clutch, which offered greater comfort going downhill, was devised by Linley and Briggs in 1894. In 1888 J. B. Dunlop gave aching bones solace by producing the rubber pneumatic tyre.

The American star model of 1880, later patented by W. S. Kelly and P. A. Maigen, was an original variation on the penny-farthing idea in that it was in fact a farthing-penny, having the small wheel in front; it worked by levers instead of cranks and the pedals were independent, so that you could push both down together for a flying start.

The first motorised cycles by Michaux were driven by steam, while the internal-combustion engine, providing the *Cycle-motor* (as distinct from the motor cycle) proliferated from the early years of the present century. The Wall *Auto-*

wheel was a popular attempt to attach a miniature one-wheel motor-cycle to a cycle as an auxiliary.

The *Monocycle*, understandably enough, seems to have succeeded only among trick riders. The *Dicycle*, with two parallel wheels of equal diameter on a common spindle, did not fulfil its early promise, while the *Pentacycle*, with one large driving wheel surrounded by four very small ones so that once in motion these could be lifted and the machine converted into a monocycle—and consequently nicknamed the 'Hen and Chickens'—does not seem to have advanced beyond the function of parcel mail delivery—if it got so far.

The *Tandem* has been around since D. Albone and A. J. Wilson in 1886 made it possible for you to have your lady friend mounted behind you: as many as six riders have been accommodated in this way.

But perhaps the most attractive form of multiple riding is that given by the *Sociable*, providing two seats side by side or with the lady sitting in front of the gentleman at such a height that he can conveniently whisper into her ear. Appropriately enough, as may be seen from our picture, while the gentleman controlled the steering, it was the lady who held the brake.

Tandem tricycle of the 1880s, complete with crew.

BILLIES AND CHARLIES   On first sight you might think they were mediaeval PILGRIMS' BADGES or primitive TOKENS of some kind—which was precisely what you were intended to think by their makers, a Mr. William ('Billy') Smith and a Mr. Charles ('Charlie') Eaton.

These gentlemen were London mudlarks or shore-rakers of mid-Victorian times, well known to readers of Dickens, who earned a hazardous living raking about in the river bed at low tide looking for articles dropped overboard from passing ships. The London Docks system was being built about that time, and the antiquarians of the day, caught up in a craze for mediaeval relics of all kinds, offered the mudlarks beer money for interesting finds.

Billy and Charlie, who worked the shore around Shadwell, found their territory remarkably unproductive of the sort of things the antiquarians wanted; but being helpful types they decided to put this right. They built themselves a little furnace and started to cast pieces of lead with vaguely mediaeval figures on them, together with vague lettering—it *had* to be vague, for neither of them could read nor write. After leaving their works of art under the mud for a tide or two they took them along to the archaeologists—who delightedly bought them and asked for more.

Soon Billy and Charlie found themselves so busy designing and casting their mediaeval badges, that they had no time either to plant their finds in the mud or to go up town and sell them: so they went into the wholesale business and distributed their 'finds' among other mudlarks for retailing. There was no likelihood of a leak: in the London of Daumier and Dickens the poor had a cast-iron security system.

Eventually one of the archaeologists smelt a rat—several pieces had rashly been given dates which didn't quite fit—and this person publicly accused a well-known dealer of selling the badges and tokens as antiques, knowing them to be fakes; whereupon a libel action ensued and Billy and Charlie were brought up from Shadwell to give evidence.

They were astonished to hear learned counsel, the accused dealer and several independent and very famous experts get to their feet and solemnly testify that the bits and pieces of lead

43

which the pair had made with their own hands in their back kitchen in Shadwell were genuine relics of the Middle Ages. If our friends had known that, of course, they would perhaps have been more careful with the dates.

The trial ended inconclusively, and Billy and Charlie went back to their work as though nothing had happened. The story did come out eventually through some detective work on the part of one sceptical antiquary: but the pieces were now sought after for their notoriety and the 'firm' prospered on until one of the partners died.

Their creations can now be seen in many museums and collections, where they are kept as curiosities. But the extraordinary thing about them is that, although FAKES, they are not copies of the real thing, for the forgers had had little opportunity of seeing genuine pieces. Furthermore, many of them have an extraordinary vigour and originality of design. In happier circumstances either Billy or Charlie—whichever it was who made the casting moulds—might have become a fine designer: on the other hand he might have remained one of those untaught 'originals', like Douanier Rousseau, Alfred Wallace or Grandma Moses, who crop up from time to time and astonish the sophisticated eye with the intensity of an entirely private vision and feeling.

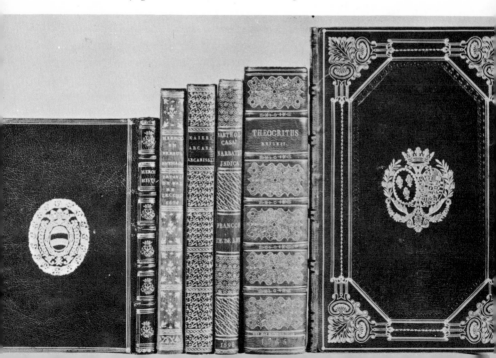

BOOK BINDINGS   There was once an ingenuous young examinee who, when asked by her examiners to define the primary purpose of cowhide replied that surely it was to cover cows. A secondary purpose for it, of course, is to cover books: and if the primary purpose of a book is to be read, surely a secondary use for it is to stand upon our shelves and look beautiful. As an old bookseller's catalogue remarked every year on its cover:

> '*For a jolly good book whereon to look,*
> *Is better to me than gold.*'

Because of this, many of these learned publications—incidentally some of the best free reading for the collector in any field—carry a separate section for 'Bindings', whereby readers may know that the works offered there are chosen especially for their merit as examples of the art of bibliopegy, or bookbinding as a fine art. The books may also happen to be worth reading; but alas! those whose bibliomania takes them in this particular direction are often led into habits of bibliotaphy, that is to say, the burying of books under lock and key.

So let us admire beautiful books, and perhaps collect them for their own sake. But since we cannot collect every kind of beautiful book what is to be our selective or limiting factor?

There are some that hold that the best binding is the most fitting one. 'Your face and figure, Sir, suggest a book appropriately bound,' says Cyril very unkindly to King Gama—although W. S. Gilbert's spiteful monarch did rather deserve it. Mr. John Carter [RL 248], that great bibliognost, has deplored the fashion in the nineteenth century and later of taking everything which needed a new cover (and a great deal that didn't) and binding it up in highly polished levant or stained yellow calf with gilt backs and sides. As he so correctly points out, such a work as *The Faerie Queene* of 1590–6 or *The Compleat Angler* of 1653, finds its most natural clothing in plain calf, sheep or vellum, while Johnson's *London* of 1738 is more at home in marbled or even plain grey wrappers. When books are inappropriately bound, moreover, they have the greatest difficulty in keeping face when placed alongside contemporaries which are in their proper clothing: as the same expert points out, your Florio's *Montaigne* of 1603, or your

45

Left: *moulded 'Gothic' binding of 1849, by H. N. Humphreys, London, of 'A record of the Black Prince'.* Opposite: *shelves of magnificently bound volumes in the showroom of Charles Sawyer.*

Tristram Shandy of 1760–7, in a shiny new morocco among friends in old calf must feel like men in evening dress at an afternoon party.

But perhaps we are still collecting books rather than bindings, and in a pretty recondite way at that. Let us go out into more popular and therefore more possible fields. Those who are charmed by the engravings or photolithography of Victorian gift books, such as the annuals or the small anthologies, will reap a second harvest in their fine, brilliantly coloured binding cloth and the lavish blocking of intricate designs in gold, sometimes signed by famous artists like John Leighton (1822–1912) who worked under the name 'Luke Limner' and, incidentally, was the first man to draw a robin on a Christmas card. A later generation of good bindings, still obtainable for shillings rather than pounds, is exemplified by two of an old Macmillan series of illustrated classics: one is Washington Irving's *Old Christmas* of 1878, the cover of which, like the illustrations, is by Randolph Caldicott; the second, Austin Dobson's *The Story of Rosina* of 1895, is in the very different mood of Hugh Thomson—and shows what a very great change there was in taste and style in twenty years.

Looking further, the bibliopegist will find it incredible that Thomson, with his fanciful, sentimental archaising, was a contemporary of Aubrey Beardsley, who designed a cover in exactly the way you might think he would.

When a few years ago that old acquaintance Mr. Ruari McLean provided his admirable chart to Victorian book production [RL 249] I did not know whether to be grateful for the light he shed in hitherto dark corners or to be irritated because he seemed likely to multiply the number of competitors who might come and elbow me from my lone and peaceful inspection of dwellers on dusty shelves in Bath or Tunbridge Wells. Mr. McLean will give many leads in the fields I have mentioned above, but strangely enough he does not seem to be interested in the fine vigorous bindings on the boys' books of the day. On the first edition of Ballantyne's *The Dog Crusoe* of 1884, which I inherited from an uncle, the runaway horses and the famous little hero make an infinitely more spirited cover than that of my own edition of 1917, for by then the deep blocking, the vigorous drawing, above all those thick bevelled edges, had gone for ever. Collectors of Henty have this pleasure as a further dividend, and for those who cannot find any more

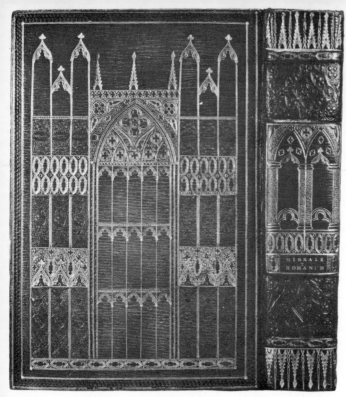

Binding in the 'Cathedral' style; England, circa 1830.

Hentys I recommend George Manville Fenn, who was just as spectacularly bound and was, in my view, a vastly superior story-teller.

But all this is personal, late in date, and, after all, but a byway of binding. For the classics of the breed, the collector must look among the early calf, the red and blue moroccos (tanned goat-skin) of the Restoration, often with inlays of other leathers; the vellum parchments of the Edwards family of Halifax (also inventors of FORE-EDGE PAINTING). Many books of that period appeared first in paper-covered boards and were bound up to the customer's taste: publishers' bindings, a profound study of its own, came in about the 1820s. Archibald Leighton, uncle of 'Luke Limner', introduced book-cloths and Sir Michael Sadleir [RL 249] has charted our way among these. Bindings can be signed in various ways; there are 'families' of bindings, such as the 'Cathedral' style, much used on works with an ecclesi-astical flavour published 1810–1840; the 'Etruscan' bindings of that era have classical decoration in acid staining on calf; there

48

are 'mosaic' bindings which offer much variety of colour.

BOTTLES AND FLASKS   'May we never want a friend
in need,' say the Proverbs of Solomon—according to Captain
Cuttle—'nor a bottle to give him.' Bottles, full or empty, are
good collecting for any man, so let us take a quick canter round
and see what we can find.

History itself is served up in the greeny brown old *Sealed
Bottles* such as were used by Mr. Pepys and also his old college.
'Went to Mr. Rawlinson's,' he noted in his Diary one day in
1663 'and saw some of my new bottles made with my crest
upon them, filled with wine, about five or six dozen.' From
this it will be seen that it was the custom in those days to buy
one's wine already put in one's own bottles, bearing one's
initials or crest, and perhaps a date. Colleges and other
corporate bodies had their bottles as well as individuals, while
some bear the initial of the vintner himself, perhaps when
serving less wholesale customers than Mr. Pepys.

From the dates on these bottles we can trace the evolution
of their shapes, from the short early 'dumpies' of the late
seventeenth century to the tall upright bottles of the early
nineteenth, by which time one had learnt to 'lay down' on
its side one's bottle of claret or burgundy, to prevent the cork
from drying out. There are FAKES about, so look for signs of
wear on bottom rims from constant travel round a table.

The delftware makers were in this field too, and their small,
white, round-bellied bottles seemed to have bridged the German
BELLARMINES and the earliest of the 'dumpies'. There is good
reason to believe that they were a seventeenth-century version
of the 'gift-pack' bottle marketed today at festive seasons: the
ever-helpful Pepys has recorded that he was given bottles of
sack on New Year's Day; perhaps they were also handed out
as wedding presents, which would account for the well-known
triple initials.

They are usually covered in the finest white tin-glaze with
hardly any more decoration than the owner's initials, a flourish
or two, a date—the earliest known specimen seems to be of
1629 and the latest of 1672—and some such description of the

49

contents as Sack, Claret, Whit or Boy. For a discussion of a common misapprehension of the significance of the word 'sack' and also more details of these famous little bottles see [RL 249].

'Leave the bottle on the chimley-piece,' Sarah Gamp was wont to instruct Mrs. Harris, 'and don't ask me to take none, but let me put my lips to it when I am so dispoged.' Sarah, whose tipple seems to have been 'mother's ruin', would undoubtedly have reached up for one of the SALTGLAZED STONEWARE spirit bottles of the early nineteenth century (see page 53), although instead of having one in the shape of the Duke of York (page 182), she may, being a stickler for appearances if nothing else, have preferred to carry her gin in the purse; she would certainly have preferred the 'Dancing Sailor' put out by Mr. Young, host of the Black Horse in Kingsland Road, London, to the fearsome bottle showing Mrs. Caudle giving her husband the benefit of her 'curtain lecture'—as retailed to us by Douglas Jerrold in ancient issues of *Punch*.

As will be gathered, these bottles, like so much pottery of the day, acted as a kind of magazine reflecting current celebrities and notorieties, political events, catch phrases and other items. You could get them in the shape of mermaids, pistols, truncheons, books, clocks, purses (as seen here). Some even were modelled as potatoes, and it is said that they would often be used for smuggling in spirits, being filled up at the coast and brought inland hidden among a load of real potatoes. The main centres of production were in London, at Lambeth, and the Derbyshire area around Chesterfield and Brampton. There is also a type with a shiny brown 'rockingham' glaze.

Passing along our bottled way, you could, if you dare, reach over to the wife's cabinet of coloured glass and filch a sealed bottle in a style made famous by the glasshouse at Nailsea, Somerset, where ordinary bottle glass was decorated by marvering in lumps of coloured enamel glass. It seems likely, however, that this particular bottle was made in one of the Scottish glasshouses, perhaps Alloa, for it bears the seal, dated 1827, of some person or institution with the initials J.S.J.M. and the place-name Stirling.

From the same domestic quarter you may also find another type of 'Nailsea' glass flask which is decorated in this

Otions of Brandy
And Rivers of Wine
Plantecion of Tea & agarle
To my mind 1794

case with red and white striations like the similar 'looped' styles. It descends from the bottles similarly decorated which come from Ancient Egypt of about 1450 B.C. down through Rome, Venice and France, and thus, apparently by way of French workmen imported by the Nailsea proprietors, to Somerset. The technique is a kind of *latticinio* treatment, whereby the glassblower takes a gather of molten glass and thrusts it into a mould lined with canes of coloured opaque glass which fuse into the clear glass: he then 'combs' down the lines of colour to produce a looped or striated effect.

51

Many of us have aspired at various times to be a pilgrim, and our next picture shows the immemorial pilgrim-bottle shape which perhaps had its origin in the dried gourd of the East. This is a specimen of the well-known but very rare Sussex pottery (of which you may see an interesting collection in the Castle at Lewes when you attend the ARMOUR and MILITARIA sales in that town). Clearly, by the touching sentiments impressed in printer's type and then filled in with darker slip—a charming decorative custom peculiar to this ware—pilgrims in Sussex in 1794 had no less exuberant tastes than those who wander o'er the downs so free in these latter days.

The United States is immensely rich in bottles and flasks, and in fact the earliest of them seem to be in this 'Nailsea' or 'country fair' glass idiom; or perhaps, having some flavour of German *waldglas,* like the attractive Pitkin bottles, with their swirled ribbing and a technique which seems to involve a dipping into a second gather. Equally attractive are the brown and amber bottles of Ohio, with moulding of broken swirls. But perhaps the most famous family in this popular glass are the whiskey flasks with symbolic or historical themes, which, like the Staffordshire blue earthenware mentioned elsewhere, record the growth and upsurge of life in the developing republic all through the century. In fact America seems to have expressed in this pressed-glass industry—in which it was far in front of

Sealed bottles, flagons and a Bristol 'square' designed for packing.

Saltglazed stoneware spirit flasks of the early nineteenth century.

the English trade—much the same interests and sentiments as did Britain in its Staffordshire figures; and domestic in inspiration as these themes are, one regrets that there was in this industry no exporting equivalent of the clockmaking Chauncey Jerome and the MECHANICAL BANK manufacturing J. & E. Stevens.

BOUNDARY MARKS First cousins and neighbours of fire insurance plaques—for they are often found on the walls of adjacent buildings—are parish, town or county boundary marks. Here again one hopes for some restraint on the part of the collector, or none of us would ever know which hundred, rape or wapentake we happened to be in. It is nice to think that all those specimens one sees in the shops were parted with by the parochial or civil fathers knowingly, when the house or wall actually came down.

Lurking in the shadows of the cellar shown here (next page) I can dimly discern some London parishes. 'St. K. Cree' is clearly St. Katherine Creechurch, whose church survived the Great Fire and the Blitz of World War II; St. Vedast, Foster Lane, which lost one church in the Fire and another in the Blitz; and among the initialed ones I would hazard guesses at St. Mary Magdalene, St. Lawrence Jewry, St. Martin-in-the-Fields, St. Dunstan-in-the-East, St. Mary-le-Bow, St. James Garlickhithe.

Like the collector of 'Signer' AUTOGRAPHS the obvious goal here is a plaque for every parish in a city or a county: the

53

More items in 'Trad' (see page 16) especially a group of Boundary marks, some identified on the preceding page.

collecting cabinet in this case is clearly the outside wall of your house.

BOWS AND SLINGS When David chose five smooth stones out of the brook and, whirling his *Sling,* sank one of them in Goliath's forehead, he was using one of the earliest long-range projectile weapons ever devised by man. The stones he selected would no doubt have been bean- or acorn-shaped, for the bullet idea was already appreciated. The Greeks cast them in lead, and sometimes inscribed them with such remarks as 'take this!' or 'desist!'; the Romans, for good measure, liked to heat up the bullets before sending them on their way.

The sling, according to Mr. Cowper [RL 255] has been described as a contrivance 'which converts circular motion into forward movement'; and there are several types. First there is the simple thong sling consisting of two lengths of cord or leather joined by a pouch, or maybe one length widening half-way along: there is the split-stick type, like the stout forked twig so widely collected by schoolmasters which we called a catapult, but having leather instead of elastic thongs, and meant

54

to be whirled by a circular motion of the arm. A third type, which is perhaps a STAFF WEAPON, is a straight stick with a thong attached in one way or another, which can be whirled round the head and the stone discharged either by letting go of the thing or using a self-releasing ring. The ancient inhabitants of the Balearic Islands used slings with such force and range that Quintus Metullus had to protect his ships by covering them with hides: the islanders, it is said, took their name from *ballein,* to throw. The Anglo-Saxons, like their cricket-playing descendants on Hambledon Down, seem to have preferred an underhand action; and their sling was used for bringing down game, mostly on unlawful occasions, down to the fifteenth century. The sling is also widely known in the New World; and it is claimed that the early Spanish herdsmen of South America could, to order, hit a bullock on either horn and so guide him.

Perhaps the next step from the sling was the *Pellet Bow,* very widely used, and capable of bringing down a bird at 30 to 40 paces with a clay pellet; this developed into the *Prodd,* or *Stonebow,* of mediaeval times.

In *Bows* of all kinds ('pent-up elasticity into rectilinear motion') we have a fascinating study in ETHNOGRAPHICA, for their range, historically and territorially, is immense. Perhaps the queen of them all is the English *Longbow*—although in discussing their capabilities users of them and writers of fiction have often drawn the longbow in more ways than one. Mr. Cowper puts the effective range of the longbow with which the English brought down the massed chivalry of France at Crécy and Poitiers at 160 to 220 yards, with an extreme effective range of 240 yards, and 280 to 290 yards for a flight arrow. There are a few longbows salved from the wreck of Henry VIII's *Mary Rose* in the Tower of London; and no doubt there is many a *cache* of them preserved elsewhere in estuarial mud, awaiting the underwater archaeologist.

With the *Crossbow* we have a much greater range and penetrating power. Sir Ralph Payne-Gallwey [RL 249], that highly practical student and collector—who as we shall see (under CANNON) could run you up a *Ballista* with no trouble at all— shot a number of crossbow bolts clean across the Menai Straits, off the Welsh coast, a distance of about 450 yards. With the

55

same weapon he put several bolts through a $\frac{3}{4}$-inch deal plank at 60 yards. Mr. G. P. Jenkinson, from whom I quote here, has a German windlass crossbow of the seventeenth century which draws at about 700 lbs pressure and could be effective at 350 yards. He tried it in competition with a longbow, and while the latter put six arrows into the target in the time that the crossbowman was attaching the windlass, aiming and pressing the trigger, the first bolt from the crossbow not only went right through the target but smashed it down altogether.

Of the various forms of the crossbow, one of the earliest is well seen in Pollaiuolo's famous 'Martyrdom of St. Sebastian' in the National Gallery, London (page 58). The weapon was surely out of date at the time the picture was painted: perhaps the artist, in telling the old story, was deliberately archaising: certainly he seems to have gone to some trouble to demonstrate how the crossbow worked, showing from two angles how the bowman bent his bow by means of a cord and pulley, placing his foot in a stirrup and using the whole strength of his body—sometimes using a claw on his belt—to pull the bowstring into position. The effectiveness of this type of crossbow was limited by the strength of the bowman, and devices were later introduced such as the *Goat's Foot* or *Pied de Biche* which worked on the lever principle and could therefore be manipulated easily on horseback. The perfected military crossbow, as used in the battles of Froissart's Chronicles, had a steel bow with a windlass. Sporting men, however, seemed to prefer the *Arbalest,* with its *cranequin* or ratchet winder, too slow and expensive for military use but handy because it dispensed with the stirrup.

Contrary to the general impression, there are many more crossbows about for the collector to find than those surviving

56

from mediaeval times, for this weapon continued in use by sportsmen and marksmen until well into the nineteenth century. Even today there exist in some Continental countries crossbowmen clubs, such as the Society of St. George at Bruges. Nothing, of course, could be handier for a poacher in search of something to put into his pot than one of the small English bullet crossbows produced by the gunmakers up to about 1840, which still appear regularly at the sales: there is at least one firm in England which is still making them. Only the other day I saw a group of brand new ones offered for sale in a shop window of the well-known firm, Lillywhites, which is just round the corner from Piccadilly Circus, London, and is famed for its sports equipment.

Intrinsically, as Sir Ralph has pointed out, the longbow was a mere stick (usually foreign, as is not usually realised); whereas the crossbow could be, and often was, a work of art. The stocks or tillers are often veneered with polished stag's horn, carved in relief with figures and shields of arms, perhaps also inlaid with mother-of-pearl; or it may be of ebony inlaid with horn, and some can be richly decorated as any firearm. This is one of the collecting items for your panelled hall.

Right: *hand crossbow of steel, spanned by a wing-nut on a central threaded rod.* Opposite: *Japanese longbow mounted packed for travelling.*

*Crossbows and longbows in action in the 'Martyrdom of St. Sebastian'
by Antonio Pollaiuolo, painted in 1475.*

BUTTONS   Once upon a time there was a man who was a collector, and he collected buttons. He was a real collector, too, for having exhausted most of the antique and junk shops in search of his speciality he then started to collect seriously.

He was looking for crested livery buttons, which the nobility and gentry and the wealthy used to order in sets for their servants; and he would go about the countryside wherever there were large houses and study the maps to see on which towns the local roads converged at the time the livery buttons were made. He would then look around these towns until he found, perhaps, a large drapery store, which had once been a small eighteenth- or nineteenth-century tailors' and outfitters'; and inside it he might find, in the very oldest part of the building, a little office or store-room with shelves; and on the topmost shelf there might be an old biscuit tin full of sets of crested buttons sewn in sets of twelve on cards in an entirely mint state. They were still there because the family for whom they had been made had moved away or died out, leaving the old tailor with stock that his successors had never bothered to throw out. And the collector would buy the whole tinful for a pound or so and go off feeling very pleased with himself.

But he had not quite yet finished his collecting, for there in the tin he had dozens of not merely duplicates but dodecaplicates (if that is the word for 'by the dozen'); whereas what he really wanted were lots of single specimens. So off he would trot with his biscuit tin under his arm to the nearest theatre where they played musical comedy in costume, or perhaps an opera house, and go round to the stage door and ask to see the wardrobe mistress. And he would compliment her on the way she had dressed the show, but say that how sad it must be for her that some of the footmen in the show had odd sets of buttons on their uniforms. And when she sighed and said yes, but where in the world can one ever get a complete set nowadays, the cunning fellow would open his tin and show her all his brand-new sets of buttons; and he would offer to change them for her odd ones: and then off he would go with his biscuit tin again, only now it was full of individual buttons, most of which were new to his collection. And both he and the wardrobe mistress lived happily ever after.

Buttons. Left to right: *mother of pearl, commemorating a son; with a classical glass sulphide head; engraved mother of pearl. All nineteenth century.*

Well, that's collecting: and in telling the story I haven't left myself much room to talk about the kind of buttons there are to collect. But books apart [RL 249] there are plenty of other people to help you, such as specialist dealers who advertise in the magazines, while in the United States there is a journal devoted to it called the *National Button Bulletin* and various societies of collectors. They collect naval and military buttons, railway, fire brigade and shipping buttons, sporting buttons, buttons of gold, silver, glass, ivory, horn, tortoiseshell, bone, china, brass, tin, copper, pewter and wood.

One of the finest collections of buttons ever to come under the hammer was that of the Duc de Meppem, which was sold at Sotheby's in 1961.

There were over 150 lots, averaging perhaps twenty buttons in each, in gilt metal, copper, brass, enamel, blued steel, wood and bone-back, glass, *verre fixé,* mother-of-pearl, ivory *decoupage,* gold-plated, painted silk, Meissen porcelain, etc.; the subjects included military and civil, classical, ballooning, animals, and much underglass painting of landscape and figures, French Revolution scenes, and the Monuments of Paris.

CANNON   These are not GUNS but engines of war, pieces of ordnance. They stand in their cradles, or on their carriages, served by their slaves; and they exist to hurl something very damaging at an enemy. They are also pleasant things to have in your garden or flanking the portals of your town house. Some are even small enough to put on your window-sill.

Among the early varieties—the 'engines invented by cunning men to shoot arrows and great stones'—you will not find it easy to collect a *Ballista,* a *Mangonel* or a *Trebuchet,* those ingenious machines operated by torsion or weighted counterpoise with which the Greeks, the Romans and the Chinese used to lob at their foes anything from stones and firebombs to, it seems, a hive of bees. You can, however, build one, full directions having been left us by Sir Ralph Payne-Gallwey [RL 249]—together with an account of the results he achieved with them in his English country home around the close of the nineteenth century (you should also try Sir Ralph on cross BOWS).

The Chinese were apparently the first to use explosive shells in their repertory of ammunition, and the first bottle-shaped European cannon, perhaps turned out by the bell-founders, hardly exist except in illustration. But there are many examples of bronze and iron cannon made by welding together strips of metal and then encasing them in bands, usually with a separate breech. If you visit the capital of Scotland you may see in Edinburgh Castle the famous 'Mons Meg' of before 1479, all five tons and thirteen feet of it, which had the temerity, and some power of divination, in bursting when it was fired to salute the arrival as viceroy of James, Duke of York, five years before he became King James II of England and eight years before he became ex-King James II of England. A sister of Meg's, the giant *Bombard,* 'Dulle Griet' (Daft Maggie), is to be seen at Ghent.

No story could be more absorbing than that of the difference in the ideas of the sixteenth-century Spanish and English in the matter of naval armament: it was the smaller but longer-range *Culverins* and *Demi-culverins* of the ships of Howard of Effingham, Drake, Hawkins and the rest, allied to nimbler manoeuvring power and superior seamanship, which out-gunned the floating fortresses of the Most Fortunate and Invincible Armada. The wider rôle played by cannon and sail in the expansion of European civilisation all over the world is admirably told by Signor Cipolla [RL 249].

61

Naval bronze carronade, 26 inch barrel, 3 inch muzzle, by J. Wolfe, Southampton, late nineteenth century.

From the above it will be observed that one of the best sources for the cannon fancier is at the bottom of the sea. Season after season the shallows of the Continental shelf yield up their rich harvest of *Periers, Cannons Royal or Serpentine, Basilisks, Sakers, Minions, Robinets* and *Falcons,* often (when not eaten away) wonderfully ornamented with Renaissance casting. One recently sold piece claimed—and justifiably so by the coat of arms cast over the breech—to have been raised from Blasket Sound, Ireland, where a ship from the fugitive storm-battered Armada foundered in 1588.

In today's saleroom it is usually the smaller type of cannon one sees. There are cast-iron and brass pieces from the late eighteenth and early nineteenth centuries, perhaps also a decorative pair of shining brass cannon of later times, or signal cannon with swivel supports for mounting in a wall, signed by such makers as Charles H. Gills, of Tower Hill, London—right outside the Tower Armouries.

For the collector without room for Mons Meg or naval fifteen-pounders, there is a fascinating range of cannon, many of them exact replicas, to be found in models. For those who like their cannon to perform a useful office, such as signalling the hour of luncheon, I recommend the *Sundial Gun* shown here—although you will have to make alternative arrangements in cloudy weather.

Sundial gun by Ling Chevallier, Paris: 5 inch barrel, 3 inch diameter lens on brass arcs, engraved with hours and months for different settings.

CHESSMEN Even if your chess is no great shakes it must be very satisfying to play with such a splendid set as that on the next page. It was made of porcelain at Meissen (Dresden) in the eighteenth century, and the chessmen are modelled as Turkish figures, the king being a sultan with a crowned turban, the queen a sultana. The castles are figures seated in a turreted elephant's howdah (is this the origin of the 'Elephant and Castle'?); the knights are figures on prancing white Arab horses, the bishops are courtiers, the pawns are soldiers differing in their colouring. The board is made as an edged tray, the chequers alternating in puce diaper and green floral sprays.

Many different kinds of craftsmen have been called in to make chessmen, and dating them is such a specialised study that it is no wonder there are dealers specialising in the sale of them. Ivory, bone and hardwood are the materials most used, but goldsmiths, enamellers and jewellers have also contributed sets.

63

Chessmen in Meissen (Dresden) porcelain, modelled as Turkish figures.

Forms of the pieces have been evolving for centuries, but the present iconology seems to have been well established by the time William Caxton published *The Game and Plays of Chesse* in 1474. He enumerated king, queen, alphyn (a kind of standard bearer), knight, rook and pawn: the knights were the king's champions; the rooks his *rocchi* or rock castles, standing along the marches of his kingdom; the bishop later took the place of the alphyn as the upholder of law and order. The pawns (peons) were ordinary taxpayers like you and me, and in Caxton's day they could comprise a banker, apothecary, notary, innkeeper, mason, wood-carver, ironworker, a keeper of the highway, courtiers and farm workers.

Some sets commemorate military victories, especially of the wars of Frederick the Great and Napoleon, with portraits of the commanders; likewise opposed are crusader and Saracen, Roman and Moor, Norsemen and French, Indians and members of the East India Company.

The 'traditional' or standard sets include the 'St. George' type, imported into Britain from France, also the 'Staunton' sets, named after the first Englishman to win the world championship. It was designed in 1847 by a Mr. Cook and issued in boxwood in natural colour and black or red. The Hastilow family made another English pattern.

Meissen was not the only factory to make chessmen of ceramics. Josiah Wedgwood had a set designed by John Flaxman in his jasper ware, used for WEDGWOOD JASPER MEDALLIONS. the pieces being actors in a performance of *Macbeth*: Kemble and Mrs. Siddons played the leading parts as king and queen. A modern version of this by Harry Barnard was issued in 1926.

At the Castleford Pottery, in Yorkshire, David Dunderdale made chessmen in his stoneware, white and black, brown and green, or blue and white; Doultons, in 1887, put out a set designed by George Tinworth which were made up of brown and white mice; for Mintons, John Bell, sculptor of many well-known statues in Victorian times, designed a set in Parian ware. There were also Rockingham sets modelled in Tudor styles, and in the early years of this century, sets in porcelain from Vienna and Sèvres.

65

COMMEMORATIVE MEDALS Of the various kinds of medals awaiting the collector, perhaps the most magnificent in artistry and craftsmanship are those which have been struck or cast—and there is a world of difference between these processes —to commemorate some person, event or cause. Here we exclude medals which have been awarded for bravery in the field of battle, or to mark service in a campaign—these are the province of persons interested in MILITARIA AND NAVALIA —also that other branch of the family, usually with no reverse and therefore probably designed as miniatures for mounting on furniture, etc., which are usually called plaquettes. Since we are dealing with metal we will also exclude WEDGWOOD JASPER MEDALLIONS

Your collecting range is still wide enough to satisfy several lifetimes of collecting. In commemorating events it can take you all the way from a Syracusan charioteer riding roughshod over his spoils to celebrate his city's great victory over Athens in 413 B.C. to the fateful Battle of Britain in the long hot summer of 1941: in celebrating famous personalities, it can take you from a Byzantine emperor to Sir Winston Churchill and President John Kennedy. On the way you will find portrait medals of the lords and ladies of the Renaissance; of the princes, bankers and theologians of the German states and the Netherlands; the kings, queens and cardinals of England and France; the defeat of the Most Fortunate and Invincible Armada; the anticipated invasion of England by Napoleon (engraved 'struck in London in 1804'); that other unduly hopeful event not to be realised for another generation, the entry of the Germans into Paris in 1914; and finally, a medal expressing the outraged feelings of theatre-goers in London when Kemble raised the prices of seats to pay for his extravagant new Theatre Royal, Covent Garden, in 1809. 'Old Prices, Open Boxes, and Deference to Public Opinion' was what they wanted, and they brought along trumpets and rattles to see they got them.

In America the celebrated Indian Peace Medals given as marks of favour to the chiefs were first used by the French in Canada, then by the English, and they sometimes had the name of the French king obliterated and that of the English one substituted. George Washington scored over both kings by producing a much larger oblong medal—it should perhaps be called a plaque —made of silver, for dies were not quickly available, and silversmiths were: the largest examples went to the famous chief Red Jacket, after whom they are sometimes called. The Jefferson Indian Peace Medals struck at the Mint usually have on their reverse the clasped hands and 'Peace and Friendship'.

Artistically the commemorative medal has as wide a range as its subjects, varying from the superb productions of the Renaissance, and some highly imaginative work of very recent years, to some quite execrable efforts in the last century and at the beginning of this.

By common consent the first of the medallists is still regarded as the greatest. He was Antonio Pisano, called Pisanello, of Verona (c.1395–1455), who has been categorised as the equivalent (though not the imitator) in the metallic art of his contemporary Donatello in sculpture. He cast his medals from wax models, combining a fine realism with skilful stylisation: he also had the first-rate designer's art of adapting his inscriptions so that they became an integral part of his design.

By way of proposing a standard of appreciation in these medals I would especially like to draw attention to some superb examples of Pisanello's work. One of them, which is in the British Museum, may have some significance in the history of the medal itself. It commemorates the visit to Ferarra in 1438 of the Emperor John VIII Paleologus, last but one of the Western rulers of Constantinople before it fell in 1453: he had come to attend a council called to try to reconcile the Eastern and Western churches.

At that time Pisanello, aged about 45, was working as a fresco and panel painter at the court of Nicolo d'Este, Duke of Ferarra; and it has been suggested by Mr. Hill [RL 249] that, having been commissioned to paint the Emperor's portrait, Pisanello was perhaps inspired by a Roman medallion of the Emperor Constantine—which was extant in his day—to produce a medal for the occasion. Certainly he followed this

67

Commemorative medals, including Pisanello's John VIII Paleologus, the marriage medal of the Marchese Leonello d'Este with Maria of Aragon, and other Renaissance medals.

precedent by putting a bust on one side and an equestrian figure on the other. Moreover the reverse of the Constantine medal, depicting the two churches or the Old and New dispensations supporting the Fountain of Life, may also have suggested a second medal of the version of the Paleologus medal: on this the cross was supported by two hands representing the Latin and Greek churches.

It may be that in this way—a travelling potentate wishing to have easily portable copies of his portrait which could be copied many times for distribution at home—that there arose the fashion for the portrait medals in which the Renaissance is so rich.

At all events the medal itself is a masterpiece, with wonderful handling of the outline of the face and the peculiar semi-oriental hat; there is also what seems to be an actual portrait of a horse on the reverse.

Then there is the utterly charming marriage medal of the Marchese Leonello d'Este of Ferrara in 1444 with Maria of Aragon, natural daughter of Alfonso of Naples. Here the austere portrait on the obverse is backed by a delightful group showing Cupid teaching the Lion—Leonello had musical tastes —to sing a song from a scroll: on the column which pulls the whole composition together is an *impresa* of a mast and sail which apparently signifies the ship of State sailing on its way. These *imprese* are a form of riddling symbolism—it has been called bastard heraldry—consisting of punning devices, obscure classical allusions and allegories, with which the artists used to puzzle and intrigue their public: and those interested in studying the matter more deeply might find some help in the works on the iconology of the Renaissance by, for example, M. Seznec [RL 249] and Professor Panofsky [RL 249], also other publications of the Warburg Society.

Pisanello was supreme among the Italian Renaissance medallists, but there were others—far too many to mention here— who produced masterpieces of the medallic art. Among them, Benvenuto Cellini, as well as telling us what a good medallist —or any other kind of craftsman—he is, has left us a useful treatise on the art, which was translated by Mr. C. R. Ashbee —himself a fine designer and worker in metal.

69

The German medal of the Renaissance has been held to have the same relationship to the Italian that Roman sculpture has to Greek. Most of the medals made there are portraits backed with coats of arms on the reverse. Dürer provided designs for medals, while Hans Schwartz of Augsburg was a fine portraitist with a large output. The German craftsmanship was superb, reaching its apogee in the first half of the sixteenth century. A century later it was the turn of France to lead the field, especially through the baroque masters Guillaume Dupré and Jean and Claude Warin.

The earliest of the English and Scottish medals are of foreign make or inspiration, but Thomas and Abraham Simon, from Guernsey, did some distinguished work, especially fine medals commemorating the naval actions of 1653, a portrait of General Monk and a brilliant Coronation medal of Charles II. These brothers were as skilled in casting as in die-cutting.

After a general eclipse in the eighteenth century, when the engravers took the stage, there was a revival in France towards the end of the nineteenth century, with Ponscarne (1827–1903) and Chaplain (1839–1909); while Mr. C. H. V. Sutherland has reminded us of the inspired portrait of Toulouse-Lautrec by André Galtié, in which the painter's vast hat is used as the actual outline of the medal. No less imaginative is the cast medal designed by Jan Pieters to commemorate the inundations in the Netherlands in 1953, which shows on one side the sea flooding in as though on to the medal itself, and on the other men pushing the waters back out of their polders. This is medal-making of a very high order indeed.

In England there has lately been some fine portraiture. At the moment of writing there is also a renewed interest in striking medals to commemorate outstanding events: the 900th anniversary of Westminster Abbey—the deaths of Sir Winston Churchill and President Kennedy—and the centenary of the climbing of the Matterhorn.

The more expensive of such medals are issued in limited editions, in the hope of an increase in value on that account. But the real criteria for any collector, I would suggest, here as always, is the artistic worth of the design and the quality of the craftsmanship. On these alone should they be judged.

70

*World War II Commemorative Series, by Presidential Art Medals,
Englewood, Ohio.*

COMMEMORATIVE POTTERY The theme is once
more commemoration; but this world is a very different one
from that of the Renaissance medal. Here we have the town
or country potter, sharp-eyed for business, watching for the
latest popular hero, the newest scandal, the current cause, the
startling event. On his pots you may read national and popular
history as though they were set out for you in a newspaper.

Here also we shall not be concerned with the niceties of
ceramics—which can be read about elsewhere [RL 254] but the
persons or events which are remembered in them. In other
words, our collecting is by subjects, not by kinds of porcelain
or pottery.

If we start with kings and queens, however, this does take us
into the very early days of English ceramic history, to the
country slipwares of the Tofts and others, with their 'trailed'
decoration. Royalty also appears in a complete gallery in the
succeeding delftware, on the 'blue-dash chargers', as they are
called from the decoration some of them bear around their rims.

In this English version of the great family of tin-glazed
earthenware (*cf.* APOTHECARIES' JARS and HISPANO-MORESQUE
WARE), these dishes, intended for display on the shelf or the
court cupboard rather than for use on the table, show in vivid
colour distinguished persons of Stuart and early Georgian
times. The earliest English monarch to appear on them is
Edward VI, and the last George II. The same picture often
does duty for more than one of them (although William III is
usually shown on a charger, following the famous portrait):

and this exchange goes on with the lesser figures, with only initials to identify them. For example, D.M. stands for the Duke of Marlborough, P.E. for Prince Eugene of Savoy, his great collaborator in the War of the Spanish Succession, P.G. is Prince George of Denmark, husband to Queen Anne, while D.O. is the Duke of Ormonde; G.M. could possibly be George Monk, Duke of Albemarle, but is thought more likely to be George, Duke of Monmouth—at all events that was the decision of a famous museum when one turned up in the hands of someone who knew neither its place in the ceramic scheme of things nor its value, which was perhaps not less than several hundreds of pounds.

Sometimes commemorations of royal persons were not particularly polite:

> George the First was always reckon'd
> Vile, and Viler George the Second
> And what mortal ever heard
> Anything good of George the Third
> When to earth the Fourth descended,
> Praise the Lord, the Georges ended.

The Fourth came in for some specific criticism, too, when popular feeling arose in favour of his wife, Queen Caroline, whom he had put on trial for adultery and treason.

> Long live Caroline
> Sing a song of sixpence
> A green bag full of lies
> Four and twenty witnesses
> All proved to be spies
> When the bag was opened
> The Lords began to stare
> To see their precious evidence
> All vanish into air.

The first Elizabethans were kinder to their monarch: nothing could be more charming than the inscription on an English maiolica-style delftware dish in the London Museum, which bears the date 1600 and the words: THE ROSE IS RED THE LEAVES ARE GRENE GOD SAVE ELIZABETH OUR QUEENE.

Commemorations of naval persons occur on most of the eighteenth-century porcelains, stonewares and earthenwares.

Outstanding among them is that Admiral Vernon who, in a dark moment in the island's affairs, earned this commendation on a bowl of salt-glazed stoneware: 'The British Glory revived by Admiral Vernon. He took Porto Bello with Six Ships only. Nov. ye 22, 1739.' The gallant and peppery admiral, who had been in retirement, had got up in the House of Commons and severely criticised the government of the day for letting the Spaniards harass our trade from their base at Porto Bello in the West Indies. Nettled, the ministers suggested that since he thought it so easy why didn't he go and take the place himself; to which the admiral retorted that if they gave him the ships he would do just that thing; whereupon they hedged and said that they had only six ships available. The admiral said that six would be plenty, and he took them out to the Chagre River and captured the hitherto impregnable fort. This feat, and per-haps even more the fact that it made the government look silly, caught the imagination of the British public, and Vernon and Porto Bello gave a name to a vast series of figures, mask jugs and views on every kind of pottery.

The saltwater-reared collector interested in a gathering of his kind will find plenty of other sailors, for example, Earl Howe and the Glorious First of June, Admirals Rodney and Hood; American naval heroes like Commodore Stephen Decatur, commander of the frigate *United States,* which captured the British *Macedonian*; also Captain James Lawrence, who won glory in the heroic fight between the *Chesapeake* and the British cruiser *Shannon.* The lower deck is represented on many a jug, mug and teapot by the intrepid Jack Crawford.

> *At Camperdown we fought*
> *And when at worst the fray*
> *Our mizzen near the top, boys*
> *Was fairly shot away.*
> *The foe thought we had struck*
> *But Jack cried out 'Avast,'*
> *And the colours of Old England*
> *He nailed up to the mast.*

Great ships had their own bowls—the large ones in delftware made at Liverpool are especially famous: Bristol also made bowls for the ships visiting the port and these have been found

73

in the other lands the ships visited. Careful search will find the *Fulton* steamboat, the *Great Eastern* and the *Great Australian Clipper Ship,* and a host of other real and imaginary craft, many of which yet offer unexplored possibilities of identification by looking out the contemporary prints from which the subjects were often taken.

English potters generally seem to have been astonishingly enthusiastic about American victories, both by land and sea. Commodore Prebble's attack on Tripoli is celebrated, so is the driving off of the British ships at Stonington in 1814, with the inscription, 'Stonington is free whilst her heroes have one gun left'. This was from the Herculaneum Pottery at Liverpool, a prodigious exporter of earthenware to the newly-born United States. Staffordshire told the story of Bunker Hill in a way their serving countrymen would not at all have approved, for it appears from the picture on one dish that it required only two solitary American horsemen to break the Thin Red Line.

Josiah Wedgwood was well to the fore here, producing in his black basalt the Rattlesnake Seal with the motto 'Don't tread on me', taken from the first American Revolutionary flag. A certain amount of sensitivity, however, appears in such a piece as a lustreware jug which, according to Mr. N. Hudson Moore [RL 250] is in the Virginia Room at Mount Vernon: it shows the victorious Lafayette on one side and on the other 'Cornwallis *resigning* (not *surrendering*) his sword at Yorktown'. Actually the potters could have spared themselves this unwonted tactfulness, for I believe Cornwallis neither surrendered nor resigned his sword at Yorktown, but left the job to General O'Hara.

Most of these pieces of course are in the exported Staffordshire blue earthenware, a colour made fashionable by early imports of Chinese 'Canton' ware, which had been favoured even on the Presidential table in Washington's time. You will need a long purse to gather in this 'American Historic' and a keen eye to see that you are not being sold FAKES AND FORGERIES.

Pots have also recorded the scientific or engineering feats of their day, though they were not always too precisely defined. There is at least one punch bowl inscribed: 'Benjm Franklin, Lld, and F.R.S., the brave defender of the country against the

One of the many views on Sunderland lustre-ware commemorating the Wearmouth Bridge; Derby biscuit figure of Admiral Vernon; teapot made by Ball Bros. at the Deptford Pottery, Sunderland-on-Tyne, in commemoration of Jack Crawford, the ship's boy who nailed the British colours to the mast of his ship at the Battle of Camperdown against the Dutch in 1797.

oppression of taxation without representation—author of the greatest discovery in natural philosophy since those of Sir Isaac Newton, viz., that lightning is the same with electric fire.' To be found everywhere on lustre and other wares is the Wearmouth Bridge at Sunderland—or rather, the two Wearmouth Bridges, for a second one was built by George Stephenson in 1858, sixty-two years after the first. In the Sunderland Museum collection there are no fewer than twenty-eight different versions, all varying in detail and made at different local factories. In America the Erie Canal and the Rochester aqueduct are similarly commemorated.

Railway collectors find much to engage them on pottery, so do those interested in coaching lore. The balloon ascent by Lunardi in 1785 took place only a few hundred yards from the Lambeth pottery, so it was natural for the occasion to be marked on wares from that establishment.

Individuals sometimes appear in history solely as commemorated on their marriage plates or jugs. 'William and Elizabeth Burges, 24th August 1632', painted in colours on a delftware mug from Southwark, marks a great day in the lives of two people we otherwise would not know. Sometimes the potters even celebrated their suppliers, as witness a delftware punch bowl with an inscription to the man who supplied the tin for their glaze:

> *John Udy of Luxillion*
> *his tin was so fine*
> *it gildered this punch bowl*
> *and made it to Shine*
> *pray fill it with punch*
> *lett the tinners sitt round*
> *they never will budge*
> *till the bottom they sound*

Perhaps the largest specialised gallery of commemorative wares lies in the Staffordshire chimney ornaments produced in huge quantities practically throughout the nineteenth century. At first there are the 'all-round figures' which followed the older tradition of Staffordshire, but as the market for these wares spread and widened there came into being the 'flatback', designed to stand on mantelpiece or shelf and look out into the

76

room. As always, Royalty dominated, ending apparently with the late Queen Mary when as a princess she was betrothed to the Duke of Clarence. Foreign royalty also appears, including the Sultan of Turkey, Napoleon III—these would have been included as our allies in the Crimean War, which produced many characters. But the last-named monarch is also seen trampled on by the British Lion a few years later when the two countries fell out again over some long-forgotten political quarrel.

Politicians, patriots and philanthropists swell the numbers, while events like the Afghan War of 1845 and Sir John Franklin's expedition were taken up eagerly. George Washington and Benjamin Franklin are included in the gallery, also Lincoln, but Americans are usually here as the result of a visit rather than as a conscious attempt to cater for the American market, e.g. such personalities as Van Ambrugh the Lion Tamer, Mrs. Bloomer, inventor of the garment of that name, Moody and Sankey the revivalists. By this time potters in the United States were doing their own commemorative work.

Murderers have their place in the gallery: there is one group which shows not only William Corder, the assassin, and Maria Martin, his victim, but also the Red Barn where the foul deed took place. James Rush and William Palmer are included, along with Potash Farm and the house at Rugely.

The intending collector will find more on the subject in SALTGLAZED STONEWARE and WEDGWOOD JASPER MEDALLIONS.

CURRENCY CURIOSA   Collectors frequently have good reason to be grateful to those museum curators and dealers who from time to time have the enterprise and imagination to mount special exhibitions which draw attention to particular fields of collecting. Not very long ago Spink and Son, the London dealers, (who were founded exactly a month before the outbreak of the Great Fire of London in 1666) put on a show of the extraordinary variety of objects which mankind in different parts of the world and at different times has used as a means of exchange. It immediately became apparent to many who had been unaware

77

*Some 'curious currency' in the form of a spear,
a bracelet, a tusk and a bean.*

of it that here was a most interesting branch of ETHNOGRAPHICA.

Some of these items were, in themselves, objects of intrinsic value, for example, the Chinese boat-shaped ingots of silver with their oval stamps and many 'chop' marks which eventually punch out the middle of the piece. There is also the well-known 'saddle' money, also named after the shapes used, circulating in China, Burma and Thailand, bearing the name of the banking house which issued it, with a testimonial to the quality of the metal used. Tin is almost as precious a metal as silver, and an obvious choice for currency in a country like Malaya, where it abounds. The fragile tin 'tree' money from which pieces are broken off as required, is, as one might expect, extremely difficult to find in its complete state. There are also square hat-shaped pieces of tin which did duty for money in Thailand.

With other types of currency, however, the value may rest in the workmanship, or some unusual quality in the material. Shells have been, and in some areas still are, a very widespread form of money, especially as strings of discs, where the red ones may be more valuable because harder to find than the white ones. There is also money made up from rattan or canes,

78

bones, whale's teeth, boar's tusks, plaited belts, bracelets made of elephant-tail hair, even sticks of tobacco.

Some types of money seem to have their origin as replicas of articles once used in barter. For example, the 'larins' of silver wire rather like hairpins, from the Persian Gulf area, and once much used in the trade of the whole Indian Ocean, are often called 'fish-hook money', for they may well derive from the fish hooks which are highly valued in those waters and played an important part in the economy there. Similarly the long thin 'Kisi' pennies, used in Liberia and Sierra Leone are perhaps based ultimately on the ancient spearheads or throwing knives, while the so-called 'hoe money' of West Africa may represent the actual implements which once changed hands in these agricultural areas. Similarly the axe money of the Congo may stand for the ceremonial axes which once changed hands as presents.

But it is not only in primitive societies that strange materials and shapes are to be found. During the disastrous *Inflationszeit* of 1921–3 in Germany, when marks were counted in millions but were worth little more than wallpaper (which some of them were used for afterwards), money was made of porcelain, iron, steel, even wood, while notes were printed on leather, silk and other materials. Still used in various parts of Russia, it seems, is the peculiar 'tea money', a form of the tea brick used, for example, in Tibet, with butter and other ingredients: its function as money also serves as a means of transporting it from the tea-growing regions.

At one time the most ubiquitous type of curious currency was the manilla of West Africa, an object like a half-bracelet, with flattened ends, perhaps weighing five or six pounds. Apparently it was first introduced there by the Portuguese as a replica of the copper rivet from the keels of rotted Portuguese ships, which the natives had begun to use as a means of exchange. There were King-, Queen- and Prince-size manillas, and most numerous of all the small Ohpoho, from two to three inches across. These were legal tender in West Africa until 1911, but the locals preferred them to the new official coinage, until in the end, about 1948–49, according to a writer in the *Antiques Finder,* nearly 32½ million of copper and brass manillas were withdrawn and exported as bulk scrap, an operation which cost the government more than a quarter of a million sterling. They can still be found, however, and in any case, shortages are likely to be amply remedied by enterprising Nigerians who have started operations using scrap metal and the old mould.

The collector of currency will sometimes find himself in the territory of the TOKENS man—for instance, the wooden nickels issued by the Chamber of Commerce of Tenino, Washington, which appeared in Spinks' show. But whether a piece is to be considered as currency or as a private token is an argument which may safely be left in the hands of both collectors— especially if they happen to be the same person.

DAGGERS In collecting, definitions must be made, and where they do not exist they can be suggested. A dagger, shall we say, is a *War-knife,* made by man for combat, private or public, with man, or for killing animals; a KNIFE is a weapon that may be so used, but also has other employment.

The Dagger can be used primarily for the thrust or it may be also designed for the cut or slash. Origins can often be seen in natural forms; for example, in the Indian *Khanjar* one has in metal the shape of the natural double curve of the buffalo horn: examples actually made from the latter, tipped with steel, are well known. There are also flints obviously made to be held in the hand, with points so long and relatively weak that they seem to be meant for stabbing into flesh: there seems no doubt about this in the case of the beautiful Scandinavian flint daggers with handgrips and pommel, which must surely have been the progenitors of the fine Bronze Age weapons tanged for insertion into wood or bone, or made with rivet holes. American Indians, as in some Ægean cultures, used copper daggers, but they were shaped by hammering rather than casting.

For four hundred years from about the year 1300, in Europe but especially in England, Scotland and Flanders, the most common kind of dagger worn by civilians and soldiers alike was the *Ballock-knife,* from the two rounded lobes on its guard: genteel nineteenth-century antiquaries called it the *Kidney-dagger.* It was also sometimes known by its contemporaries as a

Left: *European daggers;* top, right: *rondel, fifteenth century,* left, *quillon, etched with inscriptions, French, circa 1500;* bottom, right: *ballock or kidney, perhaps Flemish, 1450–1500,* right, *ear, or* daga alla Levantina *(or* Stradicta*), Italian, circa 1600.*

Above: top to bottom: *Japanese aikuchi, Cossack kindjal, Indian kukri, Indian kard.*

Below: top to bottom: *Burmese dha, Sumatran kris, Malay kris.*

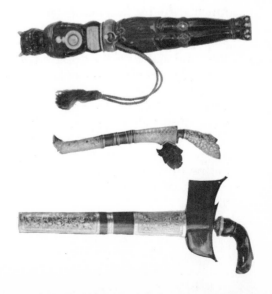

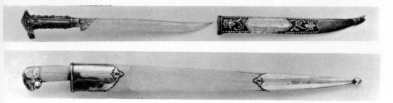

A Turkish yataghan (top) *and an Indian Prince's knife.*

Dudgeon-dagger from the boxwood often used for the hilt: Macbeth's 'air-drawn dagger' which led him on to murder Duncan was such an one.

The *Landsknecht's* type dagger was originally carried by the hard-fighting regular foot mercenaries raised by the Emperor Maximilian, who played such a large part in European fighting in the fifteenth and sixteenth centuries and who strutted about armed to the teeth in extravagant slashed doublets and ostrich feathers; their SWORDS had pierced ornaments and 'puffed' bands to match. This hilt is usually of steel, damascened or embossed.

The *Quillon* dagger covers a wide range, the common feature of which is the cruciform arrangement of the quillons, either curved or straight. A dagger with its pommel formed from two splayed discs is called the *Ear-dagger,* or *Poignart á Oreilles,* an importation from Spain in the fifteenth and sixteenth centuries, but perhaps originally deriving from the Near East through Venice. Where there is a solid disc with the blade's tang passing through its centre, and sometimes through another disc for a pommel, you have what is today called the *Rondel-dagger,* much used by knights in late mediaeval times: perhaps this was the *misericorde* of the writers of the time, used to give the *coup-de-grâce* through chinks in the armour of a fallen adversary, and also called a *Panzerbrecher,* or armour-piercer.

The *Left-Hand* or *Main Gauche* dagger has already been mentioned under SWORDS. Usually made *en suite* with its rapier, it necessarily followed the same forms; but the quillons are often arched to catch an opponent's blade. This idea is carried even further in the *Sword-breaker* or *brise-epée,* which is a left-hand dagger with the blade cut longitudinally so that it can, by means of a spring, be made to fly open and present three prongs; or it may have its back or edge cut with a series of notches.

82

Dispute reigns about the precise nature of the *Baselard,* but the name seems to be applied to a longish weapon with a hilt shaped like an 'I'; it was probably the ancestor of the Landsknecht's dagger and also the parent of the *Swiss dagger,* acquiring a more leaf-shaped blade in the process. The gilt-bronze or silver sheath had elaborate cast and pierced decoration, often with designs such as Hans Holbein the Younger's 'Dance of Death'; collectors call these *Holbein Daggers. Poniard,* as far as one can make out, simply means 'dagger', but a *Stiletto* is a small weapon with a thin, square or triangular sectioned blade used for stabbing: gunners carried them, with conversion scales on the blade for converting weight of shot into calibre.

The *Dirk,* originally the sheath-knife of the Scottish Highlanders, is not unlike the Ballock-knife, and usually has a disc-shaped pommel, a false edge and some notches in the back below the hilt. It is often carved with Gaelic motifs, but the Cairngorm pommel is a nineteenth-century affair. There is also the Naval dirk, a short weapon carried by officers, especially midshipmen, some of which have curved blades.

Of Oriental daggers, the best known perhaps is the Malay or Javanese *Kris* with its wavy or 'flaming' double-edged blade: here, too, one may perhaps see a model in the primitive deer-horn dagger. Length can vary from 12 to 30 inches, and the rough surface of the blade is due to its being made up by welding together fine steel wires. The handle is often at an angle, suggesting that it was thrust from the shoulder.

Most extraordinary of all daggers, perhaps, is the *Katar* (Khutar), quite unlike any other weapon in that it has two metal bars on the base of the blade which are joined by one or more transverse bars used as a grip in the palm of the hand, so that the whole of one's weight can be put behind a thrust. The Pattani *Jamdadu,* an elongated form, can cut as well as thrust. H. S. Cowper [RL 255] has suggested that in its shorter form the Katar may have originated as a knuckle-duster or armed gauntlet, and then, when pointed, used in the manner of a European left-handed dagger: there are certainly some forms, such as the *Jamdhar, Doulicaneh* and *Sehlicaneh*—'two- (and three-) scratcher death bringers'—which are evidently designed to catch an opponent's blade, like sword-breakers.

DAHOMEY BRASSES   One of the first pieces of ETHNO-
GRAPHICA I ever bought—to my everlasting regret I sold it
absent-mindedly when having a periodical clear-out—was the
brass group shown here of a man out hunting with a spear-
throwing bow, and a dog which really has got its eye on the
game. It hails from Dahomey, in West Africa, and it is one of
a large family of such figures and groups which one frequently
sees in the shops and salerooms, fetching no very great price—
my hunter with the football cap cost me thirty shillings. I
believe they are still being made, though not so carefully as in
the old days.

Like the well-known gold weights of neighbouring Ashanti,
they were cast by the *cire-perdue* process whereby a wax model
is encased in clay, and hot metal is poured into a hole, melting
the wax. Each piece, therefore, is an individual work.

84

Opposite and right: *brass 'cire perdue' figures from Dahomey, West Africa, used as household ornaments.*

All kinds of people, animals and events appear in these groups. Women sit beside water jars, crocodiles seize hapless humans; mothers carry huge children; chiefs are borne in litters, followed by their retinues (all mounted on a board), or are paddled down river in their ceremonial canoes. They appear to have had none of the religious significance of, for example, ANCESTOR FIGURES, but to have been designed as household ornaments, like Staffordshire figures [RL 250].

They show an interesting form of stylisation: the limbs are simplified and elongated, reminding one of Western sculptors like Giacometti and Kenneth Armitage; and on the best of them there is usually some chasing, as shown on the one here. (I'm sorry about the bent spear: the piece wasn't in my possession long enough for me to have it straightened; so I hope its present owner, if he won't sell it back to me, will have this put right.)

DEATH MASKS   Here is another highly typical story of
how a man caught the collecting bug and was led on to make
a serious and valued collection. I owe the facts to the Editor
of the Princeton University Library Chronicle.

One summer afternoon in the 1860s a young New Yorker
named Laurence Hutton was looking into the window of a
junk shop where he saw a plaster bulldog which reminded him
of an old lady of his acquaintance known as Aunt Jane. He
went inside to enquire the price, and while he was trying to
make up his mind if he could live with the bulldog Aunt Jane
a ragged urchin came into the shop carrying what appeared to
be a plaster cast of a human face. 'Is dis wort' anything?' the
boy asked the dealer, who didn't seem to think it was. He
made to send him off. But Laurence Hutton intervened and
offered the lad fifty cents for his treasure, while for another
quarter, he was led to an ash barrel in Second Street, where
were more of the curious masks. Hutton gathered them all up
and took them home.

He discovered that they had once belonged to the George
Combe, the British phrenologist, who lectured in America in
1838/40; and the finding of them set him off on a collecting
career which led him to curiosity shops and junk stores all over
America and Europe. He published a series of illustrated articles
about them in *Harper's* and wrote the book listed here [RL 250];
he also related his experiences in collecting the masks in a
biographical work edited by Isabel Moore. Hutton also
went in for GRANGERISING: a copy of *Portraits in Plaster,* extra-
illustrated by the collector with engraved portraits of the
subjects of the masks, is of value as a reference work—and an
apt example of the way in which this art can be used. Eventually Hutton provided a classical illustration of the possibilities
open to the gentleman referred to as Joe in our INTRODUCTION
by bequeathing the collection—as well as many other fine
things—to the Princeton University Library.

It should be understood that such death masks (as also life
masks, taken during a person's lifetime) are not necessarily
actual impressions from a person's face. This is usually done
in some perishable material, from which a mould or matrix
is made, after which an 'original' cast is taken.

86

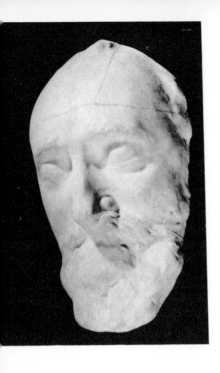
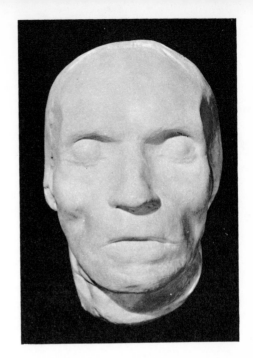

Death masks: top, left: *Henry VI of France,* right, *Beethoven;* bottom, left: *Coleridge,* right, *Walt Whitman.*

DIALS AND NOCTURNALS

'*And then he drew a dial from his poke,*
And, looking on it with lack-lustre eye,
Says very wisely, "It is ten o'clock:
Thus we may see," quoth he, "how the world wags
'Tis but an hour ago since it was nine,
And after one hour more 'twill be eleven;
And so, from hour to hour, we ripe and ripe,
And then, from hour to hour we rot and rot;
And thereby hangs a tale." '

Touchstone's pocket dial, for an hour on which he made even the melancholy Jacques laugh 'sans intermission', perhaps looked like the one shown here. If so it must surely have been a gift from his noble master, for in that day the work of the scientist had also to be a costly work of art.

There are, of course, *Sundials* on walls, on pedestals and elsewhere which can sometimes be bought and fitted up anew; but it is easier to collect the portable ones, which come in fascinating variety, in profound technical interest and often in exquisite craftsmanship. To begin with there are *Altitude Dials* with a horizontal gnomon, the tip of which casts its shadow on a surface on which curved hour lines are marked out; these are intersected by vertical lines showing the months of the year. They show the altitude of the sun (if it is visible) and they may take the form of a ring which, suspended from a shackle, is turned until light from the sun passes through a pinhole to a spot on the interior of the rim. They are sometimes engraved with a list of towns. The 'Shepherd's' dial which was in use in the Pyrenees until fairly recent times, was in column form: others are of quadrant shape, and sometimes they register 'Jewish' or 'Italian' hours—which started at different times of the day from ours.

But these dials are good for only one latitude; if you go farther afield and do not wish to buy a local instrument you need the *Universal Pocket Dial* which is adjustable for latitude. At night you may use a *Nocturnal* or *Night Dial,* an instrument by which use one of the pointers of the Pole Star can be considered as the hour hand of a clock.

With the coming of the compass there was the *Compass Dial* which used a gnomon set parallel to the earth axis, so making the same scale serve for all seasons of the year. There is also the *Analemmatic Dial* which has no compass but combines two forms of dial, one set for the season, so that it can be turned until both shadows indicate the same hour. One of the makers

Opposite: *Italian ivory pillar dial, metal gnomes within column, seventeenth century; pedestal block dial by D. Beringer, Nuremberg, late eighteenth century; German tablet dial by Leonhard Miller of unusual octagonal form, early seventeenth century.*
Below: *brass crucifix dial, engraved with towns and their latitudes, dated 1648, probably Italian; magnetic asimuth dial in wood, perhaps sixteenth century.*

was that Thomas Tuttell of Charing Cross, London, who had Samuel Pepys as one of his customers.

Michael Butterfield was a famous maker of beautiful dials, usually of octagonal shape. An Englishman who worked in Paris, he became instrument maker to Louis XIV. His are not exactly universal dials but they do usually show hour scales for 43, 46, 49 and 52 degrees latitude and are capable of further adjustment by a movable gnomon carrying a scale from 40 to 60 degrees. They could be of brass or silver, have lists of towns engraved on their backs and sport a bird-shaped gnomon: sometimes you may be lucky enough to find one in its original fishskin case bordered by silver nails.

Other makers followed Butterfield in making this type of dial; some even tried to forge his signature.

Even more valued are the ivory *Diptych dials* of the Tucher (or Ducher) family of Nuremberg and also those of *Dieppe* by Charles Bloud and other local masters. In the same sale mentioned above there was a gold and enamel finger ring with a lapis lazuli inset engraved with a coat of arms and opening to disclose a horizontal sundial with a string gnomon, the shoulders set with diamonds.

DOMESTIC MACHINERY   The date July 22, 1966, was a landmark in the history of collecting. On that day, in those venerable and stately auction rooms in Bond Street, London, owned by the 250-year-old firm of Sotheby, where the hammer has come down on such items as the Berkeley Castle Dinner Service (£207,000), Cezanne's *Garçon au Filet Rouge* (£220,000) and Rubens' *Adoration of the Magi* (£275,000), there were offered for sale an old typewriter, three nineteenth-century sewing machines, an Edison 'Gem' Model Phonograph and two Ericsson telephones.

Such items, put up in less exalted rooms, have for some time now been the quarry of males who, though never known to lend a hand with the household chores or even to offer to drive in a nail where one is desperately needed, find a passionate interest in the obsolete machinery and equipment of the home. They look for early box mangles, washing machines (now a

Table telephone by L. M. R. Ericsson of Sweden, circa 1890–1900.

century old), knife cleaners and smoothing irons—and if any-body supposes that the last-named offers no variety of interest they should visit the Troubadour Coffee House in Earls Court, London.

This is not the place to do more than suggest that those who have hitherto been interested in what are usually called 'bygones'—goffering irons, bottle jacks, tinder boxes [RL 247 and 250]—may now update their collecting into the industrial age, and fairly well on into it too, for obsolescence comes in nowadays more and more rapidly.

But it may be of interest to report what these items made at Sotheby's. The typewriter, a small, light and portable machine of the type-wheel class, invented by G. C. Blickensderfer at Erie, Pa., in 1889 (and similar to one in the Science Museum, South Kensington), went for £9. The portable lock-stitch sewing machine, patented by S. A. Rosenthall in 1880 and improved and manufactured by the Moldacot Pocket Sewing

91

Machine Company in 1886–7 (also having a counterpart in the Science Museum) made a fiver; a lock-stitch machine by William Jones, c.1879, £4; a chain-stitch machine by P. Frank, Liverpool and London, c.1875, only £3. But the Edison 'Gem', with 36 wax sleeves, introduced in 1889 and the cheapest and most popular of the Edison phonographs, whizzed the bidding up to £14, while the two Ericsson table telephones, c.1890–1900—one is shown here—designed and manufactured by L. M. Ericsson of Sweden, claimed to have been in recent use and in full working order, soared up to a final bid of £38.

Obviously Domestic Machinery is not yet in the Rubens and Cezanne bracket, but one hopes that these distinguished auctioneers will continue their pioneering.

DOOR KNOCKERS They seem to offer a perennial temptation. There is nothing quite so exquisitely funny to a boy as to watch the rage of two householders whose front-door knockers have been tied together.

They have been collected for many years: even as long ago as 1709 the *Tatler* complained of people wrenching knockers off doors at night, while by Regency times the affair had become a sport for bucks, like a modern treasure hunt.

As with opercula and fire insurance plaques, this is another trophy to be sought from those who have to do with the pulling down of old houses. Some of the eighteenth-century knockers may have heraldic arms cast in high relief; and these, of course, may usually be traced to their original bearer. Neo-classical urns or caryatids will indicate a date somewhere after about 1770. Palmettes, fruiting vines, lyres, are to be found as rappers, often in association with various other motifs: some study should be made of knockers still *in situ* to see that these are true partners.

Perhaps the greatest variety of designs is seen in the nineteenth-century brass knocker, often with its vast letter-box, both of which provide a gleam and shine which no modern material can quite match. If you propose to instal a set on your door try also to find a stone doorstep which you can have painted a snowy white.

92

DRINKING GLASSES   Like their companions **BOTTLES AND FLASKS**, these items can be interesting to the collector even when they are empty.

They can be especially interesting if he goes about collecting them in a fairly scientific way. Some years ago the late Mr. E. Barrington Haynes [RL 250]—incidentally one of the most readable writers in any collecting field—rendered a great service to glass collectors in classifying English drinking glasses of the seventeenth, eighteenth and early nineteenth centuries as a biologist might, taking their various components—bowl, foot, stem—and arranging them in species, families or genera.

If this idea sounds dull to you, look at the array of glasses I have assembled here. You will note that they have affinities or differences in the shape of each of these components, and also in their decoration or lack of it. The stems of glasses, in fact, can be *Balustroid,* like the late Stuart ones; they can have Silesian or otherwise *Moulded* stems, like the early Georgians; the stem can be *Straight*; and when it is pulled out to make the bowl it is *Drawn*; in the wake of this you will find all the family of *Air-twist*; *Opaque-white* or *Colour-twist, Hollow* or *Facetted* stems or no stems at all. Even the knops on the stems can be classified as, for example, *Acorn, Angular, Annulated, Bladed, Cushion, Mushroom, Tear-* or *Pear-shaped.* Among bowls you may distinguish between the *Bell,* the *Bucket,* the *Ogee,* the *Thistle,* the *Trumpet,* the *Cup.* There can even be variations within these shapes; the ubiquitous *Round Funnel,* for example, can be *Pointed, Pan-topped, Saucer-topped, Waisted, Lipped, Bucket-topped* and *Cup-topped,* while the *Pan-topped Round Funnel* can itself be *Waisted* or *Lipped*—and no collector could ask for more than that. Feet can have their variations no less; they can be *Conical, Beehive, Folded, Stepped, Square* or *Domed.*

After this you may consider the purposes of these glasses. Georgian *Wines* come in many shapes, and sometimes need engraved grapes and vineleaves rather than hops and bines to distinguish them from *Ales,* which, however, are usually *Flutes,* sometimes short *Dwarfs*—although there are *Giant Ales,* you didn't need a great deal of the searing stingo of those days. The flute shape helped to trap the necessary sediment—still to

93

Drinking glasses: top, left: *baluster stem, trumpet bowl, circa 1690,* right, *balustroid 'deceptive' dram, circa 1700;*

bottom, left, *'flowered' cordial with facetted stem, circa 1720,* right, *air-twist with Jacobite rose.*

be found in that finest of all beers in all time and all countries which we owe to a Mr. Worthington.

The early *Champagne* was not the wide-open *Tazza* we use today, but a sort of elongated *Pointed Round Funnel*. The *Cordial* and the *Ratafia,* used for these delicate spirits, have small bowls on long and rather thick stems, usually *Facetted*; the *Dram,* for stronger and rougher spirits, has a stem which, as my schoolmaster used to say of my memory, was short, rudimentary or absent. The *Goblet* calls for a larger bowl in relation to the height of the stem, and if you insist you can have a *Giant* or even a *Mammoth Goblet*—in Marseilles once I heard such an item called *une formidable*. *Rummers* (which were once Römers, for Rhenish wine) are goblets with shorter stems and can have *Bucket* or *Cup* bowls. Distinguish between the *Toasting* and the *Toastmaster* glass: with the first, after toasting your lady or your king, you snap its slender stem between your fingers so that no lesser cause shall ever be celebrated with it; while the latter helps you to avoid slipping under the table when, as host (or *Chairman*—another name for the glass) you have to acknowledge everybody's lady and everybody's king, president or nation. The trick is done by filling most of the 'deceptive' bowl with glass and leaving little room for drink, but making that little look a lot. A *Firing Glass* had a short stem and a great fat foot for banging on the table in response to the chairman's toasts, while with a *Stirrup Cup* you didn't need a stem at all, for you were in the saddle, hounds were threshing around below you eager to be off, it was a cold day, and you wanted some warmth under your waistcoat.

To say nothing at all, of course, of the sheer beauty of these things. Study their fine proportions, admirably adapted to their uses, note the generously broad foot made to stand firmly upon a fine eighteenth-century table, feel the rich, soft, heavy metal of the famous English glass of lead—the Continentals and the Americans never got within a mile of it, remarkable though the things were that they did with their soda-lime metal.

Do not imagine, either, that you will find these glasses only in the shops haunted by the rich: elsewhere [RL 251] I have illustrated a few such glasses I picked up in junk shops for a pound or so each.

95

Commemorative drinking glasses: top, left: *colour-twist 'frigate' cordial,* right, *'Yacht' wine, eighteenth–nineteenth century;* below: *two rummers for Trafalgar and the Wearmouth Bridge, Sunderland.*

ETHNOGRAPHICA   The 'trade' has now adopted this cumbersome, etymologically dubious, but extremely useful word ('ethno' for short) to describe what the Customs authorities classify as 'pieces of ethnographic interest'.

Neither dealer nor collector is likely to quarrel with the definition, especially if he buys his pieces from abroad, for as Mr. Philip Goldman has pointed out in the *Antique Finder,* to give them any other name, such as 'original works of primitive art' is to invite the officers of the Customs and Excise to call in. experts to prove that they are neither original nor works of art. So 'ethno' seems to be here to stay.

What does it cover? The question is really a very interesting one. Ethnology, according to most authorities, is the study of races and peoples, their physical make-up, their habits and distinctive characteristics; while the word ethnography is generally used to describe the scientific classification of these things.

But which races and peoples, and in which eras? Obviously in its broadest sense it should cover them all, so that in fact everything in this book should be regarded as 'of ethnographic interest'. In practice of course, its use is generally limited to the so-called 'primitive' societies. But which are these? The Polynesians, it has recently been shown by contemporary travellers —taking their babies with them on their way—have for unknown centuries practised astronomical navigation: highly organised societies with laws existed in, for example, the Hausa States and Benin, in West Africa, before the white man arrived there. Yet all these territories have produced what we would call 'primitive' art. How 'primitive', therefore, does primitive art have to be?

Some of the African **ANCESTOR FIGURES** described under that head are highly sophisticated creations carried out with great technical virtuosity; and such work has been deeply admired by leading artists of the West. By comparison, a painting by Grandma Moses or Henri Rousseau is indeed 'primitive' in the sense of being untaught and produced without the disciplines learned by trained artists. Similarly, in what way is a pierced and relief-carved Samoan wooden comb inferior to either a Welsh love-spoon, a piece of scrimshaw work from a New-

Anglo-Saxon scramasax, ancestor of the Bowie knife, which has as much right to be classed as ethnographica as other items mentioned on this page.

foundland whaler or any of the English bygones described in Mr. and Mrs. Scott's interesting book [RL 250]?

'Ethno' then is pretty well anything we want to make it; but perhaps it mainly covers the objects made and used in the life of the many thousands of different races and cultural units which have not—or had not until recently—been influenced by civilisations founded by Europeans and Asiatics. This is not to imply anything derogatory about such things—often the reverse—but merely to define them.

We shall therefore be interested in the indigenous cultures in Africa south of the Sahara, the Eskimos, the Indians of the Western hemisphere, the peoples of Oceania, as Mr. Wingert proposes [RL 251] and also, I would add, certain societies in Asia and North Africa.

Definitions apart, the field here for the collector is immensely wide—though there are already signs that the supply of good pieces is beginning to run short. Professional ethnologists and interested amateurs have, of course, been patiently garnering these objects for generations, helping to build up collections like those at the British Museum. All the while the cultures which produced these things have been vanishing or changing under the impact of outside influences.

CURRENT PRICES have therefore risen steeply in the last few years; and as museums proliferate, as more and more collectors find pleasure in these objects, in fact, as man gets more and more interested in the history of his kind, these prices will go higher still.

But there are many fine things still to be bought at reasonable enough prices, considering that most of them will never again be made. To be able to judge their true worth, however, I am sure the collector should take a deep interest in the cultures

98

which produced these objects. They were made in a totally different context from ours, and they must be judged in that context—which goes as much for ANCESTOR FIGURES as a piece of CURRENCY CURIOSA, for an African mask as for DAHOMEY BRASSES.

FIREARMS CURIOSA This rather curious term concerns weapons which are combined either with other weapons or with objects not in themselves weapons.

The best-known example of the latter, of course, is the *Sword-stick,* which dates from at least the fourteenth century. It is usually an ordinary walking-stick, the shaft of which forms a sheath for a thin blade, while the handle serves as a sword or dagger hilt. A variation of this device is the rare *Brandistock,* which is a staff having inside it a long *estoc* point and two shorter ones, which can be ejected at will.

Combined weapons usually bring together firearms of some sort with SWORDS, DAGGERS, KNIVES, STAFF WEAPONS, etc.; and they seem to be a means of hedging one's bets in days when no great confidence was reposed in the firearm alone. Often the efficiency of both weapons is impaired; although the astonishment produced by being able to stand one's distance

Top to bottom: *combination hanger/flintlock pistol, English, circa 1750; knife/revolver (Tranter type) and sheath; battle-axe/ matchlock pistol; dagger/flintlock pistol.*

and produce a shot out of a battle-axe, a holy-water sprinkler, an Indian katar or even a cutlass, must have been useful when facing fearful odds.

One of the most widely-used combinations was the hunting *Hanger-pistol,* which is said to have been used for giving the *coup-de-grâce* to a wounded animal: one wonders if it was also used the other way round. Even better known, however, was the *Bowie-knife pistol,* an example of which may be seen in the Wadsworth Atheneum, Hartford, Conn. A patent for this weapon, according to Mr. Blair, was taken out by George Elgin of Georgia and a number were made by C. B. Allen of Springfield, who had his blades from the Ames Manufacturing Company, and by the firm of Morrill, Mosman and Blair, of Amherst, makers of both the blades and the pistols. There was also a group of *Cutlass-pistols,* a consignment of which were ordered by the U.S. Navy in 1837 for the United States South Sea Exploring Expedition.

Mr. Winant [RL 251] offers guidance to collectors in this field. His repertoire includes such intriguing items as pistols combined with KNIVES, WALKING STICKS, flashlights, purses, ploughs, whips, BICYCLE handlebars, stirrups, keys, pipes, belts, sundials. He even shows us, as a development of the 'gonne shield' of sixteenth century England, a cuirass, to be fastened round the body, which is equipped with nineteen cartridge pistols weighing thirty pounds and capable of being fired in batteries: the maker of this human arsenal also thoughtfully provided the wearer with a pair of stirrups, each of which contained two pistols, dischargeable by pulling a strap. What one's horse was expected to do while all this was going on is not clear.

FORE-EDGE PAINTING You may one day be astonished to find yourself handling a book which until that moment had appeared to be quite an ordinary book, with a gilt edge, and then unexpectedly showed a picture on the edges of the pages.

This is an example of fore-edge painting. It is managed by slightly fanning out the leaves so that the gilt edge no longer appears, clamping it fast, and then painting your picture on the new edge thus presented.

Decoration was given to the fore-edges of books in Renaissance times, but the art was systematically revived about the year 1785 by the BOOKBINDING family of William Edwards of Halifax and his five sons. Some attractive work of this kind has been done ever since and examples frequently appear in the salerooms.

Since the collector himself, if he wishes, can add a fore-edge painting to a book it will be obvious that one of the problems facing him is how to distinguish between genuine examples from the eighteenth and nineteenth centuries and those which have been added to old books in modern times. Some do not care, of course, for a good picture is, after all, a good picture whenever it was painted. But if he *does* want old work his only real remedy is to study the kind of pictures which are likely to have been painted a century and more ago.

James Thomson's 'The Seasons' with a fore-edge painting in water-colour of Richmond Bridge, Surrey.

GONGS AND BELLS I wonder that psychotherapists have not discovered the necessity of gongs to humanity. For me any film made by the Rank Organisation is worth seeing— for the first three minutes. That opening sequence where a strong man stripped to the waist takes up a hammer and beats an enormous gong, is a deeply satisfying experience: what follows is almost always anticlimactic.

101

Presentation campanologist's set of thirty-one handbells, dated 1874.

The great gong makers lived in the Orient, especially in China, Japan and Java. Their gongs vary enormously in range of tone and volume, but they were usually of bronze hammered and hardened to provide the exact note and tone required. Not all of them are circular—there is a Burmese triangular form of polished metal; others are flat and of irregular shapes, moulded and inscribed. Many of them are not immediately recognisable as gongs, but they all obey the main requirement of the instrument, which is that it can be hung up and lambasted with a leather-covered wooden mallet.

A gong in the British Museum is four feet high and typical of those hanging under the verandahs of Buddhist temples in China, used for summoning the bonzes to service: the striker has to aim at the boss at the foot. The inscription reads:

> '*In the reign of Tao Kuang of the Great Ch'ing dynasty, in the cyclical year jen-ch'en (A.D. 1832) on the fortunate day of the first new moon, the retired scholar Miae Yin together with the Prior of*

102

the Monastery, the Bhikshu Kuo Chien, reverently made this. Vows were recited praying that the merits of the makers of this instrument might last through the whole kalpa, and that every hearer of its tuneful melody might ultimately attain the Buddhahood. Om! Tana! Tana! Katana! Svaha!'

Everyone, of course, will agree; and one hopes that its hearers responded to its call as enthusiastically as do those summoned to 'come and get it' by the iron triangle or the old beef can of the forest camp.

Of all the unofficial gongs I ever heard the most effective was one which each morning was used to restore to their barracks or their ships soldiers or sailors resting in one of those estimable places where servicemen are allowed to lay down their buzzing heads after the closing of inns and taverns. Its wielder, with malicious glee, would come stealthily into the dormitory at dawn, or a little before, bearing a large and rusty tin tray and an iron soup ladle: with these he would suddenly produce the most shattering sound that audience ever heard.

Bells have been used for every purpose from announcing the whereabouts of cows and sheep to proclaiming the Glory of God and great victories. Legends surround them and many are said to have miraculous powers, like the *Clog na Fola,* or Bell of Blood, one of fifty presented by St. Patrick himself to churches of Connaught. The O'Rorkes mysteriously came into possession of it and they would lend it out to neighbours (at a small charge naturally) for help in detecting those who had stolen their property.

There are pairs of small shrill bells for hawks, one a semitone lower than the other, as recommended by Dame Juliana Berners; flat melancholy cowbells and sheepbells; 'low bells' for catching birds by night; stridently urgent bells for fire-engines (some of them double); there are ship's bells, which sound the watches—and get so lovingly 'warmed' by liberty-men in their impatience to get ashore. Collectors of HORSE BRASSES look also for bell-terrets; and frequently seen at sales are the bells which gave way to horn and the klaxon in warning of the approach of Veteran and Vintage cars.

But all these gongs and bells if collected, must be banged or rung. I find it heartbreaking to think of the number which languish in museums eternally silent.

Or could it be that on moonlight nights, long after the last visitor has gone, museum keepers and curators steal on noiseless toe back into their galleries and hold great concerts far into the night?

GORGETS Where MILITARIA is sold you will sometimes see a small crescent-shaped piece of metal, usually silver-gilt, engraved with the Royal Arms, or perhaps a regimental badge. These sometimes very decorative articles are descendants of the piece of ARMOUR called a gorget, which, as its name conveys, was intended to protect the neck. It was still a serious piece of armour in Cromwellian times, as part of the breastplate; and this period yields the most splendid gorgets of any. When you are in Paris look at the magnificently embossed silver gorget in the Musée de l'Armée which was worn by Louis XIII of France.

In the next century the gorget gradually became smaller and smaller until it was not so much a vestigial piece of armour as a badge of rank, worn just below the high collar of an officer's

Left: *two Georgian officers' silver and gilt gorgets and two Victorian cavalry officers' silver and brass flap pouches.* Opposite: *Milanese sixteenth century gorget and breastplate, deeply embossed with battle scenes.*

tunic. The earlier types are perhaps eight inches or so deep, but by the end of their day, in late Regency times, they had diminished until they were no more than four inches long by about three inches deep. The insignia was sometimes in silver against a gilt or steel background, or in gilt on copper.

Both British and American agents gave them to Red Indian chiefs as badges of honour, but later these types degenerated into mere ornaments. In World War II, they were worn by the German *Feldgendarmerie* and other organisations, and so have become collected as Nazi relics.

A hint of the gorget is to be seen even more vestigially in the crescent-shaped variety of HORSE BRASSES.

GRANGERISING Or 'Every Man His Own Publisher'. If you like plenty of pictures in books, why not put them in yourself?

The art of grangerising, or extra-illustration, has been going on now for very nearly two hundred years. You will some-times see the fruit of it in immensely swollen volumes crammed with prints, cuttings, letters and other material, all relating, or purporting to relate, to the subject matter of the book. Some of them fetch large sums of money, others are useful only as mounting blocks to help you climb to your top bookshelves.

It all started with a Rev. James Granger, Vicar of Shiplake, in Oxfordshire, England, who in 1769 published *A Biographical History of England, from Egbert the Great to the Revolution*. The book was an enormous success, and it set a fashion for finding an engraved portrait for every one of the 2,500 or more person-ages, from Egbert downwards, who appeared in its six volumes. As a result, prices of portrait prints soared, and thousands of books were gutted for their illustrations: during the last two centuries bibliophiles coming across a mutilated book have muttered savagely, 'A Grangerite's been here, rot his soul!'

Nowadays the Grangerite may set to work with a clear conscience for, as one may see from the stacks of single prints in bookshops and on stalls, most of the books have already been gutted.

Is there a place for Grangerising today? More than ever I

106

Grangerised volume of 'Haunted London', by Thornbury, showing an interleaved engraving of 1750 of the Royal Academy.

should have thought. As modern science advances, so illustrated books, especially coloured ones, get more and more expensive. What is more fun than to take a fine travel book and extra-illustrate it with pictures from the travel magazines. How interesting to embellish biographies of stage, film and TV stars with stills. What an opportunity for your connoisseur of the fine arts to divorce the fine picture reproduction in art books from the shocking rubbish of the texts of many of them, and marry the illustrations with the work of fine critics like R. H. Wilenski?

Grangerising isn't, of course, merely a matter of sticking pictures in a book. If you do this it will look like a sack of potatoes and eventually come apart. A true Grangerite makes an elegant job of it by taking the book to pieces—two copies are needed, to show the print on both sides of the page. You paste the pages down carefully on sheets of suitable paper, preferably in fours or eights, to facilitate binding; you then extra-illustrate to your heart's content, adding 'signatures' of four or eight pages as required, finally sending your work when finished (if you live to finish it) to the binder.

The outstanding exponent of Grangerising in America was Dr. Emmet, who filled 150 books with letters, documents and illustrative materials of all kinds. He also brought into this field the associated one of AUTOGRAPHS; his four 'signer' sets, three of which are in the New York Public Library, are bound into books with prints, portraits and other associated material (in doing which, of course, he trod dangerously near the territory of the collector of ASSOCIATION ITEMS).

To achieve something really worth while in your Grangerising, always extra-illustrate a particular subject—and keep firmly to that subject. Otherwise you are compiling a scrapbook.

GUNS AND RIFLES   Neither pieces of ordnance nor any kind of artillery, such as we find under CANNON, come within this canon. Guns, as we understand them here, are missile weapons which use explosives, air or gas (on one unique occasion, steam) and which are held in the hand: rifles, in addition, have spiral grooves (*cf.* the German *riffeln,* to groove) to spin the projectile and so obtain greater accuracy of aim.

The first *Hand-gun* appeared about the end of the fourteenth century and was at first an iron tube with a rod extension behind for holding under the arm or a wooden stock bound into a socket. There was a touch-hole and a priming pan over the breech, and to this, holding the gun stock with your left hand, and tucking the butt under your shoulder, you applied a piece of smouldering tinder or a slow match with your right hand. The recoil must have been devastating; and to avoid your being thrown back over the other side of the battlements the gun had a hook fixed near the muzzle which you could clamp against a parapet or some other support: such *Hook-guns* gave us the terms *Hakenbüchse,* or 'Hook Box' in Germany. *Hackbut* or *Hagbut* in England and *Harquebus* in France A specimen sold recently is mentioned in CURRENT PRICES.

This name was, in fact, awarded to the first *Matchlock* guns, which improved the primitive means of ignition by having a pivoted 'S'-shaped lever (or serpentine) pinned to the outside of the stock, one end holding the lighted match and the other acting as a trigger. This was later made more effective by a complicated arrangement of levers and catches worthy of a locksmith or a watchmaker—which, in fact, many a gunmaker was.

By the middle of the sixteenth century the matchlock had found its widest use in the *Musket,* but this weapon was still so heavy it had to be fired from a *reston,* a 'U'-shaped support mounted on a wooden pole nearly as long as the gun; you also required a bandolier carrying a number of wooden cylinders each containing a charge of gunpowder, a bag of lead balls, a large POWDER FLASK for replenishing the wooden receptacles with coarse or 'corn' gunpowder, and a smaller one for the finer priming charge.

Thus festooned, you poured a charge down the barrel, sent a ball down after it, followed by a piece or two of wadding, and rammed all this down with a rod. You then filled the priming pan with the finer powder, took from under your cap, or behind your ear, a lighted slow match of impregnated hemp which had been burning merrily there, and placed it in the cock. Providing there had so far been no premature explosion, you pressed the trigger hopefully, there was a tremendous noise and flash, and the ball went flying off on its journey. This, roughly, was the weapon of *The Three Musketeers*—from which one realises the importance which Porthos attached to his symbolic 'walking out' baldric.

Although the matchlock musket was heavy and laborious to load, it could penetrate armour at close range with ease; furthermore, its thunder and lightning terrified the contemporary natives of the overseas countries which Europe was at that time busily conquering. Imitations of it, to the great delight of modern collectors, were made in India and elsewhere: the Japanese, having evolved a revolving matchlock with short barrels each having its own priming pan, were so proud of it that they went on making it into the nineteenth century.

But the matchlock hated rain almost as much as the old hand-gun; and as a great deal of fighting occurred in Europe, where a drizzle or a downpour is never very far off, the

109

Gun with combined match and wheel lock and walnut stock in the German fashion, inlaid with ornament of engraved stag's horn showing bear and stag hunts and antique horsemen fighting. German, about 1565. Length $46\frac{1}{10}$ inches overall.

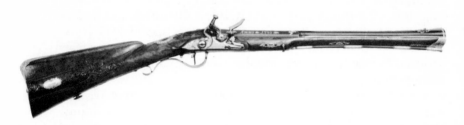

Flintlock blunderbuss circa 1780 by Johan Adolf Grecke, born 1755, a Swede who was court gunmaker at St. Petersburg. The barrel is octagonal at the breech, then round, and flares to a flattened trumpet-shaped muzzle. The oval scutcheon plate of blued steel is damascened in gold with the crowned cypher of the Empress Catherine II, by whom it was owned.

Flintlock rifle circa 1805 by Nicolas Noel Boutet of Versailles (1761–1833) one of the outstanding figures in the history of gunmaking and renowned for his finely decorated guns and rifles. This one has an octagonal barrel with multi-grooved rifling, the surface is matt blue powdered with gold stars; all mounts are stamped with a petite garantie or census mark.

German gunsmiths, then the most ingenious mechanics in the world, produced a firing device which eliminated the match-lock. The *Wheel-lock* was not unlike the modern cigarette lighter, whereby a wheel of hardened steel was spun round against a piece of iron pyrites or flint and produced a spark, which would fall into the opened priming pan and thus ignite the primer and set off the charge. At first this wheel was wound by a key or spanner (some of which are extremely decorative—see LOCKS AND KEYS), later by a self-winding mechanism: one shown in the notebooks of Leonardo da Vinci—who may well have invented the device—has been reconstructed and found to work very well.

For a long while after the *Flintlock* became the most popular weapon of the chase the Military—perhaps for reasons of economy, perhaps from conservatism—stuck to the matchlock system of ignition. Thus it is that when our musketeer friends were defending their famous breakfast in the bastion of St. Gervais at La Rochelle, they probably used matchlock muskets instead of the flintlocks which they would have taken on a hunting trip: whereas a generation later, when the real-life D'Artagnan fell with a bullet hole through his head at Maastricht—by the side of the young John Churchill, later to be the great Duke of Marlborough, and the even younger Duke of Monmouth, later to die on the scaffold for treason—it was no doubt a flintlock which took the life of the captain of Louis XIV's brave musketeers.

About this time the military arm acquired a bayonet, first the plug, tucked in the muzzle, then the socket: sometimes a sword-bayonet was preferred.

This was the great era of decoration on arms. Hunting, the prerogative of the nobleman, called for noble weapons, and these the gunsmiths provided, using all the arts learnt in other spheres. They first made use of designs by artists like Jost Ammant, Peter Flotener and Virgil Solis, produced for large standing cups and bowls by the goldsmiths and silversmiths, adapting them to the shape of lock or the sweep of a stock. Later, with the increased demand for new patterns, books of ornament containing designs specifically for firearms were issued—Parisian artists were especially productive here, as one

111

might expect from their work in other fields. Many of the engravers took working 'pulls' or prints of the designs they had carried out on weapons, and these have survived in some quantity, and may be inspected, for example, at the Victoria and Albert Museum.

In the sixteenth century the German makers were well to the fore in all this work, the products of the Munich school being especially famous; but in the next century the French masters produced work of extraordinary delicacy and refinement. The pierced and engraved work of the Italian schools at, for example, Brescia, with subjects of animals, birds, monsters and other figures, and florid baroque scrollwork, shows great skill in chiselling in high relief. This appears with even more elaboration in the workshops of Southern Italy and with charming *naiveté* in the art of the village blacksmiths and locksmiths around the main centres. Those who enjoy the beauties of wood will also find themselves attracted to the fine walnut stocks, where the figuring is heightened by slight charring over a flame, thus giving contrasts of light and dark; also in the ingenious and well-judged inlay of all kinds of materials.

In the Orient, particularly in India and Japan, the matchlock was in use long after it had been superseded here, and collectors take the greatest interest in these weapons: Japanese firearms are usually decked out in brilliant colours, making great use on stocks of the lacquer for which the decorators of that country are famous, while the russet iron barrels are often inlaid with gold and silver. In India, too, there was much use of elaborate inlay of intricate foliage and trellis work, with colourful painting on stocks.

At the other end of the artistic scale, but now a popular collector's piece, is the trade gun, made by the Birmingham gunsmiths with the local talent for exploiting the cheaper end of any market. Painted a pillar-box red to take the eye of the natives, they were shipped to Africa in great quantities in the eighteenth century for trading against slaves. Such guns were still being shipped to Kenya in this century for use by native hunting parties.

Given the wheel-lock principle the inventive gunmakers found all manner of ways in which to adapt it. One was the

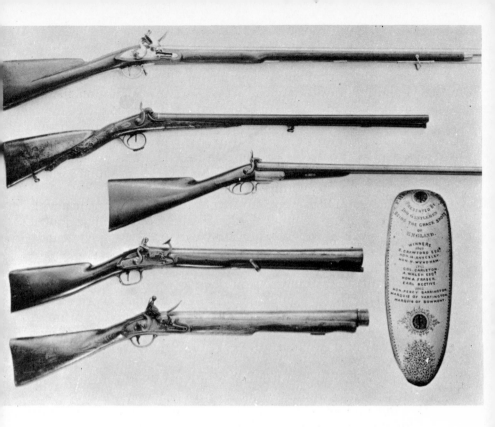

From top to bottom: 'Brown Bess' ·75 flintlock musket, 55 inches overall, barrel 39 inches with military proof marks, brass mounts.
Double barrelled 12 bore percussion sporting gun, 46 inches overall, with damascus barrels 30 inches long; by Ronge Fils of Liège.
Double-barrelled presentation 12 bore under lever pinfire sporting gun, 46 inches overall length, by J. Purdy, London, 'presented by 100 gentlemen, being the crack shots of England'. An enlargement is shown of the silver butt plate.
Late seventeenth century snaphance blunderbuss, 38 inches overall, with half octagonal bell mouth.
Mid-eighteenth century military flintlock musketoon, the seventeenth century brass barrel 23 inches long, by I. Brush; octagonal breech with strawberry-leaf engraving; lock engraved Crown and GR and 'Newton 1759'.

113

Snaphance lock, a kind of intermediary between the wheel-lock and the flintlock, which in fact was a reversal of its predecessor, in that instead of the flint being laid on the rotating steel, it was held in the jaws of a cog which was brought down on to a rough piece of steel pivoted over the priming pan. Thus its name, which seems to come from a Dutch word meaning 'pecking fowl'. This lock was used widely throughout Europe, especially in the northern countries.

The gunsmiths were also adept in combining the gun with other weapons to produce FIREARMS CURIOSA; while a double wheel-lock gave a double-barrelled gun, or a single barrel could be made to fire a number of shots in a volley. Another variation produced shots in series: you could have separate locks firing each one as you desired, or you could use balls with holes fired through them and filled with powder, so that once one had been fired all the rest would ignite and fire in turn: some poured out as many as sixteen shots. Mr. Pepys saw one of these contrivances at Lord Sandwich's one day . . . 'there were several people by trying a new fashioned gun brought by my Lord this morning, to shoot off often, one after another, without trouble or danger, very pretty.'

But multiple firing on even this scale did not satisfy some, for this series firing could be combined with mechanism for giving an interval for altering aim. The effect was rather like that of a modern machine-gun, with the exception that, since there were, as the song says, no means of stopping it, one had to be sure that hostilities had not ended before all shots had appeared from all barrels.

Most famous of the English flintlocks was the 'Brown Bess', perhaps named after its acid-brown barrel. This was England's first standard infantry musket, and it could fire at a rate of two or three rounds a minute—much faster than the matchlock. This was the weapon of Marlborough's later wars.

For sporting and military weapons, the long barrel was a necessity—although there had always been shorter pieces such as the *Petronel* and the cavalryman's *Carbine*—for other purposes length could be a handicap. In naval fighting, for example, when weapons had to be used at close quarters, something handier was required with a larger bore, and the same kind of

114

conditions obtained in providing protection to travellers by coach. Hence the *Blunderbuss,* which takes its name from the Dutch *Donderbuse,* a 'thunder box'. It was a short gun, usually with a bell-mouthed barrel, loaded with a charge of lead slugs which fanned out in a deadly fashion at close quarters.

Meanwhile the principle of rifling, which had been known and used in Germany as far back as the early sixteenth century, began to offer serious competition to the smooth-bore. At first, like the flintlock, it was used for sporting guns, where accuracy was more desirable than massed fire-power. There were initial handicaps: the bullets had to be made by the user and loading took twice as long. But with shallower grooves and standardisation, the rifled barrel gradually took over supremacy.

Among the earliest of the flintlock rifles was the hunting weapon taken to America by the German settlers in Pennsylvania: the famous native-made Lancaster Valley and Kentucky rifles which derived from these were, in the hands of backwoodsmen guerillas, to be used with great effect in the War of Independence. They eventually obliged the British Government to resort to the use of Continental troops equipped with rifles, but nothing they had equalled the Kentucky for range, accuracy and lightness.

Britain raised a Rifle Brigade in 1800, and the Baker flintlock did well at Waterloo against the French *tirailleurs.* But it was many years before the rifle was generally adopted for military use in all countries; not, in fact, until the invention of the percussion ignition—after gunpowder the most important step forward in firearms. Alexander Forsyth, a Scottish clergyman, was its inventor; his lock, as he said, 'produces inflammation by means of percussion, and supersedes the use of flints'.

There is no room here to mention all the famous rifles which have succeeded each other from the nineteenth century. Well-known in Britain are the Brunswick, with its two deep grooves and belted ball; the Minie, with its conical bullet; the Enfield, the Snider, the Martini-Henri, the Lee-Metford, the Lee-Enfield; in the United States, the great 'Models' from the National Armoury at Springfield, Mass., the Winchester and the rest. The early part of the story has been well told [RL 248, 251]; and the gaps in the later years are rapidly being filled.

HELMETS   The helmet has two functions: to protect the head and to demonstrate status and rank as a fighting man; and some of them do both. One of the fascinating aspects of ARMOUR is to note how the helmet started life in the first of these offices, then, with the development of firearms, became an expression of grandeur, pomp or authority. In the present century, however, it suddenly swung back to its original use: if the steel helmet is the last vestige of ARMOUR, it is still by no means a thing of the past.

In fact, as Sir James Mann has pointed out [RL 248] there are direct links between some of the types of mediaeval steel helmets and the 'tin hats' of today. The British-American helmet of World War I, apparently the invention of a Mr. Brodie, was clearly a revival of the broad-brimmed *War Hat* of the thirteenth and fifteenth centuries, worn by the English foot-sloggers at Agincourt and called by them the *Kettle Hat,* no doubt because they used it for that and other domestic purposes.

The French were the first to adopt the modern steel helmet, apparently as the result of General Adrian's having observed how a man's life had been saved by his wearing a metal mess bowl in his hat: but from the beginning theirs was a *Casque,* that is to say a descendant of the classical combed helmet of the sixteenth century—still worn by the French Dragoons and perhaps crossed with the French fireman's *casque du pompier.* This hat was much less bullet-proof than the Anglo-American, but it was lighter and a good deal smarter, which counted a great deal in the morale of the *poilu.*

Much more effective in results was the German helmet, which was clearly based on the *Sallet* or *Salade,* of the fifteenth and sixteenth centuries: the German versions of that day had the graceful lobster tail: one may be seen on the head of the impudent *putto* in Botticelli's 'Mars and Venus' in the National Gallery, London. The modern version was heavier than any of its contemporaries, but more fireproof and it protected a greater area; and it is hardly surprising that versions of it have since been adopted by most of the world's armies. Snipers using it were given a frontal plate—again an idea was taken from a *Siege Helmet* of the fifteenth century. The Italians

116

followed the French model, but the Belgians, later in the war, evolved a visored one on the lines of the Dunand helmet.

The American model No. 5, based on the German hat, seems to have been designed simultaneously with, but independently of, a similar model introduced by the Swiss towards the end of a war in which that nation had no occasion to use it. But space precludes our going further along these fascinating bypaths.

No modern use seems to have been found for the conical Norman helm of the Conquest, familiar to everyone who has seen reproductions of the Bayeux Tapestry; nor for the *Barbute* —so-called, not because of any beard sported by the wearer, but from the apron of mail which hung over the wearer's mouth and chin and looked like one; nor for the *Bascinet,* a development of it and the headpiece of Froissart's Chronicles and the Hundred Years' War. The *Hounskell,* or *Pig-faced* helmet is one of the most valued today because of its rarity. Magnificos like the Black Prince wore their *Great Heaulmes,* usually with an enormous crest showing their rank and lineage; and from these distinguished or disreputable heads it went into heraldry and so on to bookplates —except for a brief revival at the hands of the famous Australian bandit and outlaw, Ned Kelly, who defied arrest for a long while and continued to kill a great many men, by wearing a kind of huge iron pot with a slit for his eyes, as well as body armour.

Another stream was started by the *Close Helmet* or *Armet,* which began as an all-over covering for use in tournaments, but about the beginning of the sixteenth century developed its own lobster tail and also a series of grotesqueries. The English pikeman's *Pot* looked like, and was, a kind of *Burgonet,* with its peak and high comb.

Oriental influences are to be seen in European armour, for example, the *Turban Helmet* or *Zischägge* which the Poles and the Hungarians, in fighting the Turks, first copied from them, then discarded because of the confusion it caused in battle. There are many interesting cross-references of this kind—for example, the resemblance of the Indian Mahratta helmets to the Phrygian caps of the Greeks (and of the *sans-culottes* in the French Revolution); also the Japanese adaptation of the *Cabasset* or 'Spanish Morion .

117

Armet. Italian, mid-fifteenth century. The cheek-pieces are hinged at the top, the left overlapping the right in front, the lower edge being holed for the attachment of a camail. The sight is formed by the gap between the upper edge of the visor and the brow.

Sallet. German, circa 1450–60, ancestor of some modern steel helmets. Here the sight is provided by a horizontal slit cut in front. The rivets are for the attachment of the lining strap. There are two marks, one a fleur-de-lys, which is perhaps a guild or arsenal mark, and what looks like a crowned 'P', possibly the armourer's mark.

(Below)
Visored bascinet, probabl made in Milan about 139 1410, head-piece of Froissa Chronicles and the Hund Years' War. The poin apex to the skull and vi offered a glancing surfa The mail aventail—or cam —does not actually belong the helmet.

(Below)
War hat, German (Augsberg sixteenth century, known b its wearers, the infantry, as kettle hat, and ancestor another type of modern helme With a narrower brim it cou be thought of as a precursor the 'Spanish' morion.

(Below)
...uirassier's close helmet, with ...aked visor, early seventeenth ...ntury, probably German. ...he front is pierced with ...sette decoration, the skull ...ated with roped bands, and ...ere are four-piece neck lames ...ith scalloped edges.

(Below)
Casque, Italian, circa 1540–1560. Of classical form, with high Roman comb and chased with gadrooned ornament. The skull is boldly embossed with a lion's mask in front; the pointed peak and neck-guard are in one piece with the skull; the ear-pieces are missing.

Comb morion, circa 1600, the sides heavily embossed with foliate decoration having traces of gilding. The skull is formed in two halves.

Burgonet of the Zischägge type, Hungarian or Polish, circa 1630–40, following a Turkish style. The front of the hemispherical skull turns outwards to form a small peak and is pierced for a nasal guard now missing but for its butterfly nut. The hinged cheek pieces are in three plates, the lower two of which are restorations, as is the pointed neck guard.

HISPANO-MORESQUE WARES If pottery can attain nobility this quality is surely seen in the wares decorated in iridescent lustre and colours which were made in Spain by Moorish potters during and after the domination by the Moslem kings.

At first in Malaga, and later in Valencia and Aragon, these great dishes, some of them embellished with heraldic designs, brought the glowing fire of golden, greenish or copper lustres into the halls of the Moorish potentates, and later into those of the Spaniards who drove them back to Africa.

The wares also found their way, apparently by sea through Majorca, to the Italian potting centres of Deruta and Gubbio, where they inspired—and gave a name to—the great race of *maiolica* wares of Italy. Iridescent wares are still being produced at Manisses, in Valencia, one of the earliest centres.

The most beautiful of the old wares came from Valencia, at first showing the arabesques of Moorish work at Malaga, then a great deal of calligraphic painting with a quill pen which looks like Arabic writing. After follows the fine class of heraldic animals on grounds diapered with petalled flowers arranged in dots and circles; also creatures such as the eagle of Ycart or

Hispano-Moresque armorial dish painted in blue and yellow lustre. Diameter 17 inches, Valencia, fifteenth century.

Ricart shown here, of about 1450, with bold foliage in a blue and lustre style. There followed a rich development of many different floral styles, extraordinarily delicate and beautifully organised, with or without shields of arms. Of forms, the most outstanding are the great dishes and bowls, but there are also vases and APOTHECARIES' JARS.

If you have a dark panelled room, and a taste for candlelight, it is worth discovering for yourself what such an environment will do for these magnificent pots.

HORNS

The horn, the horn, the lusty horn
Is not a thing to laugh to scorn.

On the contrary; it is one of the most interesting and varied, and also perhaps oldest of instruments. Even at this late date you can go to the nearest slaughterhouse or abattoir, as we now call it, and begin your collection with the wreathed horn which old Triton blew as trumpeter to his father, Neptune; although no doubt his was a conch shell adapted for the purpose. The horn carried by that absent-minded shepherd Little Boy Blue was no doubt a sheep's horn with the tip removed; but it was perhaps the Cow with the Crumpled Horn which started the idea of the coiled *Hunting Horn*. This seems to have developed into the orchestral *French Horn* via the *cor de chasse* or *waldhorn*; and I gather that you could get by in a modern orchestra with an eighteenth-century model of one of these.

But the sound calculated to awaken us from the dead, which brought us all from our beds in the days of John Peel—and perhaps also that which Kathleen Mavourneen was implored to awake and hear—was seemingly quite a different affair. This English hunting horn was (and is) a simpler, straighter thing, much fewer musical demands being made upon it than in France, where huntsmen communicated with each other by an elaborate range of signals.

Straight and simple also is the English version of the *Posthorn* or *Coach-horn*—and damned difficult they are to blow, especially at the age of nine, as I discovered with the one which my grandfather kept in his livery stables and blew to announce his

121

coming up to the house for dinner.

The echoing horn which roused the rude forefathers of the hamlet was perhaps of the kind which is still blown today every evening in the Yorkshire town of Ripon, so that citizens who still don't really believe the radio time signals can set their watches right. Such ancient ceremonial horns were everywhere used in community life in former days, and they appear —alas, so often with no indication of their origin—in salerooms.

The horns of Elfland faintly blowing, sweet and far from cliff and scar, might have been the postman's horns of the last century: in those geophysical circumstances, however, they would hardly have been the horns still used by canal-boat folk as they pass under bridges—one of which I saw come up at a sale the other day. There is also, it appears, a horn which is used for recalling truffle-hunting pigs from their rooting operations. The Dor tribe of the Upper Nile area has a sideblown horn, and one sometimes sees ivory fetish horns ornamented with human skulls from juju houses in Southern Nigeria—but perhaps this is taking us too far into ETHNOGRAPHICA.

If you live at the other end of the valley from that chap, guy or *type* who collects GONGS AND BELLS you should get yourself an eleven-foot *Alphorn*. Their blowing length is actually no more than that of the modern orchestral horn, but it is to be remembered that with the latter the tube is coiled round whereas with the former it sticks straight out in front—and needs a great deal more blow. Made of wood, the alphorn unfortunately plays only the harmonics of its tube; but as it is not exactly in tune with the commonly accepted scale of today, it should make an effective riposte to almost any musical neighbour. For calling in the cows with it, however, you should learn one of the many local *ranz des vaches* or cow songs, the most celebrated of which comes from the district of Gruyère. It celebrates the story of the *armaillis,* the men who live all the summer in the high mountains, milking the cows sent there by the peasants in the valleys, and making that highly grateful cheese which goes down so well with biscuits and Châteauneuf.

If you want to play the tune on some other instrument, you will find the score in the first edition of Grove's *Dictionary of Music*: there are versions of some others in, for example, the

122

pipe of the shepherd in *Tristan* in the *William Tell* overture, and at the opening of the last movement of Beethoven's Pastoral Symphony. But it appears that it is highly inadvisable to play a *ranz des vaches* if you have a valued Swiss cook or housemaid, for according to James Boswell (in his 'Johnson') it 'instantly and irresistibly excites in the Swiss, when in a foreign land, the *maladie du pays*'. This is confirmed by Rousseau in his *Dictionary of Music* (1767) who, no doubt referring to the Swiss *landsknechts* and other mercenaries whom we meet under SWORDS, says it was 'forbidden upon pain of death to play it among the troops, because it caused those who heard it to burst into tears, to desert or to die—so much did it arouse in them the longing to see their country again'.

Perhaps it would be safer to buy a Swiss *horn*: stuff the open end with grass and it makes a milk strainer; after milking time remove the grass and through it you may sing a benediction song to the herd as it winds slowly out into the night. This could interest the neighbours too.

I have no more horns to offer—apart from those variations of it which have been used with such delight by composers of the last two hundred years, especially Mozart and Beethoven. There are a few non-horns which the purist collector will want to avoid. The basset-horn is a member of the clarinet family, perhaps so-called because it was a 'little bass' clarinet made by a man named Horn; the *English horn* or *cor anglais* is an oboe; and Browning's *Slughorn* (*cf.* Chatterton's *sluggehorn*) is an etymological misunderstanding. He (or they) mixed it up with a *slogghorn* or battle cry—which, come to think of it, would make an interesting subject for a collector of MILITARIA.

And as I go to press I make the acquaintance of Mr. Baines' learned editorship [RL 252], which adds to my list of non-horns the *Crumhorn*. It dates from the 1500s and is apparently a cross between the recorder and the bagpipes: my more musical readers will be delighted to know that some modern German makers are now reviving it.

HORSE BRASSES Here survive the amulets and other adornments with which men of classical, mediaeval and

123

Renaissance times proudly decorated their horses. While the GORGET is the last remnant of steel body-ARMOUR, the face-piece with a raised boss is perhaps a memory of the projecting spike in a rosette on the forehead of the warhorse shown on page 27.

There are real horse brasses made for horses to wear and there are also souvenir brasses, stamped out in their hundreds of thousands for the tourist trade; and the collector who seeks the genuine article will need to educate both his eye and his hand.

With the first true horse brass the face-piece, or face-brass, either had a boss or was a plain disc or 'flash'—some held that it was there, like the ancient amulets, to protect the horse from the 'evil eye'. There were also crescents, and other simple shapes, perhaps having some similar significance.

Then, somewhere about the eighteen thirties—one wonders if there is significance in the fact that makers of gorgets for the Military went out of business at about this time—there began to appear a whole range of brasses cast in moulds. Most of them were in calamine brass, showing pitting and a coarse texture: better sorts were in Prince's metal, an alloy resembling pinchbeck which is said to have been invented by Prince Rupert, the Cavalier leader. They could be cast in sharper relief and given a fine golden finish, and were used for the horses of owners of estates, or for commemorations, for example of the coronation of Queen Victoria.

Cast brasses may usually be identified by traces of the 'gets' on their backs. These were small projections allowed for in the mould which enabled the finisher to fix them securely in his vice so that he could file away excrescences and generally sharpen up the casting: after this he either filed down the 'gets' or removed them altogether—though there is usually some trace left. When copies are taken from old brasses these files marks are no longer sharp and clear.

These were the early days of brasses, heavy in weight and bearing the handwriting of the craftsman. There is not much difficulty in distinguishing them from the much lighter ones which the brassfounders started stamping out by machine in thinner-gauge metal about the year 1870. They show the

*Double fly terret, with ring of
bells and coloured plumes;
martingales, 'composed' with
horse subject brasses.*

pattern in relief on the back and have a much finer texture
than the old, the alloy having been improved.

This was the era of the greatest expansion, when all kinds of
new patterns which would have been too expensive to produce
by the old method were now available to the carter and the
drayman, which he could buy from his saddler made up on
leathers or laid out for his choice on stalls at country fairs.

Other metals were sometimes used. There are 'brasses' of
silver, which were specially popular for the carriage horses of
gentlemen in Denmark and Sweden; they were also made in
'German silver', an alloy of copper, zinc and nickel similar to
the later nickel-plated silver—sometimes they have a boss of
copper. There are also bosses of porcelain or tinted glass.

As to the designs, it has been calculated by a well-known
collector that there may be about 2,000 patterns in all, with
minor variations and possibly about the same number of
souvenir designs.

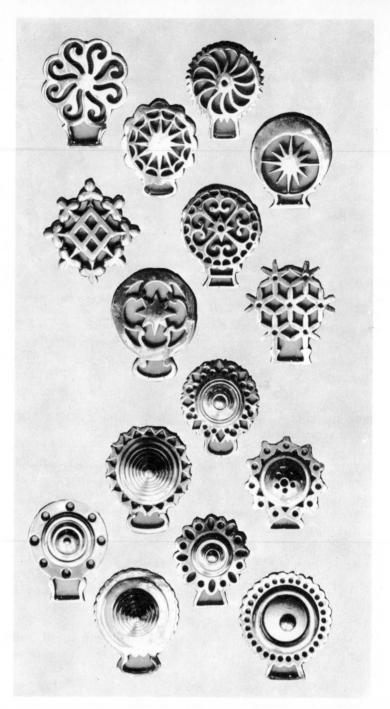

Horse brasses with 'bosses', star, diamond and wheel motifs.

Some account of them, with illustration, is given by Mr. Hartfield [RL 252]. Perhaps the most numerous are the various 'pattern' or geometrical designs where enormously varied play is made with the circle and its segments and derivations like the trefoil and the crescent; the diamond, the square and the cross; the lattice, the wavy line of heraldry and the zigzag; the polygon, the scroll and many others.

Of the subject designs, animals—and obviously the horse—predominate. The latter appears heraldically—as, for example, the Invicta and the winged horse of St. Mark—also as every version of the noble beast from a cart-horse to a racehorse; the horseshoe and the hoof are other lively motifs. The deer family is well represented, with the stag's head of the Dukes of West-minster, the white hart, with crown and chain, of Richard II, the hind and the chamois. The bear appears muzzled, collared and chained, presumably finding its way on to brasses by way of inn signs near a bull ring. But these animals may well have been taken from heraldic arms with a canting charge or rebus, i.e. a play upon the name (Beresford, Hogg, etc.).

The lion appears very frequently in all his poses, also the monkey badge of the Marmion family. The herd of elephants is led by the celebrated Jumbo. He and his consort Alice were popular figures in the London Zoo; and it took a long time for Londoners to recover from their grief and shock when he was sold to the American showmen Barnum and Bailey: this was expressed in a popular song of the day which went:

Jumbo said to Alice 'I love you,'
Alice said to Jumbo 'I don't believe you do,
If you really love me as you say you do
You would not go to Yankeeland and leave me in the Zoo.'

There are bulls and cows and many kinds of dog, including the talbot and the greyhound, while fish are represented by the dolphin. Trees, especially the oak, with the oak leaf and the acorn are often found, as well as flowers of various kinds, especially the lily. There are many kinds of birds, the swans being perhaps the most attractively designed. Of various 'objects' one may mention the sun (usually 'in splendour'), playing cards, skull and crossbones, the wheatsheaf of the corn country and the windmill of the flat lands, castles and towers,

127

bells, agricultural features such as gates, ploughs, wagons, the locomotives of railway companies, ships and anchors of dockyards and the barrels of brewers.

Of the many commemorative brasses the largest single class mark the Jubilee of Queen Victoria of 1887, but royalty appears a great deal, also many political and national figures.

Sets of brasses are still to be found on their original martingales (and many FAKES have been put on old ones). There are also various other appurtenances which the brass collector often takes into account. These include the fly terret or swinger, set with brass or bell, holding a tall brush with white or coloured bristles, also nosebands and hame pieces.

But beware of FAKES. When a wheelwright makes a wheel for a cart he 'dishes' it so that it is hollow from the outside. As George Sturt so interestingly revealed [RL 252] this is because a horse sways slightly from side to side, and if the wheel were dead vertical it would break under the strain. The wary connoisseur of horse brasses bears this fact in mind—that the horse, like a ship, rolls as well as pitches, and this leaves a characteristic kind of wear on brasses which have actually seen service on a horse. He will also look at the bottom edge of the back of the brass, where it bounces against the leather, and see if there is wear there as well.

No signs of wear at all do not necessarily indicate a fake: it may have been a perfectly genuine brass which was bought and for some reason or other never used. But there are clever fakes of the old cast brasses which sometimes puzzle even a knowledgeable collector: the only solution here is to become *very* knowledgeable.

ICONS An icon is an image: the iconology of works of art covers their subject matter or meaning, their images or symbols—as distinct from their form, colour or technique of production.

But an *Icon,* as a work of art in its own right, is a religious PICTURE—and to many people it is something considerably more. Recently and quite suddenly, and not a little mysteriously, they have aroused interest in a wider circle than that of the ordinary art collector.

First of all, what are they? The Icon, as a portrait, first

128

appeared in Byzantium, probably having developed from the tomb pictures of the Egyptians; and it followed the Christianity of the Greek Orthodox Communion as spread through the Balkan lands into Russia.

Originally icons showed representations of Christ and the Virgin Mary, and told the Bible stories in the manner later adopted by the Italian primitives. But in the Greek Church a much tighter control was exercised over the subject matter and its treatment. The artists, unlike those of Italy, were not allowed to deal with secular subjects: they were also expected to remain anonymous, to obey the rules laid down in manuals, and to live according to the precepts of the Church, so that this selfless spiritual behaviour would find expression in their work.

Image painting in this spirit, in fact, was one of the issues on which the Greek Church finally parted from the Latin: one party in Byzantium in the eighth century, who in their zeal destroyed these representations, gave us the term *iconoclast,* or image-smasher. To their opponents these images were actually holy. They argued: 'If God in his mercy could decide to reveal himself to mortal eyes in the human nature of Christ, why should he not also be willing to manifest himself in visible images?'

Physically, the icons are usually painted on wooden panels with a gesso support, perhaps on a canvas foundation. They vary a great deal in size, some being in dyptich (double), or tryptich (triple) form. There are also icons of bronze. Some of the wooden ones are large enough to be carried in processions, others are quite small, for hanging above a bed or in a corner of a room. As with contemporary PAINTINGS in the West, the medium used was egg tempera, the colours afterwards being varnished to give them depth and intensity. In the early ones the picture would have a gold or silver background, later followed by white, red, blue or green, some areas favouring one colour, and some other colours.

Their greatest development (the story of which has been well told by Tamara Talbot Rice, RL 252) was in Russia, starting from the times when Vladimir, Grand Duke of Kiev, became converted to Christianity and imported artists from Constantinople. Many of the early Russian icons were destroyed in the Mongol invasions of the thirteenth century; but the art developed strongly at Pskov, Yaroslavl and other centres, and especially at Novgorod, where named artists like Theophanes, Andrei Rublev and Dionysius became famous. Important stylistic changes came in with the Moscow school, including landscape compositions and greater naturalism. The Stroganov school, founded by a family of merchants, stemmed the tide with a return to traditionalism, and as developed in the Imperial Court circles, the movement gave rise to later miniature-style icons of great delicacy and beauty.

Professor Gombrich (whom I quote above on the apologia of the icon-makers—RL 252) has asked if the beliefs which surround the icon are magic ones, if the image on the wall really comes to life (perhaps like the ANCESTOR FIGURES mentioned under that head). The similarly hieratic and detached art of the Italian 'primitives'—Cimabue, Giotto, Duccio di Buoninsegna, Simone Martini—which are so highly regarded today, share the non-materialism and spirituality of the iconic art.

The renewed attraction of the icon, especially for the young of this generation, may well be a manifestation of the strong drive, as Professor McLuhan has noted which exists today towards 'religious experience with strong magical overtones'.

JAPANESE SWORDS AND FITTINGS

> *'Treasure swords of Japan are obtained from the East by merchants of Etsu. Their scabbards are of fragrant wood, covered with sharkskin, gold, silver; copper and metals adorn them, hundreds of gold pieces is their cost. When wearing such a sword one can slay the Barbarians.'*
> Thus Oyo Eishuku (1007–72), of the Sung Dynasty.

No race has given its SWORD so much symbolical significance, or lavished upon it so much loving craftsmanship as the Japanese. As an instrument of death it is perhaps the most deadly and effective weapon ever made by man: as a work of art it is one of the most beautiful. It is itself collected, but so are its smallest fittings; and for this reason the sword and its furniture is dealt with here apart from other SWORDS.

The various blades of Japanese swords, the forging of which

130

is always a matter of high ceremony, found their forms six or seven centuries ago, after which they did not substantially change—there was no need. The names and dates of no fewer than twelve thousand Japanese swordsmiths have come down to us, and we can read many of their signatures on the tangs of the blades they forged. We also know either the names, or the schools or families to which they belonged, of four thousand of the artists who provided the swords with their furniture.

The Japanese connoisseur usually finds his first delight in examining according to a set formula the twelve different sections of the subtly forged blade, handling it vertically in front of him and looking for flaws, form and workmanship in the forging, the sharpness of the hardened razor-like edge, and the *mei* or signature on the tang. Then only does he turn to the sword furniture—which holds the greatest interest for Western collectors, mainly for the forms of its decoration.

Swords made before 1600, at the end of the long period of civil war, are called *Koto* ('old swords'); those of rather later date *kinkoto* ('near-old swords'); and those made after this *shinto* ('new swords'). The *samurai,* or professional warrior, wore two swords when in action, the longer *tachi* and the shorter *tanto*; when without his armour he wore the long two-handled *katana* and a shorter 'companion sword', the *wakizashi*. Sometimes there is a short dirk called *aikuchi*.

The component parts of the furniture are explained in the caption to our picture; but there is a whole range of terms to identify the different forms of decoration. *Sentoku* is an alloy of copper, tin and lead, and zinc, which may be a yellowish bronze and gold but comes out after treatment as a very beautiful and unique black. *Shibuichi* is an alloy of copper and silver which after pickling can turn from a yellowish hue to shades of silvery grey.

Great attention is paid to various kinds of grounds: *nanako* (fish roe) shows a series of raised dots; *ishime* and *tsuchine* show a roughened surface produced by beating; *yasurime* are marks made with a file.

The new collector, either of the swords themselves or their furniture, will need to familiarise himself with variations in the

131

Top: *tsuba, or sword guards.*
Below: *Parts of a Japanese sword:* (left to right) *hilt (tsuka),
collar (fuchi), pommel (kashira), washer (seppa), guard (tsuba),
washer (seppa), rivet (mekugi), blade (Hon-tsukuri type), tang
collar (habaki), scabbard (saya) with tying cord (sage-o), and
scabbard knife (kodzuka).*

work of the different masters and their schools and periods. It will help him enormously—as in collecting any other form of Japanese art—if he studies the national approach to æsthetics, which differs entirely from that of the West. He will also find it necessary—and extremely rewarding—to learn something of the iconology of the subject—the literary and religious symbols and allusions which are so richly expressed in Japanese art. In this he may find some help from Mr. Turk [RL 252].

KNIVES

A Schefeld thwytel bare he in his hose,
Rond was his face and camois was his nose.

In fact the Sheffield *Whittle* as worn by Chaucer's character with the camois nose, seems to have been at once the descendant of the Anglo-Saxon *Scramasax* (which we also meet in its longer form as a SWORD) and the ancestor of that type of all-purpose stabbing, slashing, dissecting blade, equally useful for cutting up an onion or *whittling* a stick, which culminated in the world-famous, notorious and extremely beautiful American *Bowie knife* (it was a snub nose).

The story of Colonel James Bowie of Texas has been told many times, but new ears are constantly arriving in the world ready to hear old tales. He was born in the 1790s in Logan, Kentucky, of Scottish emigrant stock and grew to be a strapping man six feet tall and 180 pounds in weight. After a career of lumbering, hunting, fighting, land-speculating and slave-running, he turned up in Texas around 1828. It is said that one day in an argument with a sheriff he was wounded when he himself was unarmed: whereupon he resolved never again to move without a thwytel in his hose. Perhaps he actually saw a Sheffield whittle and adapted the form to suit himself—George Wostenholm, the Sheffield maker, was selling them in the south-western states at this time—perhaps he invented the shape all over again, by instinct, like the Anglo-Saxons. But in this knife he gave the world two highly versatile WEAPONS: in its larger form (14 to 16 inches long) a sword with which you could cut off a man's head or run him through, and in its smaller (8 to 9 inches) a combined dagger, throwing knife and

133

The 'American bowie knife', by Edward Barnes and Sons, Sheffield, circa 1830–40.

general-purpose blade suitable for most of the chores of frontier life. Sheffield did, it seems, actually make knives to Bowie's orders, for Wostenholm is said to have been responsible for a dozen with pearl handles which the Colonel bought to present to his friends.

It was perhaps one of these which featured in the romantic end of Colonel James Bowie. In the war for Texan independence from the Mexicans, Bowie was in the famous Alamo fortress where the garrison of San Antonio had taken refuge from the forces of the Mexican general, Santa Anna. Although on his back with pneumonia during the battle itself, Bowie is said to have shot down assailants from his sickbed; but when the fight was over, his dead body was thrown, ignominiously and dishonourably, on a funeral pyre; and it is said that it was one of these pearl-handled knives which survived the flames to rest for many years in the collection of the Alamo Museum— from whence it disappeared, apparently by theft, only a few years ago.

After Bowie's death the fame of his knife spread far beyond the Texan country to which he also gave his name. Schools sprung up to teach the use of this knife as the finest kind of life insurance, but by about 1840 so many citizens had got into the habit of settling arguments with it that heavy fines were imposed upon those who even showed signs of drawing one out of its sheath.

We are not here directly concerned with tableware, but some of the knives used at the table in mediaeval and renaissance times seem to be the progenitors of many of the interesting shapes used in various trades and crafts. The *Matchet* or *Sword knife* found enormous use in the nineteenth century in clearing tropical forests as well as in fighting enemies, native-born and immigrant, especially in South and Central America.

A branch of the family is the *Panga* used by the terrorists (or liberators, whichever way you look at it) of the Mau-Mau in West Africa. Special knives were evolved for the glazier, the butcher, the shoemaker and other trades.

There have been *Clasp knives* or *Shut knives* since Roman times; they were of ivory or bone and by the decorative motifs seem to have been designed for the chase. The *Pen Knife,* as its name signals, was evolved for sharpening quill pens; and it is perhaps in this difficult field that the art and craft of the knifemaker receives its most exacting tests; for each blade must 'walk' easily when opening or shutting, and yet stay firmly side by side with its fellows.

That they came in infinite variety is seen in the fact that one American merchant in his catalogue of 1893 claimed to stock 1,500 different kinds of pocket knife; the volume weighed 15 pounds. Of the various implements one expects to find alongside the blades there are, to mention some only, button hooks, corkscrews, stonehooks, leather borers, tweezers, nailfiles, gimlets, saws, prickers, fleams, castrating blades, erasers, scissors, budding and grafting blades, cartridge extractors, screwdrivers, cigar forks, shackles and openers. The beak-shaped *Wharncliffe* blade apparently owes its origin to a sixteenth-century Earl of that title.

Those interested in studying the processes of making a Sheffield knife will find the whole thing set out in *The Sheffield Dialect* of Abel Bywater (1839), quoted by Mr. Himsworth [RL 252]. In Abel's account of 'ivvera thing ats dun to a knoif throot furst tot last' after describing all the processes Jooa Crocus summarises thus: 'Wa mun o did'nt owt to loise for that bit; bur o avver, let's just reckon hah menny toimes won part or anuther on em gooas throo us hands. Wa then, we'll begin wit blade makker, furst:

Blade maker	toimes	4	
Scale and Spring maker	toimes	4	
Groinder	toimes	8	
Cutler or Setters in	toimes	23	total 39

besoides a menna mooar little jobs, stitch as wettin and woipin, etc.'

135

The unquenchable collector, however, will not rest content with knives of metal. He will go to Virginia and seek out one of the reed splinters which Captain John Smith found being used by some Indian tribes there to cut up feathers for their arrows; he will visit the opposite ends of the earth to find shell knives used by the eskimos of Greenland and the inhabitants of Tierra del Fuego; he will search back in pre-history for flint knives used for ceremonial and sacrificial purposes. He will perceive the prototype of the modern serrated bread knife—which burst upon the world as a tremendously new idea in the last few decades—in the tooth-edged tusk of the sawfish, extensively used in the South Seas; he will discover in his wanderings around the pleasant valleys of ETHNOGRAPHICA knives edged with glass, with the teeth of fish and with flint.

LOCKS AND KEYS When Penelope proposed to the suitors that they should decide her fate by an archery contest, using the famous BOW of her long-lost husband Ulysses, she first had to unlock the inmost chamber where she kept the treasures of her lord.

The key was of brass, with an ivory 'grasp'. The lock was evidently a quite different affair from any we have, for to open the door:

> *'She loosed the ring and brace,*
> *Then introduced the key, and, aiming at them from without,*
> *Struck back the bolts.'*

Homer gives us here a pretty fair description of the mechanism used for a lock at that date—according to Eustathius it was the invention of the Lacedemonians. It consisted of a leather thong, having a loop ring or hook at the end, which was passed through a hole in the door, and, catching the bolt, moved it either backwards or forwards.

Locks with wooden pins on the keys to correspond with holes on the bolts—which sound to be nearer our own—were used in ancient Egypt, but since they were of wood few have survived. Something like them is known from much more recent times in Scotland: the Society of Antiquaries of that country have a wooden lock from Ronaldshay.

Collectors of today have perhaps to decide if their interest is æsthetic, mechanical or a mixture of both. Perhaps nobody has done a more thorough job in this respect than Charles Courtenay, President of the International Locksmiths Association, whose collection of 2,000 locks and 10,000 keys offers items from the world's castles and cathedrals, palaces and privies, houses and harems.

The early iron locks worked either with wards, whereby the key could not enter or turn unless it fitted these projections, or with tumblers, which the appropriate key lifted. These *Plate locks,* as their name suggests, simply had the works rivetted on to an iron plate fixed to the door or inside of a chest. The *Stock lock* improved upon this by being let into a block of wood, often reinforced with a metal plate, while with the *Rim lock* all was placed within a metal casing, to match the striking plate. The *Lever lock* with its pieces of flat metal, offered a more complicated mechanism.

Those in search of fine craftsmanship will find it here, especially in the work of the Renaissance locksmiths—many of them, no doubt, the same people who were responsible for work of ARMOUR, an industry in which there must by then have been some redundancy.

Indicating or detector lock by 'Johannes Wilkes de Birmingham' circa 1680, which registers the opening of a door.

The steel locks of the Elizabethan smiths would have their cases softened for engraving, chiselling and damascening with gold or silver wire: these, like so many other things of the kind, were imitated in the archaising spirit of Victorian times. In Carolean days openwork patterns in latten brass would be laid over blued steel, giving a rich and handsome effect. There was also a good deal of applied work in high relief like that on the *Detector lock* shown here. Crests, cyphers and coats of arms are to be found on such locks, and an ESCUTCHEON may well help to fix a date of manufacture.

Keys, apart from opportunities for brooding over the exact type of lock from which they have long been parted, offer an endless variety of patterns—and another collecting item which lends itself to display upon a flat surface: I have seen them mounted on coloured velvet in picture frames with striking effect.

Steel lock in case of pierced and engraved brass, English, circa 1650–1700, with key of a later eighteenth century style.

MAPS   Old maps make fine PICTURES. In the early ones monsters, sea gods, tritons and ships share the waters of the oceans; hills rise like sugar cones on the land and rivers sprout gods and goddesses. Later they have elaborately designed cartouches containing the titles, armorial bearings, views, town plans, vignettes of battles by land and sea, groups of persons going about their avocations.

But there is another and a deeper interest for the collector. It is difficult for us to understand how our ancestors looked at the world until one is aware of the way in which it looked to them. Old maps show us this; and a well-chosen portfolio often increases our apprehension of the unfolding of history and geography more easily than books.

They have risen in value during the last few years, but considering their age and interest they are hardly over-valued even now. For example, those of Sebastian Munster, printed from woodblocks in the sixteenth century, can still be acquired at reasonable cost. They are not great works of art but they have the charm of the primitive. The opposite may be said of the contemporary work of Abraham Ortelius, who published his attractive maps (including some fine miniatures) from the printing house of Christophe Plantin at Antwerp, which you may visit today and see exactly how a prosperous sixteenth century man lived and worked—and come away with a piece newly pulled from his press. Of no less importance was Gerard Mercator (1512–1594), Flemish mathematician and geographer, author of the famous planisphere for use in navigation, the first map 'on Mercator's projection'; and the first map-maker to give a systematic collection of maps the name 'Atlas'.

First of the great English map-makers was Christopher Saxton, a Yorkshireman born in about the year 1542, who was engaged by Queen Elizabeth to survey the counties of England and Wales. They are beautifully decorated, and collectors seek the early impressions with the 'grapes' watermarks —a lozenge of small circles. A few counties were covered by the regrettably short-lived John Norden (1548–1625), while successors of his were William Hole and William Kip. But perhaps the most popular of these early English map-makers is John Speed, a Cheshire man born in 1552, whose maps are positive mines of information, for in addition to the usual monsters and ships he gives a great deal of relevant heraldry, battle scenes, plans of towns. There were many issues of these famous maps, published from 1611 well into the eighteenth century. There are also good modern reproductions, which collectors distinguish by the difference in the kind of paper used and the impression made upon it by the effect of a copper plate in a hand-press, compared with modern photographic methods.

William (or Willem) Blaeu of Amsterdam made some maps based on Speed but showing great originality: similar work, often copied from Blaeu, was done by John (Jan) Jansson (1596–1664).

John Ogilby, to whom fell the task of mapping London after the Great Fire of 1666, produced a famous series of strip

Sea chart of the north Spanish coast by Lucas Jansz Waghenaer, issued in 1588.

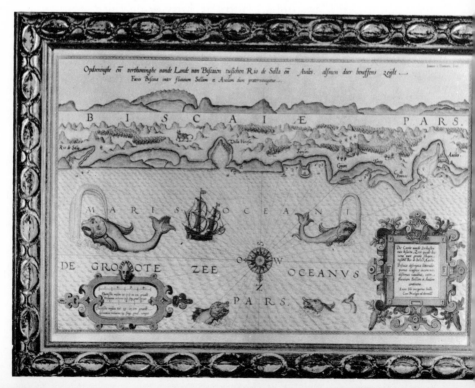

road maps in 1675: some of them show the roads being measured by a waywiser wheel. Richard Blome was another decorative map-maker of this era. With the last of the great decorative map-makers, Thomas Moule (1784–1851) we have a typical High Victorian quality which will appeal to devotees of the age, whether they are serious cartophiles or not.

Seafaring men will be interested in the early charts, some of which were done by the map-makers. But many were made by specialists like Lucas Jansz. Waghenaer, who produced the earliest charts of the British sea-coasts, lettered them all in Dutch, but made up for this by including more monsters and ships. Sir Robert Dudley made the first set of sea charts based on Mercator's projection in 1646, while Captain Greenville Collins, a Brother of Trinity House, began his seven-year survey of the coasts of the British Isles in 1681.

'A Map of New England, being the first that ever was here cut,' obviously elects itself as the first American-born map: it appeared in a book by William Hubbard in 1677 and was apparently printed by John Foster at Boston. Benjamin Franklin put out a woodcut showing the boundaries between Maryland and Pennsylvania.

The names of Peter Pelham, Lawrence Herbert and James Turner stand out among the earliest of the American copperplate map-makers, the last named having been the author of the deservedly popular *General Map of the Middle British Colonies in America,* made by Lewis Evans in 1755. After the Revolution and with the opening up of the West there was an enormous spate of map-making, both general and local, recording the changing of frontiers and state lines, the driving of roads and railways, as well as American-made charts of the waters surrounding the new republic.

Town plans make an interesting byway of map collecting: many of them—such as those of Braun and Hogenburg of Cologne—are bird's eye views, which make them all the more interesting as records of buildings which have long since vanished. Those of Wenceslaus Hollar, for example, show us pre-fire London in fine and exact detail. The American cartographers were also exceptionally prolific in this field.

The buyer of old maps is as interested in margins and plate

marks as the lover of PRINTS, and he particularly watches the colours, sometimes finding them useful in dating. According to Mr. Radford [RL 253] there is much bad amateur painting which has been applied to, and spoilt, many a good print. In his student days the serious collector will accordingly do well to turn to authorities like Mr. Tooley [RL 253] and to accept the advice of the specialist dealer, such as Mr. Radford. In England he may also find it useful to join the Map Collectors' Circle (Durrant House, Chiswell St., London E.C.1).

MECHANICAL BANKS Sometimes called Toy Banks, because they added to the sublime virtue of thrift the perennial childhood joy of seeing a piece of machinery do something surprising or amusing. You put your coin in the place indicated and something happens . . . a footballer kicks it into a goal, a negro swallows it, a soldier fires it at a pigeon or a tree, children slide down a chute, horses ride round a circus, dancers dance.

Most of these engaging pieces of automata were made in the United States and many bear the names of actual American banks. But they turn up surprisingly often in Britain: I usually see three or four each year without actually seeking them. This was because English manufacturers began to copy some of the models such as those of the Creedmore Bank—e.g. the 'Volun-

pposite: '*Tammany*' *mechanical* *nk*. Below, left; '*Chief Bighorn*' *echanical bank. When you put a* *in in the slot in front of the Indian* *frog jumps up from the swamp.*

teer' and the 'Grenadier'—whereupon to protect their interests American makers like the J. and E. Stevens Company of Cromwell, Conn., patented the designs. From then on they took advantage of this to export thousands of these banks to England—with the result that many a British child, without realising it, invested pennies in an American 'bank'.

The toy banks first appeared in about 1870 and continued in production on a considerable scale until about 1910, after which only a few were made. Most of them are of cast iron but they can also be in lead or tin. This is particularly true of the banks actually made in Britain, in Germany and France. Mr. Griffith [RL 253] has distinguished between American and other banks, differentiated the mechanical from the semi-mechanical and the 'pattern' banks, and listed a number of obvious FAKES and also some of 'uncertain' origin.

Most useful of all, he has graded the genuine banks in order of rarity and quality. From this we learn that the most desirable of all, from the collector's point of view, is the very elaborate piece of automation called 'Clown, Harlequin and Columbine'; the 'Freedman's Bank' (which is of wood, metal and cloth); the 'Merry-go-Round'; the 'Old Woman in the Shoe'; and the 'Shoot the Chute'. Of the models shown here, the 'Tammany

143

Bank' is one of the most common, while the 'Chief Bighorn' is about half way down the scale. Both were sold in England recently. Among the more desirable non-American banks, it seems, are the 'British Lion' in tin; the 'Tommy', showing a British soldier firing at a tree from the prone position and the 'Giant in Tower'.

MILITARIA AND NAVALIA In the county town of Lewes, a few miles from the spot on the Sussex Downs where Simon de Montfort fought a battle against his king and helped to found the English parliament, there foregather nine times a year collectors of and dealers in things which are usually called Militaria. The second word in my heading has been added from respect to former naval persons, hoping that, for once, they will waive their right to precedence.

The collectors are at Lewes to attend what is perhaps the biggest sale of its kind in Europe: and for three days they sit, tense and sharp-eyed, while lot after lot is knocked down to

A collection of 300 yeomanry cap badges and buttons, with rare Colonials, including British American.

them or to the perhaps even larger number of people who have entrusted their instructions to the auctioneers.

Under these heads are most naval and military relics— trophies from the world's battlefields, uniforms, badges, BUTTONS, brooches, shoulder-belt plates, pouches, documents, books, pictures, naval and military stores, and equipment of all kinds. Then there are all those items which, as explained in my INTRODUCTION, seem to offer themselves as collecting subjects in their own right. For example, GORGETS and HELMETS may exist without ARMOUR, while among WEAPONS, SWORDS and STAFF WEAPONS are large enough affairs to require special attention. Some have civilian or decorative as well as warlike use, such as BOWS AND ARROWS, CANNON, DAGGERS, GUNS AND RIFLES, KNIVES and POWDER HORNS, while JAPANESE SWORDS AND FITTINGS are surely recondite matters needing separate consideration.

Left to right: *Crimean officer's Royal Irish Dragoon Guards gilt helmet; lieutenant's shako of 89th Foot (Royal Irish Fusiliers) 1869–78; helmet of officer in 2nd Life Guards.*

Full-dress sabretache of the 10th Hussars (Prince of Wales' Own Royal); brass model field gun with recoiled fitting and limber.

But if you range around in the sections of this book you will find there can be military or naval affiliations in almost any of them. I have deliberately excluded campaign awards from this volume, but COMMEMORATIVE MEDALS often mark a battle, a conquest or a defeat, while COMMEMORATIVE POTTERY, as will be seen there, has its heroes, from Jack Crawford to Lafayette, and also its occasions, from Portobello to Yorktown.

Sometimes a lot at the auction will tell the story of a young officer fallen in battle whose accoutrements, returned to a mourning family at his death, now appear in public at *their* death; sometimes, amidst the hackles, plumes, pom-poms, epaulettes, sporrans and sabretaches, there appears another kind of 'trophy', say, an 'Eastern Lady's Yashmak'. A more sinister note comes in with the large number of so-called Nazi relics— standards, insignia, the fateful long knives of history—but one notes that this term is also taken to cover items from Germany's Imperial past: so apart from any interest in Hitlerian horrors, one finds here the age-old impulse for victors to gather trophies of the vanquished.

146

A collection of military headgear from early eighteenth to late nineteenth century.

MODEL SOLDIERS From their earliest days men have made models of other men; and since men have always been fighting there have always been models of fighting men. In the Cairo Museum you may see an Egyptian army of about 2300 B.C.; Greece and Rome had their model cohorts; the young chivalry in mediaeval times learnt the trick of jousting and battle with manoeuvrable toy knights in ARMOUR; Louis XIV had cardboard cut-outs in his nursery—which later must have stood him in good stead when his generals tried to argue with him.

But today, when we speak of model soldiers—or 'military miniatures' as some call them—we are referring to what we once knew as 'tin' or 'lead' soldiers, some of them *Flats,* or metal cut-outs, some *Semi-solids* (or *Semi-flats*), that is to say in low relief; and some *Solids,* or moulded all around—*ronde bosse,* as the French say.

147

Apart from the cardboard figures for which Strasbourg was such an important centre, the first sheets being issued there in 1744, the flats seem to have come first. In them the toymakers of Nuremburg, especially J. G. Hilpert from about 1775, bodied forth the contemporary regiments of Frederick the Great, that Prussian king who was celebrated quite as much as any English hero on our COMMEMORATIVE POTTERY and glass. The range of subjects offered by Nuremburg and the other German centres soon covered most of the soldiery of Europe, also classical and mediaeval figures and—for the first time extending beyond the merely military—peasants and townsfolk, tradesmen and trolls. They continued in production right down to World War II, and may still be seen in many collections on the Continent. At first these *Zinnsoldaten* really were made of tin, but as time went on the term persisted but the makers found it expedient to alloy their metal.

A second outstanding figure in German production was the celebrated Heinrichsen, who started business in Nuremburg in 1839 and a few years later standardised the size of his figures to

148

the 30-millimetre scale: it became known as the 'Nuremburg' size. A descendant of his was still in business until World War II.

The first semi-solids and solids must have appeared very soon after the flats. The solids were made in much the same way as porcelain figures, the limbs and other parts being cast separately and then assembled by the equivalent of the potter's 'repairer'.

While the Germans led with the flats the French seem to have preferred to develop the solids. From the 1820s onwards the firm of Mignot, now the oldest manufacturers of model soldiers in the world, built up a wide range of figures, and later bought the models of the fine figures made by the fine modeller, Lucotte. They include many British regiments, bivouac scenes from the American War of Independence, Red Indian camps.

But the Germans quickly took up the challenge, and by the 1890s British and American boys were playing their games mainly with model soldiers of German origin. In the meantime, however, a British manufacturer was beginning to com-

Opposite: *Diorama of Napoleon and his staff in the field;* and right, *detail of the officer, circa 1812.*

pete with these imports; producing a hollow cast—and therefore cheaper—figure which these lads began to prefer to the rather larger types from the Continent; it also had the advantage of full standardisation. This was the appropriately named William Brittain, whose catalogue for 1939 included every regiment in the British Army and representatives of most foreign armies. After World War I Brittain extended his range to animals, farm workers, vehicles, etc., and by 1960 the firm was making a million castings a week. The United States seemed to have depended largely on imports up to about World War I, when a firm called Barclay made some solid figures of American troops.

Collectors of model soldiers are happy folk in that their quarry goes on accumulating. They often also make their own pieces or convert acquisitions from others. They will take some quite ordinary model and give it a twist—a variation in the angle of a tail or a head which gives it more drama and character. They also buy from firms like Brittains unpainted castings, spare limbs, weapons, etc. Nor have these arts been

Opposite: *Royal Scots Greys rallying to the guidon after a charge,* and, left, *detail of a corporal.*

killed by the advent of the plastic model soldier, which is able to show much more fidelity of detail than the metal one. Here, the collector-modeller puts away his hacksaw, file and soldering iron and does things with more delicate tools to the heated model, as though he were working in sealing wax.

There are also 'connoisseur' pieces made by outstandingly skilled modellers and painters like Roger Beroud of France, who specialises in mounted figures of the First Empire. Richard Courtney's mediaeval figures are very fine, and so are others by the Americans, Brady, Bussler and William Imrie; the latter has done a great many figures around the War of Independence.

There are many fine collections to be visited by the travelling collector: some descriptions of these, and much other lore, is to be found in the literature of the subject [RL 253].

MUSICAL AUTOMATA   There are automata, or animated figures, and there are musical boxes; in Musical Automata you have the two together: figures moving to the sound of (more or less) sweet music.

Perhaps the earliest and most delicate (and also the most expensive) of them are the very small singing bird boxes which were among the luxuries the eighteenth century produced for

its pleasure. At a touch on a spring, a bird appeared, turned its body, fluttered its wings and uttered a shrill roundelay before disappearing again. These tiny songsters were also to be found in cages, watches, hand-mirrors, the handles of **WALKING STICKS** and even bracelets: and the more ingenious the arrangements the more you had to pay for it. The trick was done, basically, by the operation of a spring mechanism on small bellows with a reed outlet. Many of them came from Geneva, but London watchmakers had a hand in some.

The singing bird idea developed into the full-size cage with a reed organ in its base and they frequently come up for sale today. But this was still piping stuff; for the full orchestra one had to wait until Regency times and the revolving brass cylinder with steel pins striking a comb. There was a shaft which also revolved and worked the figures above by a system of wheels and cogs operating rods.

From then on the inventiveness of the automaton maker knew no bounds. There were dancing dolls, sometimes on a revolving table, quizzing monkeys, marching soldiers, performing acrobats. From this developed the full *scena,* sometimes associated with a clock. There was also the handle-turned hurdy-gurdy or street organ with figures, as shown in

152

the illustration. This was evidently intended for the export trade, for as well as the 'Sailor's Hornpipe' it plays the 'Green Hills of Tyrol' and the 'Bonaparte March'; and it has seventeen figures, including Napoleon hinself, Turkish musicians, a clown and a lady playing a spinet. In good working order and condition (and very similar to one now in the Metropolitan Museum in New York) it was sold in Lewes recently for £550.

NEFS Only a tolerably wealthy man could make a large collection of nefs; but whoever takes pride in his festive board, and proposes to spend a reasonably long lifetime at it, owes himself at least one.

The nef is a large table-piece in the form of a ship, usually in silver or gold, with masts, yards, shrouds and even sailors climbing the rigging. They were also made in glass: there are Venetian ones with the hull in brilliant blue glass and the

153

The 'Burghley' nef, a nautilus shell mounted in silver parcel-gilt, with figures of Tristran and Iseult, 1482–83.

rigging of clear *cristallo,* supporting fabulous dragons. Filled with sweetmeats the nef was sometimes put on wheels, like a wine wagon, for navigation along the lord's table.

Often the nef is a perfect replica, to scale, of an actual ship, in which case they could become the ultimate quarry of the collector of ship models.

They can sometimes be bought for sums less fabulous than the money which would be made, if it ever came on to the market, by the celebrated Burghley nef shown here [RL 253].

PAINTINGS Highest place in this hierarchy is usually accorded to *Oil Paintings,* presumably because most important works since the Renaissance have been in this medium. But there are other kinds of paintings using quite different media.

The technique of applying pigments mixed with oil of varying kinds on to the slightly absorbent surface of a *Support* (usually primed canvas or wood—or in modern times hardboard, aluminium and other materials) is traditionally associated with the Flemish fifteenth-century painters Jan and Hubert van Eyck, though it is now generally considered that they merely produced more efficient materials than had been used by their predecessors.

If you walk around the galleries and look closely at oil paintings you will find that there seem to be two quite different ways of using oils. In one you can hardly see the brushstroke; and in fact the picture has been carefully built up over a (possible) initial outline by first laying in the tones or values in monochrome then gradually building up the colour by the use of transparent or opaque glazes. This was the usage of the older of the old masters. At the other extreme is the method called *Alla Prima,* wherein the brush is loaded with pigment already mixed to the exact tint and tone required, which is then put on with more or less dexterity and necessarily a good deal of bravura—as well as the brains which James McNeil Whistler said he found the best thing to mix with his colours.

Many painters used a combination of these methods, for

155

example Rembrandt and Rubens, adding to their original groundwork *Scumbles* or opaque glazes and heavily laid-on *Impastos,* or slabs of solid paint, to secure variety and drama: note, for example, a nose on a typical Frans Hals and see how this whole feature comes into existence by a flick of a brush. But also reflect that, simple as this seems, it may have cost him the whole morning, and absorbed a great deal of drinking time, to get that flick exactly right. Between attempts, of course, he had recourse to the *Palette knife,* that useful instrument which makes oil painting technically far easier than *Water Colours.* All the same, exponents of the latter type of painting such as Turner seem to have done much the same thing with a razor and a thumb.

When people speak of *Tempera* painting they are usually referring to egg tempera, which preceded oil painting for easel pictures. You took fresh egg-yolk thinned out with water, mixed this with your colour powders and applied it to a *Gesso* ground or *Priming.* It dried extremely quickly (which oil does not) but stayed put for centuries, drying a lighter tone than when it was wet. Painters found that there were advantages in adding to tempera a thin film of oil, and from this '*Mixed-Method*' there developed oil painting *tout simple.* Some contemporary painters have gone back to the tempera method, for the paints can now be bought ready mixed. As already noted they have also in recent years adopted a great many other media and supports.

In collecting paintings at the salerooms or the galleries you will at this late date find that a great many people have been there before you, and have either taken the best pictures or pushed the prices of the remaining ones out of your reach.

But it is important to note that they have only done this with the kind of paintings which have already been appreciated for a long time. People are snobs about painting as about most other things: there are also a great many people who buy paintings as they would stocks and shares, and seldom look at them or even take them out of their bank vaults. In the same way, only a very few people will venture to buy a painting by an unknown artist whose wares no dealer is pushing.

So that one infallible way in which collectors in all ages have

156

Collection of still-life paintings of fruit, made by Mr. Gerry Richards, designer and fashion illustrator; an example also of Subject Collecting.

been able to buy good pictures at no very great cost, thus forestalling the market, is to forget all about schools, signatures, attributions and the rest, and buy those you like, only making sure that if it is a painting you want, it is neither a *Chromolithograph* nor any other kind of PRINT or picture reproduction. If, after a time, you find your purchases palling on you, or becoming downright distasteful, this is fine: it means you are educating and refining your taste in the best possible way—at the expense of your pocket. All you have to do now is to sell the damn things to someone who is in the state of innocence in which you once were (you may even make a profit) and start all over again [RL 252 and 253].

PEWTER TANKARDS One of the reasons why foreigners do not like the best beer in the world—which is to say British beer—is that it is so often served to them in a glass, instead of in pewter. What is more, it should be in old pewter, of the illegal poisonous sort, with plenty of lead in it.

In collecting pewter tankards you could try to make a sequential collection, starting at the beginning, coming down to about the end of the last century, and then firmly and definitely stopping.

You should begin, if you can possibly afford it, with the finest of all shapes, as shown on page 160, with all the restrained grace of the English Renaissance, yet sitting more firmly and decidedly upon the table top—which should be of oak, not mahogany—than any other tankard before or since. Here is the flattened 'bun' shaped top and serrated lid edge, the skirted base and filet, the pronounced *entasis* or taper upwards from bottom to top, the fine outward sweeping handle, its tail nearly touching the table, the great 'double-volute' thumbpiece standing up vigorously and pleading for the lid to be raised. All these features would proclaim its date even if it did not bear the cypher and portraits of William and Mary.

Styles overlap, and one finds about this time the beginning of the domed-lid types, still with the tooth-edged serration in front, but later to lose it; afterwards the 'double-domed' type, the curve starting from the outer edge. At this time one looks also for the 'swan-necked' handle, perhaps with a fishtail, shield or ball terminal.

From now on one finds that the straight lines of the Restoration and Queen Anne begin to get competition from the curves of the baroque; the 'bell' and the 'tulip' body shapes come in, getting themselves up on to feet; there are 'S' and double 'S' curved handles, with one or both handles standing out from the body on struts—a form that perhaps consorts better with pewter than with silver. There is often a dished top to the handle, with a 'tuft'. Thumbpieces now seen include the 'chair-back' and the 'open', like a gate. The lidless tankards follow this same progression of shapes, but on the whole are slimmer and seem to retain their elegance until a later date.

The nineteenth century saw all the types of the eighteenth

Pub tankards with glass and engraved bottoms from The Chequers Hotel, Lamberhurst, Kent.

in characteristically 'blown' versions, also such features as bottoms of clear or tinted glass, sometimes cut with a star or engraved with hops and barley. This, too, is the era of the 'pub' tankard, one of the collecting items which still come to light in some numbers whenever a foundation is re-dug or an old wainscoting pulled down. In shapes they are ageless, but a good many were used as measures, and you can sometimes date them from the successive excise marks around the rim.

As far back as the reign of Charles II, pubkeepers would mark their expensive tankards ('Edward Hill at ye Red Lion in ye Poultry, 1670'), and sometimes add some such imprecation as 'If sold, stole'. But in Victorian days there was an almost standardised system of marking, the name of the pub and perhaps its landlord being punched in separate script letters round the bottom just inside the rim. Most of these inscriptions have a family resemblance, and one concludes that they were the work of the travelling tinkers or pewterers who came round repairing the pewter pots. I still have a sandstone bath, now full of plants, in which my grandfather had his pewter pots sanded.

Tradesman's Card of Edward Quick, London, circa 1740–50.

A highly disinterested form of collecting—though one which might make you many friends—would be to gather such tankards and, wherever these named hostelries still existed, restore them to their ancient homes. To the remainder, the orphans, you should give a good home, with proper grooming and regular exercise [RL 253].

Tankard engraved with a cypher and the portraits of William and Mary. Maker's touch 'R.S.' crowned.

PICTORIAL NOTEPAPER This is a department of PRINTED EPHEMERA, but it seems to call for a corner of its own in that it also provides us with a story of how a collector found a new field for collecting.

When we have our notepaper printed nowadays we tend to limit ourselves to a bare recital of our addresses and telephone numbers, sometimes going so far as to add our names, and if necessary, our titles—although in the latter case it is usually considered better form to throw in a coronet or a coat-of-arms and hope that our correspondents will be bright enough to catch on.

There was a time, however, when people liked their letter-heading to be embellished with pictures—landscapes, animals, genre scenes, seaside motifs. If they were very grand persons, like Queen Victoria, they would have views engraved of their own residences—Windsor Castle, Osborne House, Balmoral, sometimes even showing members of the family moving about in these august settings.

Topical affairs of the day would also be pictured on this letter paper. The lively engravings shown here of the Fall of Bomarsund, an incident in the Crimean War, is from a heading in the collection of the late Mr. Scott of Manchester, to whose daughter, Miss Elisabeth Scott, present owner of the collection, I am indebted, not only for permission to reproduce this example from it, but for the story of its genesis.

It appears that Mr. Scott possessed a lady's writing case which had belonged to a member of his family who died in 1869, and which contained seven or eight pieces of notepaper with views of the Lake District, Derbyshire and Wales. He had never taken any special interest in them, but one day in 1944 there appeared in *Country Life* (August 14) a letter and some illustrations which a correspondent had found in an old scrap-book. Mr. Scott sent in one of his and from then onwards, readers began exchanging their duplicates, as collectors so helpfully do; so that Mr. Scott was able slowly to build up a representative gathering totalling 175 examples. Some of them were complete sheets, large and small, some simply the cut-down pictures. There are views of country seats, halls, castlès, cathedrals, river scenes, etc.

161

Notepaper heading depicting a scene from the Crimean war (see this page).

Most examples of this pictorial notepaper seem to come from around 1840–60—the era, be it noted, of travel books with wood or steel engravings, also of the great outburst of underglaze printing of such subjects on Staffordshire earthenware: no doubt there are many correspondences.

But the picture-headed paper seems to have continued in use down to the 1880s, by which time of course the picture POSTCARD had appeared, and perhaps became the major factor in ending the vogue. The discovery of these interesting items is one more argument in favour of never allowing a scrapbook to pass one by unexamined.

PIPE CASES The collector, both of smokers' sundries and of wood carving will find common ground in the fine workmanship of the carved wooden pipe cases which were made in Europe in the seventeenth and eighteenth centuries.

Rarest of them, made to carry the forward-sloping clay pipes of the early days of the weed, have tapered sliding shutters on the underside. Later, when pipes acquired a 'spur', they were given hinged lids at the bowl end. Most of the elaborately carved ones of the eighteenth century, came from the Netherlands, France and Austria.

Pearwood, boxwood and olivewood, among others, are used, and specimens are often engraved with initials and a date. One case in the Pinto collection [RL 254] has a combination lock, to prevent unauthorised use by another person other than the owner.

PISTOLS AND REVOLVERS These very important WEAPONS, a self-contained department of MILITARIA AND NAVALIA, are, by the usual definition, firearms which may be carried and fired in one hand.

The German potentates of the sixteenth century, who were among the earliest users of the weapon, started by favouring a pistol with a butt which followed the line of the stock or ended in a fishtail. But gradually the grip was set at a sharper angle, and since the weapon was used mainly by horsemen, carried in a holster, the ball terminal easy to grab in an emergency became the most widespread form.

There were, however, pistols which could be carried in the belt. At first these had short barrels and wide bores, but more slender versions appeared towards the end of the fifteenth century, with straight, flared or curved butts, sometimes cut off straight. Later these had a more pronounced downward curve in the butt and perhaps a ring terminal, while later again this was replaced by a dome which extended further and further up the grip. Of special types one may begin with the *Turn-off* pistol, in which the barrel could be unscrewed just in front of the chamber, into which the ball could be loaded directly and therefore more tightly, so reducing the loss of gas and increasing the firepower. It also made rifling more feasible, and in fact there were rare *Screwed Turn-off* pistols of the seventeenth century. An adaptation of around 1750 whereby the cock was moved from the side to the top of the lock and held between two plates, the pan and cover being also moved up, gave the *Box-lock*.

Pocket pistols, at first a smaller version of the holster model, usually had a turn-off barrel and after 1750 a box-lock. The *Deringer,* a small light pistol with a bore of 0.48 in., first produced by Henry Deringer of Philadelphia, and much copied

163

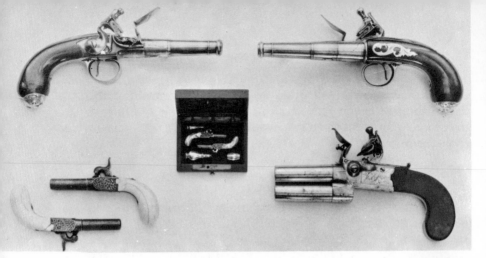

Above: top, *a pair of Queen Anne type silver-mounted cannon-barrelled flintlock pistols, 9 inches long overall, by How of London;* centre, *a pair of miniature percussion boxlock pocket pistols, the barrels only ½ inch long;* bottom left, *pair of Belgian percussion boxlock muff pistols, 4½ inches long overall;* bottom right, *double-barrelled over and under tap action flintlock, boxlock pistol 7½ inches long overall, Birmingham proved.*

Opposite: top to bottom: *six shot ·44 Colt first model Hartford dragoon percussion revolver, 14 inches long overall, marked 'Address Saml. Colt, New York City'; Continental style percussion duelling pistol, 17 inches long overall, 50 bore, by Joseph Lang, Haymarket, London; six shot ·44 Remington New Model 1874 single-action army revolver, 13 inches long overall with engraved Turkish silver muzzle sheath and Turkish butt; cannon-barrelled flintlock pistol.*

elsewhere, will be familiar to all students of the American West. Mr. Blair [RL 248] says that purists reserve the spelling *Derringer* for these imitations.

The *Duelling* pistol was a special type, for it called for special considerations. First, since a gentleman's life and honour depended upon his marksmanship, it had to be as accurate as possible; so instead of putting value into lavish decoration, it was invested in perfection of mechanism. Perfect balance was sought, so that the pistol might feel like a prolongation of the arm itself—duellists were expected as a point of honour to point rather than to aim. All parts were carefully finished, and not only was there very little in the way of silver mounting—which could glint in the sun—but the metal mounts were usually blued. The pistols were usually bought in pairs in a case, with compartments for POWDER FLASKS, bullet-mould, wad-cutter, flints, etc., and may still be found offered in this way.

Scotland has its own model in the *Highland* pistol, which comes in a number of forms, all of them with brass or steel stocks, sometimes engraved with Celtic strapwork, and they have a long flat belthook. They are classified according to their butts which can be *Fishtail, Lemon, Heart, Scroll, Ramshorn* or *Lobe-butted.* There are inferior specimens from Birmingham.

There were *Revolvers,* on the revolving-cylinder system as long ago as the late German sixteenth century, but they had to be rotated manually. The earliest single-action six-shooter appears to be one of about 1680 by John Dafte, of London. Its mechanism was very similar to that of the first commercially viable revolver, patented in 1836 by that almost legendary

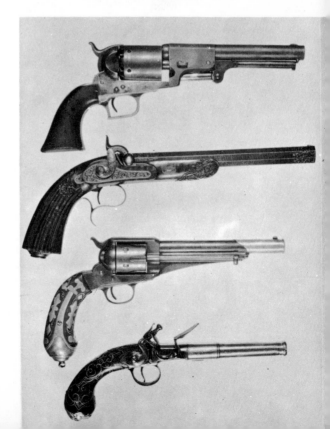

Top, left: *double barrelled ·41 over and under Remington Derringer,
5 inches long overall, ebony grips, nickel plated overall, with front
sight added to the barrel;* centre: *ten shot ·22 centre fire protector
palm pistol, 4 inches overall length, by Turbiaux;* right: *seven
shot ·22 Reid's patent 'My Friend' knuckle duster pepperbox
revolver, 4½ inches long overall.* Bottom, left: *double barrelled ·28
rimfire Woodward's patent turnover Derringer pistol. 5 inches long
overall, by McNaughton;* centre: *small six shot 5 mm. pinfire
revolver, 5¼ inches long overall;* bottom, right: *eight shot ·22
rimfire pepperbox revolver, 5½ inches long overall, by Fletcher,
London.*

figure Samuel Colt, who founded at Hartford, Conn., one of the world's leading firearm factories. Every movie-goer has seen how a single-action six-shooter may be fired very rapidly by holding the trigger back and 'fanning' the hammer, so that all shots could be fired in less than four seconds.

There are revolvers with clusters of barrels, as we have seen in GUNS AND RIFLES, which are called *Pepperboxes,* and many other oddities, which Mr. Winant also classes as FIREARMS CURIOSA such as *Double-ended pistols,* which fire both ways, but fortunately not at once, so that the owner cannot actually commit simultaneous murder and suicide. This can be achieved, however, by the *Double header,* and also with a GUN which fired cartridges with powder in the middle, a projectile which went out one way and a charge of shot which went the other: the idea was to reduce recoil—in which it must surely have been highly successful.

Top to bottom: *flintlock pistol, Neapolitan or Brescian, but with Spanish type lock. Length overall 15⅘ inches; wheel lock pistol, with lock of French fashion but decorated in Spanish style; small wheel lock pistol, Dutch, circa 1610, with different makers' marks on barrel and lock-plate.*

POSTCARDS I wonder that more people do not collect old postcards. They have come—and still come—in enormous and fascinating variety, they provide miniature galleries of pictures in every conceivable style and subject, and they are the easiest and most convenient things in the world to keep: all you need is a supply of empty shoe boxes.

They are very easy to find, and very cheap when you do find them. Time and again I have seen in some old junk store an album full of cards dating from the eighties and the nineties. A box of oddments will often yield a bundle of them, and of course there are stalls and barrows at certain fairs and markets which show a good display of them classified in types and subjects. There are several, for example, along the *quais* of Paris opposite Notre Dame.

Serious collectors, as usual, select; but since there is apparently no highly organised system for selection by traders, the specialist is just as likely to find his speciality in the junk shop as anywhere else—just as there may be lurking in Uncle Joe's old stamp album that extraordinary rarity which no schoolboy would have recognised. So it is that you may easily find for a shilling or so one of the incunabula—the early Austrian postcards of 1869. There are also the many early commemorative series: events like the death of Verdi, the Kaiser's visit to Constantinople, the assassination of King Humbert of Italy were all marked in this way.

Perhaps most collectors go for subjects. Venerable persons will remember the lovely ladies who appeared on cards in late Edwardian times—Phyllis and Zena Dare, Lily Langtry and other idols of stage and society. There are some who collect places as much as cards; and indeed there must be very few media in which the almost day by day changes in street scenes and even landscapes is recorded in more detail; one could almost write the history of a town by gathering together a succession of views of it.

The student of social life also finds much interesting material here. There are, for example, all those seaside comic cards of Donald McGill's, which so intrigued George Orwell, with their 'endless succession of fat women in tight bathing dresses . . . mother-in-law, baby's nappy' [RL 254].

168

Cowhorn flask, scrimshaw engraved with U.S. Eagle and shield, and trophy of flags with 13 stars.

POWDER FLASKS They are sometimes called powder horns, for the primitives of the species, made right down to the mid-nineteenth century and even later, were actually cowhorns, provided with a base at the wide end and a pouring hole in the pointed end. They were also sometimes made from antlers, large nuts and even ostrich eggs.

Basically, a container for one's gunpowder had to be light in weight and easy to sling about one's person; above all, of course, it had to keep one's powder dry.

From cowhorn, or other natural materials, the user of a powder flask could move all the way up the decorative ladder, by way of carved wood, bone, ivory, tortoiseshell, enamels, silver, even gold encrusted with jewels. Flasks usually have a nozzle ending in a cap and fitted with a cut-off contrivance whereby a charge can be measured off into the nozzle. When the finer priming powder came into existence there was a smaller flask or touch box, sometimes made *en suite* with the larger one, perhaps also matching the firearm itself.

The very splendid flasks of the earlier period, made for the great persons of the time, will appeal to connoisseurs in the same way as do the firearms of the day. But I must confess that I find high romance in those simple cowhorn flasks engraved with some old trapper's name, or perhaps a pioneer sketch map of good hunting territory.

Even some of these can cost money. At a London saleroom recently there was sold a simple horn, engraved with the name of the owner, David Stubbles, but also the Hanoverian Royal Arms, the date 1760, a view of New York and a map of the Hudson Basin and representations of the fortifications as far as

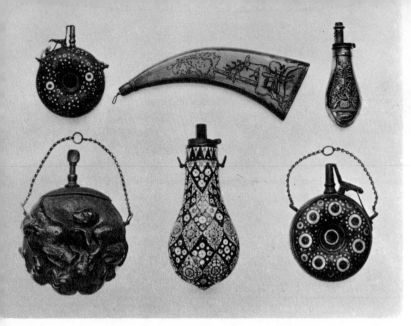

Powder flasks: top left to right: *German late seventeenth century wood and staghorn; Scottish eighteenth century flattened cowhorn, carved; French embossed copper;* bottom left to right: *seventeenth century Italian carved wood; Indian eighteenth century overlaid engraved ivory; German seventeenth century wood and staghorn.*

Lake Ontario. Knocked down for 140 guineas, it has a companion, I believe, in the Metropolitan Museum in New York. Who was David Stubbles, one wonders, and why did he carve that map on his powder horn?

PRAYER WHEELS   Tibet, the land where until recently the wheel was largely disdained, is said to be the home of the prayer wheel, although many examples are known from Japan and other countries where Buddhism flourishes. It was also once not unknown in the West; Aethelwold, a Bishop of Winchester in the tenth century A.D., had a wheel hung with bells in his cathedral which he spun on saints' days—but perhaps this was just because he liked the sound of BELLS.

170

Many prayer wheels are fixtures, built securely into the walls of Tibetan monasteries, and the traveller is expected to spin them as he passes on his way. They are also found high up in the mountain passes, turned by wind or water—rather like those engaging home-made little musical waterwheels one sometimes comes across in German woods.

The hand prayer wheels which sometimes appear at sales in the West are usually of bronze, though a few are of silver: they consist of a shaft around which revolves a cylindrical box, and inside this are coiled paper ribbons printed with symbols of prayers. The one most often seen is *Om Mane Peme Hum* ('Hail the Jewel in the Lotus'). A metal weight hangs on a chain attached to the cylinder, which it spins round by centrifugal force, and the wheel can thus be spun by a flick of the wrist. Amulets were made from the worn-out ivory or stone base of the handles of prayer wheels, and these are objects of great veneration.

To a Buddhist the purpose of spinning these wheels is to ensure that in their next incarnation they are not born into a lower form of life, but that with each one they acquire more merit and thus reach Nirvana.

PRINTED EPHEMERA Here we have that vast and varied flood of unbound pieces of paper or pasteboard, usually destroyed as soon as their practical purpose has been served, which society has found necessary to it ever since the emergence of what Marshall McLuhan has called Gutenberg Man. In fact the grandfather of printing himself produced ephemeral printing in the shape of the Mainz *Indulgence,* or Pardon, shown here. Produced in 1454 two years before Gutenberg put out his first Bible, it is the oldest known dated piece of jobbing printing.

In case you feel that a modern collector, even in a lifetime of collecting, is unlikely to come across fifteenth-century rarities of this sort, you may like to know one of the reasons why Mr. John Lewis [RL 254] started to collect printed ephemera and eventually came to write his classic on the subject. In buying an album of old printed matter from a bookseller in

171

The oldest known dated piece of jobbing printing (see previous page).

a country town in Suffolk he became the owner of a similar
Indulgence printed by Thierry Martens at Antwerp in 1497:
it was granted for the repair of the hospital at the cathedral
of St. Santiago de Compostella. After that anything seemed
possible.

But the range takes you all the way down to the latest
baggage check. Manufacturers of playing cards were plying
their trade even before Indulgences were printed, as were the
printers of ballads and broadsheets, almanacks and other items.

Programmes, menus, wine lists, even sauce labels, can stir
our taste buds still; billheads and receipts inform us about the
commerce of the past; travel bills and tickets take us on
imaginary journeys by early locomotive, diligence and sailing
ship. History is to be found in Royal and Presidential, Mayoral
and other proclamations, decrees, petitions, licences, election
notices, offers of rewards and summonses to appear before
one's temporal judges.

Typophiles, or lovers of good printing, find enormous interest
in these things, for many of them are the work of untutored
printers totally unaware of the principles of typography or even
of elementary design; yet they produced some astonishingly

172

Above left and below right: *watch-papers, from the back of a pair case watch to stop chafing.* Above right: *tobacco label, late eighteenth century.* Below left: *sauce bottle label, nineteenth century.*

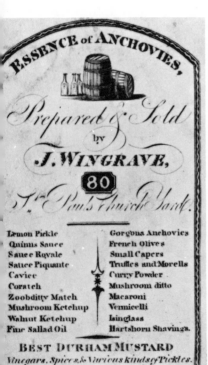

effective results. It cannot be held against them, for example, that they fail to convey their message—the main purpose of print. So here you may revel in typefaces from the Gothic or Black Letter of the incunabulists, based on the contemporary handwriting in Germany, and watch its adaptation in English and American printing down even to the present; the Roman and Italic based on the obliquely stressed handwriting of fifteenth-century Italy; the Fat Faces of the early nineteenth century for display; the shadow and ornamented letters; the Egyptian, French Antiques of High Victoriana down to the austere sans serifs of today.

These 'papers of a day, the Ephemerae of learning', as Dr. Johnson called them, are by definition short-lived and transitory. Yet also by definition the class as a whole is immortal: a child of mine recently collected several hundred printed orange wrappers merely by eating the oranges and not throwing away the wrappers. She was following the example of such thoroughgoing collectors as the shoemaker

BOSTON,
Plymouth & Sandwich
MAIL STAGE,

CONTINUES TO RUN AS FOLLOWS:

LEAVES Boston every Tuesday, Thursday, and Saturday mornings at 5 o'clock, breakfast at Leonard's, Scituate ; dine at Bradford's, Plymouth ; and arrive in Sandwich the same evening. Leaves Sandwich every Monday, Wednesday and Friday mornings ; breakfast at Bradford's, Plymouth ; dine at Leonard's, Scituate, and arrive in Boston the same evening.

Passing through Dorchester, Quincy, Wyemouth, Hingham, Scituate, Hanover, Pembroke, Duxbury, Kingston, Plymouth to Sandwich. *Fare*, from Boston to Scituate, 1 doll. 25 cts. From Boston to Plymouth, 2 dolls. 50 cts. From Boston to Sandwich, 3 dolls. 63 cts.

.N. B. Extra Carriages can be obtained of the proprietor's, at Boston and Plymouth, at short notice.—
☞STAGE BOOKS kept at Boyden's Market-square, Boston, and at Fessendon's, Plymouth.

LEONARD & WOODWARD.

BOSTON, November 24, 1810.

Boston Mail Coach notice, 1810.

Greenwich, 11th June, 1825.

LOSS

OF

Mr. GRAHAM,

THE AERONAUT.

From the Statement beneath, it will be perceived that the above named Gentleman, in affording Amusement and Gratification to the Inhabitants of Greenwich and its vicinity, by his Ascent on Monday last, and thereby in some degree benefiting the Town, has Sustained a

Loss of £50.11s.2d.

and it having been Suggested to him by several Gentlemen of the place, that provided the same was made known and accompanied by an appeal to the well known liberallity of the Public here, they were coovinced it would have the effect of at least alleviating, if not altogether clearing him of so great a Loss. He therefore upon these conditions respectfully informs the Public, that Subscriptions for that purpose will be received at Mr. COLES, Bookseller London Street, Greenwich, and at the BAR OF THE MITRE TAVERN.

EXPENDITURE.	RECEIPT.
£. 91 : 12 : 2	£. 41 : 1 : 0

Printed by J. COLE, London Street, Greenwich.

and bookseller, John Bagford, who was collecting material for a never-to-be-written history of printing and whose albums are now in the British Museum; of Dr. John Johnson, sometimes Printer to the University of Oxford, whose gatherings are now in the possession of the University Press; of Mrs. Bella C. Landauer, whose immense collection is in the care of the New York Historical Society, and those with collections in other universities and institutions.

There will always, one hopes, be new men coming forward to put slips of paper into files, who, like Mr. Lewis, are not above ransacking garbage bins, waste-paper baskets and even peering down into a muddy Ipswich gutter to find a hardware label of satisfying beauty.

PRINTS Here is an enormous and exciting field with great opportunities for the new collector. Printmaking has been going on for hundreds of years now, and in spite of all the new

175

mechanical processes which have come into being, continues as vigorously as ever. If in some departments only the wealthy can compete for the rarities, the possibilities outside this are immense: prints in general, I believe, are still undervalued compared with the rise in price of other things and also with the fall in the value of money.

How to begin? Some people buy a print ot two, framed, simply because they want some nice pictures on the wall, such as a seascape, a landscape, or a farmyard scene; and buying a print is one of the cheapest ways of getting a good picture. Others buy them because they may be interested in some special subject, like MILITARIA, or a particular profession. Some of these may become involved in GRANGERISING books with the prints they find.

But *print* collectors, whether they go in for a particular artist, or a special kind—bird or flower prints, English mezzotints, town views, historical subjects, portraits, Currier and Ives lithographs, sporting or marine prints—keep them in special cabinets and portfolios: and it may be worth pointing out here that to enjoy prints it is not at all necessary to have them framed and hung on a wall. The Chinese often keep theirs in boxes or rolls and bring them out when they feel so disposed, or want to show them to their friends. There is sense in this: leave a picture on your wall, and there may come a time when you never look at it.

The subject is so vast that in this piece I have space only to outline the technical differences between the various kinds of prints; to explain the difference between an etching and an engraving, a mezzotint and an aquatint, a lithograph and a serigraph. In CURRENT PRICES I have given some indication of the prices at which they can be bought, all the way from Albrecht Dürer to Picasso.

First of all, a print, though it may copy or reproduce, say, an oil painting, is not a *picture reproduction,* which is a photographic affair—though not necessarily to be despised on that account. A print, in the sense we are using the word here, is a *picture* in its own right, which has been printed by one or other of the various processes available. No matter if it is an original design, or if it is based on some other artist's original work in some other medium, *it must have been worked on in some way* by an engraver or an etcher, a mezzotinter or a lithographer, or whatever process it is, so that it again becomes an original work of art.

Technically, prints fall into three main categories, *Relievo, Intaglio* and *Planographic.* In relievo, or relief, as its name suggests, the parts of the picture which are to appear dark stand up in relief, like pieces of type, and the picture is printed in an ordinary letterpress printing press such as you will find still being used in old printing works for taking hand 'pulls'. It acts on the same principle as a wine press, and in fact was probably adapted from it, wine having presumably been fancied long before prints were. The result is the *Woodcut,* perhaps the oldest of all processes, and much used for book illustration, for the block sat very happily alongside moveable type when that came along in the fifteenth century. A woodcut will tend to show through a magnifying glass, or from the touch of a finger, indentations in the printed lines and an embossed effect on the back.

In true wood *cutting* (as distinct from the *Wood-engraving,* we shall be discussing this later), the wood is cut 'on the plank', i.e. with the grain, in some soft wood like sycamore, cherry, maple or white holly, and it may show this grain as a 'texture'.

Of the intaglio processes the earliest is *Line engraving,* deriving from the art of the goldsmith and ARMOURER: it is said to have originated in what is known as *Niello* work, where engravings on the surface of silver or bronze were filled with a black sulphur composition (as in Indian *bidri* work); and it was found that the paper proofs of these designs, taken from time to time to let the engraver see how he was progressing, were in themselves interesting productions.

Taking a 'graver' or burin, and moving his work around on a cushion as he needs, the engraver ploughs little furrows to create his lines: if any 'burr' stands up along the edges of his cuts he removes it with a scraper. Variety of tone and texture can be obtained by close engraving or cross-hatching; but the characteristic of the method is clean bold line.

Drypoint is a kind of engraving, but instead of using a graver, the artist takes a tool of pointed steel which gives freer line, and

177

*Engraving of the Fall of Icarus, by Frans Huys after
Pieter Brueghel the Elder, first state.*

having ploughed his line he does not remove the 'burr' with a
scraper but allows it to stay and impart a rich velvety quality
to the line which has great attractions.

Mezzotint takes this even further by abolishing the line
altogether and giving something very like the tonal quality of
an oil painting. Here a copper plate is given a roughened
surface by means of a 'rocker', with teeth-like serrations in the
lower edge: the design is either drawn or transferred on to the
'rocked' surface, the burr of which is removed with a steel
scraper, working, of course, from dark to light. By this means
all gradations of tone are given from the deepest up to white.

Still with the intaglio processes, we next come to *Etching*,
which gives a much freer line than either line engraving or
drypoint. The plate is covered with an etching-ground with a
waxy composition, then blackened in smoke, after which the
design is traced with etching needles of various sizes drawing
in reverse, thus laying bare the surface of the copper. The plate
is immersed in an acid bath which eats away the exposed metal;
and the results are produced by varying the time the plate is left

in the bath, and alternately 'biting in' and 'stopping out' with varnish. Etching, as noted elsewhere, was used by the decorator of ARMOUR, GUNS, SWORDS and other WEAPONS. In *Soft-ground Etching*, tallow is added to the ground and the design is made with a lead pencil on a piece of grained paper stretched across the ground, and the impressions thus made are later etched in the same way as described above. This process naturally gives a much softer look, and more broken line, and can produce the effect of a drawing by pencil, chalk or charcoal.

Aquatint is akin to mezzotint, and etching, in that a ground is laid and then subjected to 'biting in' and 'stopping out' processes, but a more translucent effect is produced by using a ground of resin which can be applied as sand, or as a spirit and left to evaporate, when the acid (or aqua fortis) eats into the surface and produces a minute pitting. As a mezzotint gives the effect of an oil painting, so aquatint is closer to a water colour.

Stipple Engraving makes use of a needle point, or a roulette, to build up a tone in much the same way as is done nowadays by a half-tone process.

From time to time artists combine these processes to achieve the desired results, so that sometimes an etching can only be distinguished from a line engraving by deciding what proportion of the work is done by each method.

An entirely new method with the wood block was worked out in the early nineteenth century by Thomas Bewick (1728–1828), using the harder boxwood and engraving it with a graver on the end of the plank against the grain: this became the *Wood-engraving* as distinct from the woodcut, and its main feature was the greater use of the 'white line' as contrasted with the black outline of the woodcut. In the meantime, with the enormous increase in the demand for copies of prints both separately published and for use in illustrated books, printing from copper was replaced by *Steel-engraving*.

In the *Planographic* process, namely *Lithography*, the print is neither in relief nor in intaglio, but, as its name suggests, flat. It is a print made by drawing on to a stone or a metal plate—or transferring it thence by means of a transfer paper—in ink which has some kind of grease in it, like soap or tallow. The stone absorbs the grease, and it is 'etched in' with nitric acid:

179

after which the other parts of the stone will absorb water but not fatty materials: the process thus depends on the natural working of the antipathy between water and grease. The virtue of lithography is that it is an actual drawing, whether it is with chalk, brush or scraper, and displays exactly the artist's hand. The legend goes that Alois Senefelder, its inventor, made his discovery by happening to write out a laundry list for his mother using materials like this, which he had been experimenting with in learning to do engraving to save money: it seems a roundabout way of providing one's mother with a laundry list but boys have been known to do things in a roundabout way.

So far we have been discussing only monochrome processes: but colour can be provided by relievo, intaglio and planographic methods. Colour blocks were used in woodcuts from the earliest times and of course were highly developed by the Chinese and Japanese—though this is a department we hardly have room to pursue here. In general, line engraving and etching do not lend themselves very happily to colour, though coloured inks have been used on copper plates, and prints made from them have quite a different quality from photographic work: but better work, sometimes quite delightful, is seen where monochrome prints have been tinted by hand. It is in mezzotint, aquatint and stipple engraving, however, that colour shows to best advantage.

Various efforts at combining wood colour blocks with engraved or etched plates preceded the method patented by George Baxter in 1830 of using a succession of wood blocks, sometimes as many as twenty, for various tints, printing in oil colours, and, in fact, aiming at something like an oil painting. Lithography developed into *Chromo-lithography* and permitted much printing after the Old Masters, such as those published by the Arundel Society. Today much fine original work is being done in colour lithography, as also in *Serigraphy* or *Silk-screen* printing, whereby complicated mosaics of colour can be built up by the use of successive applications with screens blocked out in the required patterns.

In buying a print you will find that values depend very much on what is called its 'state'. A print passes through several,

180

perhaps many, stages before the artist is satisfied with it, each embodying new work; there are also variant impressions arising from the amount of ink used on a particular print. Moreover, the markings on the plate are in time worn down, and a 'late' impression may be a mere shadow of an early one. There is a story of an old collector in Paris, of great sensibility but limited resources in the way of cash, who, when prints were being pulled from plates made by one of his favourite artists, would hover around waiting for the exact moment when the impression was not so far worn that it displeased his taste, but sufficiently far on the run to bring it within his price range. But in general this question of states and impressions is something the tyro will perhaps find it better to pick up as he goes along: there are many who feel more attention is given to such considerations than they deserve. Certainly the beginner will find it more interesting first to familiarise himself with the subjects and styles of the print makers.

Of the meaning of abbreviations found on prints, the following selection may be helpful: *Delin., (deliniavet),* drew; *exc., exud., (exudit),* printed or published; *f.,fec., (fecit),* etched or engraved; *figuravit,* drew; *inv., (invenit),* designed; *pinx., (pinxit),* painted; *sc., sculp., (sculpsit),* engraved.

SALTGLAZED STONEWARE This entry is made, not with the idea of offering any detailed survey of this most interesting field of ceramics, but to define it, and also to list some fields of it.

Stoneware, of which porcelain is a variety, is clay pottery which has been fired to a temperature exceeding that of ordinary earthenware (such as a breadpan or an old Staffordshire blue plate), say 1200° to 1400°C., so that it becomes vitreous and impervious to liquids. In ancient China, through the use of two forms of felspathic rock, this developed into porcelain; but in Europe, where the Chinese secret remained unknown until early in the eighteenth century, potters wishing to offer a product with many of the qualities of porcelain stayed with stoneware.

It chiefly developed, however, in the northern countries,

181

Saltglazed stoneware: spirit flask representing the Duke of York, uncle of Queen Victoria and right, *Staffordshire 'Pew Group', early eighteenth century.*

since firing to such a high temperature called for vast quantities of the timber with which these countries were richly supplied. Since the lead glazes were unmanageable in kiln at such temperatures, but since for practical purposes such as cleanliness, some sort of glaze was required, it was found most expedient to use common salt, throwing it into the kiln at a certain moment of firing so that it combined with the alumina and silica in the clay to form a thin hard vitreous film on the surface.

Germany, and especially the Rhineland, was the great source of fine stonewares in post-mediaeval times, and BELLARMINES made around Cologne have already been mentioned.

From Höhr, in the Rhineland Westerwald (often called the *Kannenbackerland,* as the Staffordshire equivalent is called the Potteries) comes the jug of perhaps mid-nineteenth century date which continues the tradition.

Large covered pots and a great variety of other types, come

182

from Raeren near Aix-le-Chapelle, and are perhaps the finest of all German stonewares, flourishing principally in the second half of the sixteenth century. Saxony was another important centre, likewise Kreussen near Bayreuth, some of which had reliefs in the Rhineland style, others bright opaque enamel colours—the first appearance of this kind of decoration in Europe. Characteristic of Kreussen ware are great tankards with metal covers and a speciality was the *Schrauflasch,* a four- or six-sided flask with a metal screw stopper.

Derivations of the German product were made at Fulham, in London, by John Dwight (who called his product porcelain), in Nottingham and in the Potteries just mentioned.

In Staffordshire, however, an attempt was made to offer competition with Chinese porcelain by producing a delicate white stoneware which has now become high collecting— and no wonder, for with its delicate applied reliefs and mould- ing it is among the most delightful of wares, even if its hard pitted orange-skin surface was apt to wear away silver spoons. Teapots in the shape of kneeling camels, of houses and ships lead us to the enchantingly primitive bandsmen and horsemen, and also to the humour of the famous 'pew groups' where

Two mugs, one as a boot, another as a man in a dressing gown, and an annular vase, in Rhenish stoneware; Höhr-a-Rhein, nineteenth century.

ladies and gentlemen of the day (around 1740) are brought to life merely with adroit and witty use of rolls of clay and the potter's knife.

Saltglaze continued in production on the Continent, and had a lively rebirth in England in the early nineteenth century with the stoneware spirit flasks.

A variety of similar wares was made at Lambeth, and in Derbyshire, around Denby, Belper and Brampton and Chesterfield, the last two names often being used to describe these rather undercollected wares—perhaps because so many of them are hunting jugs and other items which have a largely male appeal.

The early American potters made white stoneware of the Staffordshire kind, while TOBY JUGS appeared in buff and brown, as well as many household crocks, much of it using clay from the rich deposits around Amboy, New Jersey: there

Stoneware figure vases by the Martin brothers, Southall, late nineteenth–early twentieth century.

is also some very attractively 'primitive' painting in blue on grey salt stoneware [RL 254].

In High Victorian days the tradition was kept alive by potters like Doulton, who among their art pottery made fine stoneware, some of them in the Rhenish tradition, some with incised decoration by individual craftsmen like, for example, the free sketches of animals and trees by Hannah Barlow.

As one has noted in the INTRODUCTION there are probably many items in this book—for example, the wares we have just been discussing—which could appeal equally well to the ladies as to the gentlemen, especially in the department of ceramics; but one could scarcely number among these the grotesque figures and mask jugs of the Martin Brothers of Southall, Middlesex. In a sense they represented a breakaway from the Doulton tradition, and they developed a family of fine vases in various natural forms, with skilful use of surface textures and colouring.

But quite what set them off on the track of these strange leering birds, grotesquely depraved human faces and the rest of the oddities is difficult to imagine. Until just before the last war scarcely anybody remembered the work of these brothers; but perhaps helped by the catalogue of Mr. F. J. Nettlefold's collection—he rented premises to the brothers—the London shops were scoured by collectors and dealers for specimens, so that they have now arrived at the final canon of collecting, the Sotheby, Christie and Parke Bernet class.

Which only goes to show that it is to the snapper-up of trifles when they are as yet unconsidered that the honours of collecting must always go.

SAND-GLASSES There are those of us who still find a sand-glass egg-timer to be the only reliable equipment for boiling an egg, for it neither gains nor loses, nor does it need winding.

There are hour-glasses which have measured out interminable sermons in churches and chapels; their age may be determined by the quality of the glass, which is darker in hue and oilier in the older types. There are ship's sand-glasses, measured

185

in half-hours to determine the striking of the bells, also *Log Glasses* for timing the running out of the log line which measures the ship's speed through the water.

Some glasses hold actual sand, but more accuracy will be given by ground marble dust, boiled in wine and reground. Large ones are marked with twelve hourly divisions; there are sets of four, each of them designed to mark the quarters, some of them splendidly inlaid and engraved. You might think that as the upper compartment emptied the sand would run out more quickly, but the makers have taken care of this: 'The angle of the double cone connecting the two chambers at the aperture is made equal to the angle at which the sand lies in repose.'

The collector of medical antiques will look for the small sand-glasses carried by doctors for timing your pulse.

SHIPS IN BOTTLES

> *Whither, O splendid ship, thy white sails crowding,*
> *Leaning across the bosom of the urgent West,*
> *That fearest nor sea rising, nor sky clouding,*
> *Whither away, fair rover, and what thy quest?*

Even more important, how, with all those white sails crowding, did it get through the neck of that light bulb?

The answer is, of course, that it didn't, at least not with all gear and tackle rigged. The sea goes in first, a mixture of materials such as sand, putty, cork and glue, roughed up and painted with long brushes and wires. Then the hull is inserted and glued into position in the sea. Masts and spars are pre-fabricated, folded into a neat package and again pushed into position where they can be stepped. Then the sails are raised by means of threads, and spread athwartships, after which a great deal of poking around and gluing makes all secure.

This ship in a light bulb is a fairly modern variation in an art which has been going on for many generations among sea-going men, using up the bottles which are never totally absent from the lower deck, and the hours of the watch below, which sometimes seem much longer than those of the watch on deck: they can also be a plentiful source of beer money after the

Sailing ships in a light bulb and a bottle.

anchor has been swallowed. The connoisseur in this field, of course, seeks out models of ships which did actually sail the seas, or of their types.

But ships are not the only things which have been magicked into bottles in this way. There are railway engines, which by the cut of their jib seem to have been made a very long time ago; and it would be surprising if there were not aircraft.

From Sweden in this *genre,* there are little weaving dolls; while another variety mounts bells which seem to be admirable concomitants to the tiny HORNS of Elfland.

If you want to make your own ship-in-a-bottle, there is a book about it [RL 254]. There is even a way to get inside it yourself: one ingenious person has put into a bottle a fisherman with a miniature bottle in his hand, inside which is a tiny replica of an early paddle steamer.

SHOP AND STORE SIGNS In the early years of the eighteenth century a man named David Wishart, a Scot, kept a shop in Coventry Street, London, in which he sold snuff and smoking tobacco. In those days, of course, before the houses in a street were numbered, everybody identified their place of business with a sign of some sort, which could be either a painted board or a figure. Since the Great Fire of London—it was claimed that the swinging signboards with which the streets were festooned, dried to a tinder by a long hot summer, had helped a great deal to carry the flames through the city—a restriction had been put on them, and tradesmen now preferred to use an effigy in the round.

Being a true Scot, David chose a figure of a highlander in doublet and trews: and by way of warning the Sassenach not to take the recent Act of Union too seriously, he armed the bonnie man with a targe and a claymore (though not of course, as we have seen in SWORDS, the *claidheamh mor,* which he might have wielded at Bannockburn).

The story goes that after the catastrophe of the '45 when Bonnie Prince Charlie had fled for his life and his supporters gone underground, Jacobites met in David's house to toast the 'King-over-the-water' in secret: and thus it is, according to the legend, that the big Highlander has become one of the signs and the tokens of the snuff merchant—though now, as you see from the picture, he is armed with nothing more dangerous than a SNUFF MULL.

But he who starts to collect such effigies will find—as collectors of TRADESMEN'S CARDS know full well—that there is no very hard and fast ruling about the things they stand for. The tobacco and snuff men did not, for example, remain faithful to the Jacobite cause, especially when they braved the dangers of the New World. They would sometimes use historical figures like *Sir Walter Raleigh,* or *Uncle Sam;* also when offering tobacco from the Old World, the *Turk. Blackamoors* or *Pompeys* were an echo of the Bristol trades, which we have seen on the labels in PRINTED EPHEMERA, and there is also the *Princess Pocohontas,* though often she is simply a *Squaw.* The most ubiquitous figure in America, of course, well known to an older generation in Europe through the educational work of the late Mr. Mack Sennett in his Keystone Comedies, is the *Cigar-store Indian.* There are many types of Indian, with a wide range of stylisation; and that the searching out of them has been going on for a long time is evidenced by the fact that even in 1911 a lady named Kate Sanborn thought it fun to go *Hunting Indians in a Taxicab,* and published the results of her quest.

There are a number of known carvers of these figures: Mr. Erwin C. Christensen [RL 254] mentions a certain Thomas Brooks of New York who carved *ships' figureheads* and these

188

Right: *an eighteenth century wrought iron sign of a posting station, and* left: *a wooden cigar-store figure of a Turk, nineteenth century.*

Indians for thirty-five years. No doubt the one took over from the other in his workshop, and indeed it does seem likely that the larger type of effigy used in America, with the remote and distant gaze as though surveying in vast waters, derived from the seafaring types rather than those smaller figures which perhaps followed the English tradition.

Sometimes, indeed, an actual figurehead has been adapted for a sign; there is, or was, a fine one of a Swan outside an hostelry of the same name on the Folkestone-Ashford Road in Kent; and of course there are many antique dealers who choose this way of advertising themselves; notably the *Post Boy* on the London to Hastings road. That the latter proved a good investment is shown by the fact that a few years ago it lured in an American dealer who bought the entire stock.

Tobacconists apart, what signs are there, and what do they signify? The red plaster jars of the oil and colour merchant, the huge padlock of the ironmonger, the golden trout of the fishing-tackle seller, the mortar and pestle, the tea canister, the pair of spectacles, the razor, the open umbrella, the top hat, the hanging boot or shoe—all these explain themselves adequately enough and many may still somewhere or other be seen *in situ*. As in the case of *fire insurance plaques* and *opercula,* there

189

are no doubt many local collectors and dealers bivouacked nearby and waiting for them to be dismantled by the house-breaker. Others of course are not so easy to place, perhaps because a man may have moved from one shop to another and decided to retain the familiar sign, or he may have combined it with his own. Such pairings as the *Bull and Mouth*, the *Lamb and Dolphin*, the *Bull and the Bedpost*, the *Three Nuns and the Hare*, seem to invite this explanation. Innkeepers, who in England have by law been obliged to show a sign since at least the fourteenth century, preferred on the whole to use animals or heraldry of one sort or another; the *Bear and the Ragged Staff* has perhaps been seen around Tewkesbury ever since the day that Queen Elizabeth Tudor's Leicester owned land there. The royal coat of arms of various reigns is often seen splendidly carved, gilded and painted; for example, outside the *Rose and Crown* in Tonbridge, Kent.

Considering the disdain with which these examples of popular or folk art were treated in Victorian times it is surprising that so many have survived, either in their original places or in collections. Readers of Dickens will recall his reference in *Dombey & Son,* to one of the 'little timber mid-

Snuff and tobacconist's sign of a Highlander, with snuff mull, from a shop in High Street, Lewes, Sussex.

shipmen in obsolete naval uniform eternally employed outside
the shop doors of nautical-instrument makers, taking observa-
tions of the hackney coaches': the one outside Sol Gill's shop
bore 'at its right eye the most offensively disproportionate
piece of machinery'. He also poked fun at the fine lively horse
which still stands outside the *Great White Horse* at Ipswich,
scene of Mr. Pickwick's nocturnal appearance in the widow
lady's bedroom, as a 'stone statue of some rapacious animal
with flying mane and tail distinctly resembling an insane
carthorse'.

The smaller figure already mentioned which stood on the
counter or in the shop window, is perhaps a tradition on its
own. To this genre the Staffordshire potters contributed giant
tea-pots, bull's and pig's heads for butcher's shops, swans and
cows for dairies—and apparently still do so for supplies may be
bought by the dozen. The glassmaker made the huge coloured
bottles found in chemists' shops; and there are many others of
the type.

Today, unlike the great Charles, we find character, charm,
spirit and naive vigour in most of these things, many of which
are, in the phrase of Nina Fletcher Little [RL 255] 'tangible
expressions of the average man's creative impulse': others are
simple craftsmen's shapes, totally repetitive. Still others, however, betray more than a passing acquaintance with schooled
art; someone was producing naval figures around New Bedford, Mass., of a much more sophisticated type than the one
Dickens satirised; there are some fine bold carvings of animals;
some echoes of Hogarth and Rowlandson; some lovely
Pocohontas; and also some baroque decorations which show
fascinating correspondences with the work of the decorators in
other fields.

One does not look only in junk shops for these things: your
true collector, as we have already seen elsewhere, will look
everywhere. For example, in tapping on the door of a house in
a country village to ask my way recently, I noticed on the edge
of a garden rockery three cast-iron high relief heads of a bull,
a pig, and a sheep, which had no doubt once graced the shop
front of some local butcher. They were not for sale, but I found
they could be bought.

191

SILVER SNUFF BOXES Snuff boxes are made in so many different materials and in such diverse forms that an account of all of them would become a mere catalogue—and hardly, unless you own a large mansion, a very feasible collecting possibility. So should we not limit ourselves to one material: and since there is little about silver in this book might we not choose that metal? And as there is no need to be disobliging to those near relatives of ours who collect TOBACCO BOXES AND JARS, could we not use a little of our space here to show an argentiferous box or two in their line of country?

Among the earliest tobacco boxes we find are the small simple oval ones with a pull-off cover, like that shown here which commemorates the martyr's death of Charles I in 1649. They often bear heraldic crests which, with a little research, may lead you to their original owner. A generation later, in Restoration times, one has the small rounded or 'cut-corner' box with 'scratch' engraving of, perhaps, mythical birds or foliate designs—perhaps even this odd design of a heart in flames upon a rooftop.

The oval box with rayed bright cutting spreading out from the monogram and shield, which is by Samuel Hennell, 1795, typifies the more restrained styles of the Adam era at the end of the eighteenth century. No less simple, and almost a reversion to the earlier shape is the slender waistcoat pocket box of the same decade which is only $\frac{1}{4}$ in. in depth. The strongest possible reaction from this austerity, however, is seen in the magnificent table box by John Bridge, which bears the hallmark for 1822 and is very much in the French taste of the period. Even deeper relief decoration than this, however, could be used twenty years later, as is seen in the other table box by Nathaniel Mills of Birmingham, 1846. It shows a view of

Above: *a selection of silver and silver-mounted snuff boxes, dating from Charles II to William IV.* Opposite: *silver gilt George IV table snuff box with a pastoral scene in the Louis Quinze manner.*

Buckingham Palace; and visitors to London (for Londoners themselves never look at their own city) will be interested to note that it shows the Marble Arch on its original site, before it was moved to the north of Hyde Park at 'Marble Arch'. Mills and others made a great many of these boxes, with views of great houses and castles, and florid as the style may be to our present tastes there is no denying their superb craftsmanship.

Some collectors like to specialise in subjects, for example commemorative ones, or they may like sporting motifs with hunting scenes, horses' and hounds' heads, prize fighters, etc. There are also reproductions of famous pictures, either landscapes or views, painted in enamels or upon an ivory mount. Others like *fantaisies,* such as a silver mouse with eyes of red garnet and a hinged head to permit the insertion of a snuff spoon; while those who extend their range to silver-mounted wares will find boxes made from shells of terrapins or turtles, the box underneath having a head and flippers; mussel shells are used in this way, also stag cowrie shells with silver lids. Scrolls, shell and diaper work came in strongly with the Georgians, as in every other kind of silver, together with a

193

good deal of repoussé work; the bombé shape appears as it does in sideboards, while the cartouche so beloved of the Chippendalians is frequently seen.

Snuff boxes should open smoothly and gently, then shut with a hermetically satisfying 'pfft' sound. Why, then, do nosologists tap their boxes three times before opening them? Some say that they are making sure the snuff is shaken away from the edge of the box and the hinges; others that there is here an act of appeasement to the gods, analogous to the reluctance of smokers to light three cigarettes in succession from the same flame. Perhaps by this elegant and sometimes expressive gesture they are showing the rest of us how far we have fallen from grace.

Small items of English silver are sometimes unmarked, others have had their marks worn off by use: in these cases, the collector will have to be guided by his judgment and knowledge if he wants to date his pieces. But if the marks are readable, there is a little book [RL 255] by Frederick Bradbury, obtainable from most silversmiths, by which one can interpret the assay office, the maker's mark, the annual date letter, the standard mark and the sovereign's head, etc., and so learn precisely where the piece was made, by whom, and of what standard of metal.

SNUFF MULLS AND RASPS There was a famous drawing by Charles Keene in *Punch,* during the eighties, which showed a Scot in a railway carriage proffering his 'sneeshin miln' to a fellow traveller who rivalled even 'Snozzle' Durante in the size of his nose.

'Tak' a pench!' says the first Scot. 'Na, I'm obleeged t'ye— ah dinna tak't,' replies the large-nosed one. Whereupon the first one sighs and says, 'Man—that's a pity! Ye've gr-r-raund accaummodation for't.'

The mull offered was not so grand an affair as the one shown here, obviously made for the messroom or the baronial hall—a complete ram's head mounted with silver and engraved, and set with cairngorms. It was much more like a small pocket one, which a curious collector bought, photographed and sent

Snuff mull in the form of a ram's head, mounted with silver and set with cairngorms.

to me asking what I thought it was.

Some of my readers may not be aware that the Scots have a certain reputation for frugality, or shall we say, caution in laying out their 'bawbees'; and at a time when the rest of Europe was buying snuff and carrying it in neat little boxes, the Scots preferred to buy their tobacco in the *carotte,* or plug as we would call it, and use a sort of portable snuff factory. It was usually made from a ram or cow horn, or perhaps a hoof, or half-hoof (all of which, of course, cost nothing) and the inside was cut with sharp ridges from top to bottom, so that the owner could scrape his plug of tobacco in it and produce his snuff.

The properly equipped mull had accessories in the way of a small miniature hammer and pick to break up caked snuff, a rake to smooth the surface, a spoon or 'nose shovel' and a brush to sweep the surplus snuff from moustache and beard.

Snufftakers more extravagant with their pennies went in for a *Snuff Rasp,* something like a nutmeg grater, with a compartment behind to catch the grated snuff and a hole to pour it from. In a more sophisticated form this became a box of carved pearwood, boxwood or walnut, often inlaid with ivory, coloured woods, or gold or silver piqué. Dean Swift had one entirely of ivory. Very large ones were made for shops or inns.

In France the *rappoir* (snuff= *tabac rapé*) became a most elaborately carved affair, often with religious subjects, and similar boxes were made in Italy and the Netherlands.

SPURS AND GOADS *'Then came unto the knight seven noble maidens attired in white, and girt his sword unto his side. That being done four knights of the most honourable in that presence put on his spurs.'* Thus the author of *The Booke of Honor and Armes,* printed by Richard Jones, at the sign of the Rose and Crown, near Holborn Conduit, in the year 1590.

Collectors have to thank this emblematical and ritual significance of the spur for the finely wrought specimens which have come down to us from the mediaeval workshops. But its history is much longer [RL 255]: at first, it seems, the spur was part of the stirrup and this practice has persisted down to modern times in some parts of the East. By the time of the writer Theophrastus (*fl.*350 B.C.) the two had evidently parted company for he writes mockingly of the kind of men who show off by walking around in their stirrups.

But apart from what you can find with the spade, collecting will start with the mediaeval *Pryck Spur* with a single spike, perhaps conical in shape, mounted on a rising moulding or ball so that it would not cause unnecessary pain and damage to the horse. The *Rowel Spur* seems to have appeared in Europe sometime in the early thirteenth century and in the next century it gradually took over. The early rowel spurs had deeply depressed sides passing under the ankle bone without a crest. The points of the *Star Rowel* are divided up to the centre, those of the *Rose Rowel* only part of the way; when made in some other fanciful pattern they were *Foliated.* You may see fully developed spurs of this type, as worn by Edward the

196

Black Prince, hanging over his tomb in Canterbury Cathedral.

The spur was deeply affected by changes in the development of **ARMOUR**. The transition from mail to plate, especially the adoption of *flanchards,* or iron valences, round the horse's side, called for elongation of the neck, sometimes requiring the spur to reach a length of as much as fourteen inches. During the fifteenth century the neck shortened, but the rowels themselves lengthened, perhaps up to three inches. With the gradual disappearance of the horse-armour in the seventeenth century much plainer rowels were used, while the Cavaliers of the seventeenth century used a large and heavy type not unlike that of the Mexicans. 'Jingles' came into fashion at this period.

By late Stuart times the curved sides had straightened and so much width was required to cover the heavy boot of the period that they were often hinged. The eighteenth century saw

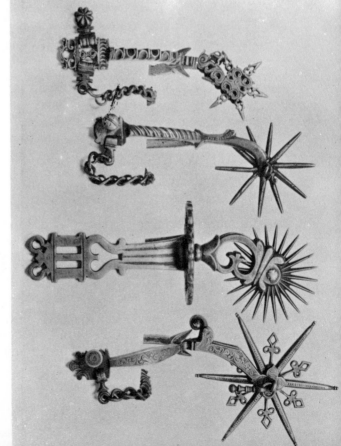

Spurs: top to bottom: *South American, with pierced and engraved plates; Moroccan; Spanish; Brazilian, engraved and with pierced rowels.*

smaller rowels still, with much less elaboration.

The interesting and very distinctive Mexican spurs with the large circular heel-plate seem to have derived originally from the Moors through Spain; similar traces of their styles are seen in the kidney-shaped opening in the neck.

The *Hunting Spur* changed very little between early Georgian and modern times; but with the coming of 'trowsers' in the early nineteenth century, there arrived also the military *Box Spur* with its short spike driven into the back of the boot heel and screws holding the sides fast: wearers of them had either to defy Theophrastus or change their boots.

Goads are perhaps gruesome collecting for their own sake but they have sometimes been regarded as **WEAPONS,** a collector of which will perhaps want one of the Syrian ox goads eight to ten feet long with a prick at one end and a paddle at the other for cleaning the plough; for it was presumably with this weapon that Shamgar and his fellow husbandmen slew six hundred of the Philistines. Charles Darwin was struck with the fighting potential of the twenty-foot ox goad of the South American pampas, with their projecting spur for the leaders and middle pair.

Goad is rather a derogatory term for the *Ankus* used for the Rajput elephants: its rich inlays and exquisite damascening make it one of the aristocrats of metal work.

STAFF WEAPONS   It must have occurred to man very early in his career as a thinking animal that if he lashed a stone or a sharp piece of metal to a length of wood, it would make a very useful **WEAPON** with which to bring down his enemies or the animals he lived on, either by striking them or hurling it at them. It could also make a very useful agricultural implement. Today, it offers collectors one of the finest kinds of decoration for an interior stone or plaster wall, as many an owner of a raftered hall or barn has discovered.

These *Pole-arms*—as they have also been called—come in wide variety, they often have the most confusingly inter-changeable names, but they can be grouped into families.

The *Club* started as a means of crushing or bashing, and as a striking weapon ought to be distinguished from the *Throwing Stick.* Some are made entirely from one piece of timber, hardened and often carved for piercing like the bird-headed clubs of New Caledonia; others have points of materials like nephrite and bone (the Maoris) and rhinoceros horn (the Bechuanas). The many-bladed throwing knives of African tribes is the same idea expressed in metal.

One line of development of the club led it towards bludgeons and truncheons, another in the direction of the mediaeval *War Hammer,* which gave a surname to Charles Martel, who drove the Saracens from France in the first Battle of Poitiers in 732. At Hastings, the *fyrdd,* a kind of county militia of enlisted men, had in their repertoire a heavy long-handled stone hammer which they threw in the manner of modern athletes. These objects would come spinning over your forward lines in a great arc, and a volley of them could be highly disturbing to infantry massed in any kind of close formation.

When the increasing power of the longbow and even more the crossbow called for tougher and more completely enveloping plate ARMOUR, the hammer was found a useful means of breaking it open. But it needed greater sophistication in the way of pointed faces, spikes and flukes—and duly received it, as we can see in the *Martel-de-fer* or *Reiterhammer* (as seen on page 200).

In the fourteenth to the sixteenth centuries the foot soldiers' long-handled hammer, at first called a *Maul,* was in more knightly hands—but still on foot—given a spike and a face channelled into points, also a curved beak, thus earning the name *bec de faucon* or *rabenschnabel.*

Another derivative of the club was the *Mace,* a weapon said to have been used by the prelates who fought alongside the land-hungry warriors in the Conqueror's army. As holy men they were expected to spill as little blood as possible in chastising their enemies: but to judge by the edge on the six or seven wings of steel brazed on to many of them these instruments were capable of producing a rich enough flow of gore.

Certainly no such tender feelings could have been in the minds of those who used that variety of the mace called the

199

From right to left: *mace of the 'Morning Star' type, with 22 spikes, the head inlaid with gold scrolled foliage, the haft damascened in gold with delicate arabesques on a russeted ground. Milanese, circa 1580. War hammer of the* martel de fer *type, the precursor of the* bec-de-faucon *or* rabenschnabel, *handy for breaking open plate armour.*

Mace in the Gothic fashion, the head with six small flanges, south German, circa 1470.

War hammer of hollowed diamond section balanced by a sharp bec-de-faucon, *minutely decorated with Italian etched floral work, as practised between 1480 and 1520. Italian, circa 1490.*

Mace of Milanese type of blued steel damascened with finely executed floral arabesques in silver and gold.

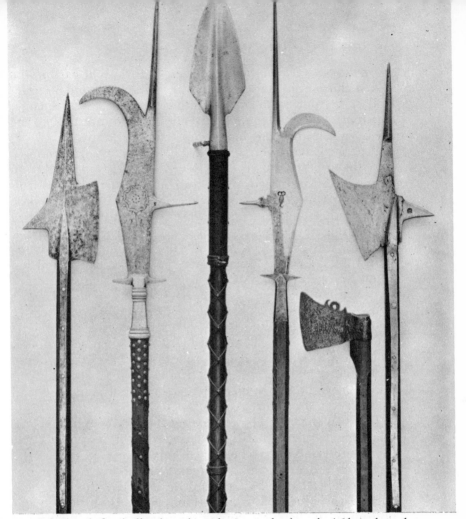

From right to left: *halberd with maker's mark, length* 16¼ *inches, late fifteenth century.*

Axe head with modern halve. Engraved with letters I.H.S. German or French, circa early sixteenth century.

Bill, the face incised with a double rose with thorns on each side and crescent shaped ornament. The maker's mark is clearly visible. Because of the Tudor-style rose the weapon has been described as English, but the form is typically Italian of about 1515.

Boar spear, the staff plaited with leather thongs secured by round-headed nails. Length of blade, including socket, 10 5/16 *inches.*

Bill, with spikes of strong diamond section, stamped with maker's mark. Length, including socket, 35¼ *inches. Italian, sixteenth century.*

Halberd, typical of the kind carried by German and Swiss infantry at the end of the fifteenth and first half of the sixteenth centuries.

Morgenstern or *Morning Star,* for here we are right back to the spiked club of the caveman. Popular in Germany and Switzerland in the fourteenth and fifteenth centuries it owes its name, apparently, to its usefulness in wishing 'Good morning' to the enemy when surprising him asleep before cockcrow.

Place a chain between the spiked ball and the handle and you have the military flail, or *Holy Water Sprinkler,* so named from its resemblance to the ecclesiastical *asperge*; there are also flails like the agricultural ones, but with iron or steel arms and spikes.

So handy an implement as the axe could hardly have escaped being translated into the *Battle-Axe,* which, as a striking weapon, was extensively used in the age of the Great Migrations by the Celtic, Germanic and Slav tribes who wandered about Europe in search of new lands and in doing so founded some of our modern nations. At Hastings, King Harold's housecarles, or professional soldiers, carried spears and swords, but they also used the heavy Danish axe, like a domestic hatchet, with a shaft about four feet long. When near enough to use it you stuck your kite-shaped shield into the ground, took hold of the axe with both hands, and if you went about things the right way you could kill a horse with one blow and its rider on the return swing.

This was the type of axe liked by the Franks and therefore called the *francisca.* Charles Martel, apart from his predilection for hammers and javelins, used this axe—not unlike the American Indian tomahawk—against the arrows and darts of the Saracens. Later the Germans developed a throwing axe with sharp points before and behind, and also on the top and bottom of the haft: the correct spinning action was deadly.

Another line of development took a hint from the hewing spear of the Vikings, a cutting weapon which could be used while keeping out of the way of the enemy's axe or sword. By the fifteenth century this had been elaborated into the *Pole-Axe.* Handsomely decorated and elevated to knightly rank, it was popular with gentlemen trying their strength against each other on foot in the lists.

A lighter form of Pole-Axe was the *Halberd.* Generally speaking, it had a longer shaft and was lighter than its predecessor, and perhaps at first had a crescent blade, and later

202

various cleaver-like shapes, with pointed flukes and pike tops.

It was originally, of course, a peasant's weapon like the English *Bill,* which it greatly resembled; and when swung by a strong man it could cut through mail as though it were wool. It brought down Charles le Temeraire, the last of the Dukes of Burgundy, to die in a muddy ditch at Nancy.

The *Bill* and its derivatives, especially the *War-Scythe,* obviously stem from the butcher's cleaver, the hedgeman's slasher, the harvester's sickle. The bill specialised in curved prongs rather than an expanse of blade, while the *Glaive* offered a broader space for decoration, which eventually turned it into a ceremonial arm. The *Partizan* is really a spear, with lengthened and broadened blade, which lends itself even more to display. The Yeomen of the Guard and the Yeomen Warders of the Tower in London still carry it today on their occasions. It was borne by officers of the infantry until the nineteenth century, but for this purpose it is perhaps more correctly described as a *Spontoon* or half-pike. The name *Spetum,* as used by collectors today, seems to imply a *Corsèque.*

To return for a moment up the family tree to the *Throwing Stick,* as distinct from the *Club.* This gave us the throwing *Dart, Arrow* or *Javelin,* in fact, the *Spear.* The blade is usually shaped like a broad leaf, though there are versions which are arrow-shaped, like the German *Wurfpfeil.*

After the *Spear* the *Lance,* that most romantic of weapons, the arm of the horseman from time immemorial, though presumably one had to wait for the stirrup to be invented before it became fully effective. A long slender shaft of ash or bamboo, a piked or a leaf-shaped blade socketed on to the shaft, and a sling of hide, and nothing could be better devised for the swift onslaught—but after that you needed a SWORD.

With the lance and the long straight swords of the Migrations, the Goths won that extraordinary battle which changed the whole course of military tactics in A.D. 378 at Adrianople, and established the superiority of cavalry over infantry for a thousand years.

The Assyrians and the Egyptians used the lance. In the hands of the fifteenth-century knight it took on a tapered form, with a narrow hand-grip near the end, protected by a steel disc

203

called a vamplate. The tilting lance usually had a rebated head. The fifteen-foot pole tipped with steel never really went out of use. One of the answers to the cavalry charge in the sixteenth century was the foot soldier's *Pike*. The great specialists in this weapon were the Swiss, their highly organised tightly-knit formations of infantry being armed with pike and halberd. From the battle of Mortgarten (1315)—for two hundred years, the sturdy men from the free cantons resisted and even dominated most of the European armies of the day.

Their pike had an ashen shaft eighteen or more feet long with a steel head another foot long. Holding it in both hands at shoulder height, with each successive rank pointing it at different angles, a body of pikemen could move swiftly forward for a mile or more, hiding their halberdiers behind something like a moving hedgehog. The moment contact was made the ranks of the pikemen would open and the halberdiers would emerge to do their deadly work, followed by bearers of two-handed swords, morning stars and *Lucerne hammers*—a fearful variation on the halberd with curved prongs instead of the hatchet blade, with which you could drag a horseman from his saddle. No wonder the Swiss Confederates managed to keep their mountain homelands inviolate for centuries.

One hopes that nobody will take the foregoing as more than a brief summary of the family of staff weapons and their uses and some of the effects they have had on history and politics; nor expect the present writer to delve into the implications of the many names which have been offered to describe the various genera and species. It is for the new collector to take his pleasure in these fields, with help from the READING LIST [248, 255], and find his fascinated way among such items as the *Bardiche* and the *Brandistock*, the *Gisarme* and the *Godendag*, the *Lancegay* and the *Langdebeve*, the *Rawcon* and the *Runka*. This will keep him busy in Europe; after that he has the rest of the world.

SWORDS The sword is the symbol of power, authority, protection and justice. Perhaps the finest of them all, both aesthetically and in fighting power for its day was the sword of the middle Bronze Age in Europe. It has a blade shaped nearly like a willow leaf, with a short, clubbed tang, the point is long and deadly for the thrust, the blade thickens exactly where it should for the most terrible of sweeping cuts; and there is a reverse curve towards the hilt for that back-handed slash which completes what the forward swing has begun. It is so beautifully balanced that Mr. Oakeshott [RL 255] recommends you to use only three fingers to hold it, the forefinger lying down the shoulder, the thumb on the other side. No wonder men have given personal names to such swords.

But the men of the Great Migrations, the huge-handed Burgundians, the Almains, the Franks, with their more highly developed skills, knew how to forge weapons from iron, and so were able to arm themselves with a longer and slenderer sword having nearly parallel edges tapering slightly to a rounded point. With this they struck down everywhere the beautiful sword of the bronze founders, especially in Gaul and Britain, where it lingered long after iron was worked in other ways. As the wandering tribes increased in power and settled in their new homelands they encrusted their swords with jewels and decorated them with elaborate engraving.

This sword, shorn of its luxurious trimmings, then became the austerely beautiful sword of the Vikings of the Norse epics. They also had their names—the *Durnadal* of Roland, the poisoned *Hrunting* of Beowulf, the *Excalibur* of King Arthur, the English *Quersteinbeis*, with which, as its name indicates, its owner, by a single stroke, split a large millstone in two.

The chivalry of the Middle Ages took this sword, gave it a quillon, or cross-guard (it made the weapon look like the Cross) and balanced it with a larger pommel. For the *Bastard,* or Hand-and-a-Half sword, they added 10 inches of length, making it 45 to 55 inches, so that you could use it with one hand or two as circumstances warranted: there was also a six-foot version which really did need two hands.

These swords would cut through mail and even plate, and a man's legs could be sliced through with one blow—this actually happened at Visby, as we can see from a body buried there. The German soldiers of the early fifteenth century preferred the *Two-Handed sword,* covering the base of the blade with

205

leather so that one hand could work beyond the quillon: there could be another shorter quillon beyond.

The Romans had generally preferred the point of the sword to its cutting edge, as used by the people they called barbarians. St. Louis told his men to use the point; and in late mediaeval times the point was revived in the *Estoc,* or *Panzerstecher,* with a blade of square or triangular section, which perhaps started life as a short lance—and in its heavier form continued to do so. But as a lighter weapon it began to supersede the very long sword with a thin, but two-edged blade which—now that trial by combat in the lists was out of fashion—gentlemen had taken to wearing and using to settle their quarrels. From

Viking sword, the thrusting weapon of the West. Ninth or tenth century. Incised on the forward face of the quillons are the letters H L I. Length 30⅛ inches.

Above: *Mediaeval knightly sword, descendant of the above and the weapon of Froissart and the Hundred Years' War. The wheel pommel 'is heavy enough to give good counterbalance. The two-edged blade has a broad diamond section, stiff and strongly tapering. Maker's mark, a small cross. French, circa 1375–1400. Length 30 inches.*

Below: *Two-handed sword, having a two-edged flamboyant blade. Maker's mark of the Christolph Stantlers, father and son, of Munich, circa 1580. Beyond the forward curving quillons, strong side lugs protect the second hand when extended to grasp it.*

Garniture of rapier and companion left-hand dagger, chiselled and pierced, the hilts signed by Antonio Cilenta of Naples. Circa 1650.

Italy came the art of fencing and from there and France the *Epée Rapière*, or *Rapier*; and the Estoc form of this became anglicised as the *Tuck*.

At first the parrying was done with a cloth wrapped over the left arm; then a DAGGER was used in the left hand: both sword and dagger were made as a *garniture* and decorated *en suite*. By middle Stuart times the rapier had developed into a light weapon which could itself be used for parrying, and the dagger *á main gauche* survived only in Spain for another century.

There were still fighting swords, of course; the two-handed and the hand-and-a-half swords continued in use, though in much greater sophistication. The true claymore of the Scottish Highlands was not the basket-hilted broadsword of popular legend, but the *claidheamh mor* or Great Sword—a big two-hander, usually with upward-sloping quillons.

As the rapier developed, the straight wide cross-guard gave place to the *Swept Hilt,* having a continuous knuckle-guard and sweeping quillon; then either the flat *Dish Hilt* or the deep *Cup Hilt.* As might be expected, these swords were given lavish decoration, perhaps the most interesting of which is the chiselling in steel, which often reaches considerable heights of sculptural artistry.

Even more elaborate and costly decoration was given the *Smallsword,* which took the rapier's place in the mid-seventeenth century. As the weapon now worn day by day on social occasions it expressed the refinement and the extravagance first of the late Renaissance, then of the eighteenth century. Here, as much as in any china cabinet or on any snuffbox, one may find in chased gold and enamel work, even in Dresden porcelain, the luxury of the baroque and the rococo. By easy stages the smallsword declined into the modern *Courtsword,* as degenerate in its race as Mr. Flint's bowler hat is in that of the HELMET.

But military fighting had still been going on. Cromwell's men used the *Broadsword,* a weapon with a wide double-edged blade having a basket or shell hilt and a heavy round pommel. The Scottish variety (misnamed the claymore, as noted above) had a conical pommel; and the Scots also favoured a *Backsword,* with a single edge and a blunt back. The so-called *Mortuary Sword* was another variation, used by the Cavalier or Royalist cavalry in the Civil War, who saw in the chiselled human face on the hilt a remembrance of their martyred king, Charles I.

That great innovator, Gustavus Adolphus of Sweden, made much use of the slightly curving *Sabre,* with its characteristic stirrup-hilt. It had been successfully used by the Hungarian and Polish light cavalry when they drove the Turks back from Vienna in 1683, and he gave it to his own new highly mobile light cavalry squadrons, proving it to be more effective than arming cavalry with PISTOLS, carbines or musketoons. Seventy years later Marlborough used the weapon magnificently at the crisis of the battle of Blenheim, when he sent on his cavalry not at a gallop but 'at a quick trot' in a series of thin lines: the manoeuvre took nerve, but it succeeded.

The all-purpose *Hanger* (a name later used for its attachment) was also usually slightly curved, though straight ones are known. This was useful when meeting villains armed with bludgeons and truncheons on shipboard (where it became the naval *Cutlass*) by infantry and by hunters: it is sometimes called the *Couteau de Chasse.*

208

But generally speaking it is in the Orient that the heavily curved slasher became most fully developed. The Turkish *Yataghan,* though often only very slightly curved, and having no guard, looks more like a long carving knife than the sabre with which it is usually compared; the Japanese version of this has a sharply curved point. The *Scimitar* is found from Venice, exhibiting the mingling of East and West in the great maritime republic, but in its Turkish form the points of the guard generally turn down towards the blade, which is chopped off across the bottom: the Chinese scimitar or sabre resembles this but has no quillons. Oriental varieties of the hatchet sabre are difficult to identify precisely to a place or time; and here one must leave the specialist student to make his own way.

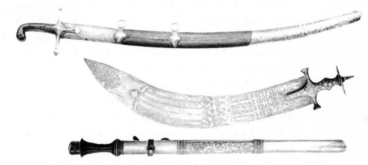

Top to bottom: A long sabre; Indian curved dagger; Tibetan dagger.

There have been regulations about swords ever since the beginning of national standing armies in the mid-seventeenth century, but these varied enormously from country to country and even from unit to unit and also in the way they were interpreted by different commanders and even individual men: no kind of summary of them can be attempted in this place. Here again is a field for the specialist willing to venture into fairly untrodden paths [RL 248, 252, 255].

TIN BOXES   Collectors have been known to undergo conversions. A friend of mine, having spent many years putting together perhaps the finest collection of **HORSE BRASSES** in the world—then stowing them away in chests—began to make an equally unique gathering of livery or crest **BUTTONS**; and having exhausted that field he set about getting together about five hundred different lace bobbins.

If any of my readers have reached such a climactic they might well allow their jaded eye, as it travels along the shelves of junk shops, to rest upon the first printed tin box seen there. It will not at first, perhaps, arouse any particular interest, but as is usual in collecting, once you start looking at a particular kind of thing it starts turning up in great variety and quantity.

We are looking, of course, for tin boxes which are decorative or informative in some way, and we will find them first in the special 'gift' packs put up by tea and tobacco blenders, makers of chocolates, candies and sweets and the like, but especially biscuits. Once emptied they lived a second life, perhaps being refilled from less spectacular purchases in packets, or doing duty in humble homes as money or trinket boxes.

It is by no means surprising that they should have been preserved in this way, for in fact they represented not only a kind of industrial folk art but were also an expression of the very latest industrial techniques of the day. The Staffordshire potters, especially Felix Pratt of Fenton, had already shown how to print in colours on earthenware by means of a multi-coloured paper transfer. In some such way the earliest of the boxes, perhaps dating from the 'sixties, seem to have been printed; but later the makers adapted an older method using a 'bat' of glue, as developed for china by the Flights and Barrs of Worcester. By 1875 this had developed into the offset lithographic process, using a glazed cardboard (afterward a rubber) 'blanket' for transferring the design to the tin. With the earliest of the boxes—which were of tinned iron—the parts had to be soldered together, which accounts, of course, for their longevity: with the coming of tinplate or tin-coated steel the greater ductility reduced the need for stout soldering.

At first the boxes assumed fairly orthodox shapes; but as time went on the manufacturers vied with each other in stamping out patterns in high relief, on letting the boxes assume all kinds of shapes—fishermen's creels, caskets, etc.

TOBACCO BOXES AND JARS Here is an enormous

210

Three vest-pocket tobacco boxes, early eighteenth century, one commemorating King Charles I as a martyr.

field, and unless the collector is prepared to heave wife, family and the household chattels into the street (which was once done by a collector of books I knew) he must specialise.

Perhaps, to begin with, he may decide to distinguish between a *Box* and a *Jar*. In the eighteenth century you might call a porcelain tea container or caddy a 'jar'—the makers certainly did—and this title is surely earned by those items of stoneware, earthenware and china which stand upon our mantelpieces holding shag or best Virginia—or did once when we had mantelpieces. But other kinds of receptacles for tobacco, made in gold, silver, enamel, iron, pewter or wood, and having a lid, ought, I think, to be called boxes.

Specialising again you might decide on boxes of lead, the favourite material for this purpose ever since the coming of the weed for whose sake Charles Lamb would 'do anything but die' and which Sir Arthur Helps thought to be the greatest blessing that Europe owes to the discovery of America. Perhaps no material better maintains humidity and fragrance. Of these again, one might elect to concentrate upon those with decoration of the kind which one found under COMMEMORATIVE POTTERY. They celebrate, often in moulded relief—which in many was originally coloured—battles fought by the war heroes of the eighteenth and nineteenth centuries, with lively scenes of the goings-on there, and perhaps on the knobs of the lids features of the commanders—Washington, Nelson,

211

Wellington and Napoleon. Most often, however, one sees there the famous Negro Head which has been associated with tobacco from the beginnings.

Brass tobacco boxes offer another field, and here the Dutch, their boxes embossed with all kinds of subjects, have left an indelible mark. There are the *genre* scenes of which this nation was so fond in its painting and tile-making—smokers in taverns, carousals, bear-baiting and other sports, battles, townscapes and seascapes. Many Scriptural subjects are used, such as Jonah and the Whale, the Judgment of Solomon, Noah and the Flood, even the Crucifixion. One shows a couple driving to market; inscribed in Dutch: 'Is it not good to have a cart and horses in this world?'

If the collector prefers pottery to metal he will have to rationalise himself even more severely. A gathering of ceramic interest alone could be made from the immense race of tobacco jars related to the stoneware spirit flasks dealt with elsewhere and coming from the same makers. Most of the famous Staffordshire potteries tried their hands here, in earthenware or stoneware, in bone china and the rest and exported a great deal overseas, where it may still be found.

Coin-in-the-slot tobacco boxes were made for inns and taverns—there are two in the White Lion Hotel at Banbury, Oxon.

They often bear a rhyme on the outside inviting one to buy a pipeful:

> *The custom is before you fill*
> *To put a penny in the till;*
> *When you have filled without delay*
> *Close the lid, or sixpence pay.*

TOBY JUGS   Toby, familiar now to all of us for more than two centuries, sprang into existence quite suddenly. He has often been fathered upon one or other of the noted topers for whom England was famous in the days of large draughts and unquenchable thirsts, notably Harry Elwes who is said to have tucked away 2,000 gallons of it in his lifetime (which was perhaps on that account not a very long one) or Paul Parnell, a

212

Toby jug in the Ralph Wood style decorated with coloured glazes.

Yorkshire farmer and grazier, who managed to consume nine thousand pounds' worth of the local stingo.

But most authorities concur in identifying the old toper with a fictional character called Toby Fillpot, who first appeared in a song called *The Brown Jug,* 'imitated from the Latin of Hieronymus Amaltheus' by the Reverend Francis Fawkes, a minor poet of the day, who not only tried his hand on Theocritus and Anacreon, but also, very bravely, on the Lowland Scots of Gawin Douglas. This song which appeared in a book in 1761 was used for an engraving by Robert Dighton, published by Bowles and Carver, showing Toby

> *'In his Flow'r woven Arbour as gay as you please*
> *With a Friend and a Pipe, puffing sorrow away,*
> *And with honest old Stingo was soaking his clay.'*

I have set out the whole poem elsewhere [RL 256] but the gist of it is that after Toby had died suddenly 'full as big as a Dorchester Butt' and his well-matured flesh had turned again into clay, a potter chanced upon this exceptional piece of earth and made of it a brown jug which was thereby made sacred to 'Friendship and Mirth and mild Ale'.

Be all this as it may, there was already a prototype in the early seated figure-jugs attributed to John Astbury, and representing midshipmen, army officers or fiddlers. The true Tobys, made after the publication of the print, are in time to have been made by or under the direction of the elder Ralph Wood (1716–1772) in his fine liquid colour glazes. After this,

213

most of the potters tried their hands at the *genre*, and production has not yet ceased.

Apart from the original Toby, who even in the standard version appears in all kinds of variations, there are other members of the family, about fifteen of which may be dated to the eighteenth century. They include Admiral Howe, with his King Charles spaniel; the Sailor who sits upon a sea chest labelled 'Dollars' and holds a jug which is sometimes inscribed 'Success to our Wooden Walls'; the Thin Man, who, however, looks very cheerful about it; the Parson, a standing Toby from the famous 'Tithe Pig' group, where he is being offered the tenth child rather than the tenth pig from the litter; the Welsh Country Gentleman, with a Welsh goat between his legs; the Unfrocked Parson with a coloured coat and a full-bottomed wig, sometimes called Dr. Johnson; the Hearty Good Fellow; the Planter, with striped trousers, and others which were added to steadily during the nineteenth century.

There were two ladies among the original characters, the Gin Woman, perhaps inspired by Hogarth, with her heavy moustaches, and Martha Gunn who kept a bathing machine at Brighton. Punch appeared in the nineteenth century, together with a Judy, John Bull and Santa Claus; while later characters included military and political figures of World War I, such as Jellicoe, Lloyd George, Foch and Kitchener. Sir Winston Churchill has recently been elected to the gallery, in a model by Leonard Jarvis.

Coloured glazes apart, Toby has also appeared in earthenware and stoneware, especially as transplanted into the United States, where he was made in quantity at Bennington, Vermont, and the Salamander Works at Woodbridge, New Jersey. There is also at least one version of him in wood, made I know not where.

TOKENS The collector who likes each of his pieces to tell its own story will hardly find a richer or more inexhaustible field—nor one where so many items can be crammed into so small a space—than the token.

Once again it is necessary to offer definitions, for there are

214

*ly nineteenth century tokens, issued by firms in Stockton-on-Tees, Barnsley
York; by the Bewick Main Colliery, Northumberland; the Middlesex Mail
ach; the Priestfield Furnaces, Staffs.; Cox's Iron Foundry, Taunton, Somerset.*

tokens classified as such which ought more properly I think, to be thought of as COMMEMORATIVE MEDALS. There are also those issued solely as advertisements, without the necessary implication of redemption.

A token proper, I suggest, is the equivalent of money or currency (even if it is CURRENCY CURIOSA), but it is currency, not of the realm, having the force of law, but of the private person or trade, the club, the society, the public (or rather private) enterprise. Even so there are some border-line cases: what, for example, of those pathetic emblems of suffering and endurance, the siege coins, cut out of church or secular plate, stamped with a value, and made into temporary, though illegal, currency by the commander of a beleagured city?

Let us, however, take some examples from the excellent Montague Guest Collection in the British Museum [RL 256]. A gold token there would have taken you, around 1603, into the Swan Theatre at Bankside, where Ben Jonson acted and Fenner and Middleton produced their plays: an engraved ivory one, perhaps bearing the name of Mrs. Siddons or Mr. Sheridan, would have admitted you to the second Drury Lane Theatre ('All performers whose salaries are above £6 per week are entitled to four ivory tickets for Free Admission of their Friends. . . . All performers whose salaries do not amount to £6 per week are totally excluded from any similar privilege.').

A token which was 'Warranted Pure Silver; Intrinsic Value 25 cents', would in 1857 get you into the New York Temple of Minstrelsy, 561/563 Broadway, to hear Wood's Minstrels give their 'select and varied entertainment'; a silver token showing Euterpe in a chiton and pelos would admit you to the famous Ranelagh Gardens, which Horace Walpole thought 'totally beat Vauxhall'; another would ensure you a riotous evening with the 'Order of the Beggar's Benison and Merryland' at Anstruther, Fife: and it would perhaps bear what the catalogue of the collection calls an 'indecent subject' and such exhortations as 'Be Fruitful and Multiply' and 'Lose No Opportunity'. On the other hand you could further your interest in Sunday schools with a token proclaiming your membership of the Hampstead Philoinvestigists' Society, inscribed 'BROTHER ★ DO ★ ALL ★ THE ★ GOOD ★ YOU ★ CAN ★'.

216

Boxing matches, cockfights, curling, gambling, all had their tokens. The signs of hundreds of inns perished in the Great Fire of London in 1666, yet the subjects painted on them are often preserved in the tokens issued by the innkeepers. But for a token, for example, we would not know that the sign of the famous Bel-Savage Inn ('La Belle Sauvage') on Ludgate Hill showed a figure of a beautiful Indian woman holding a bow and arrow.

Tokens also mark changes in the social life of a district; for example, local industry might create a demand in a particular area for coinage where, lacking a country banking system, it was difficult to get coins distributed. One of the largest issuers of tradesmen's tokens was Thomas Williams, owner of mines and smelting works; another was John Wilkinson, one of the leading eighteenth-century ironmasters.

Such tokens may proclaim their purpose: a Cornish mine-owner inscribes his 'For the Accommodation of the County'; a Hereford ironmonger issues them 'For Change not Fraud'; another token is 'A Remedy For the Shortage of Change'.

Most of the tokens issued in this entirely reputable way are from the seventeenth and eighteenth centuries, and may be of lead, copper, porcelain or brass—hence possibly the North Countryman's use of this last term for money, even when it is in the bank. Shopkeepers had to keep boxes with partitions for sorting out the tokens issued by their neighbours and redeeming them by exchanging them at their local banks.

America had its unofficial currency in the form of the 'Hard Times Tokens' issued during the depressions in the thirties of the nineteenth century. Most of them are in the large cent size. Another type was issued by local traders, redeemable like the English ones, to remedy the shortage of coinage during the Civil War. They are mostly of the small cent size and there are thousands of varieties.

TRADESMEN'S CARDS No collecting item takes us more graphically into the everyday working life of bygone times than the cards or bills on which tradesmen and professional men once offered the public their goods or services.

217

These pieces of PRINTED EPHEMERA, sometimes quaint and primitive, sometimes beautiful specimens of engraving or typography, preserve for us enchanting pictures of, for example, gunmakers illustrating how their weapons can be used not only in sport but in protecting life and money from highwaymen (they sold STAFF WEAPONS as well); how a MAP and print seller at the sign of the Hogarth's Head also offers and illustrates a ZOGRASCOPE; how Henry Hastings, the Nightman, comes all the way from Southwark with his discreetly covered carts to deal with His Majesty's Offices, and 'being at the work himself could assure gentlemen that their business would be decently performed'.

They were, of course, the earliest form of display advertising, for in that age the newspapers usually carried only what we would now call lineage—rather after the style of that famous one in the *Mercurius Politicus* for the week ending September 30, 1658, which, next to an announcement offering a reward for a lost bay gelding, proclaims also the arrival of tea in England:

> '*That Excellent, and by all physicians approved, China Drink, called by the Chinese Tcha, by other Nations Tay alias Tee, is sold at the Sultaness Head, a Coffee House in Sweetings Rents by the Royal Exchange, London.*'

On your pictorially engraved card, on the other hand, you could show the range of products you sold, the kind of factory in which they were made or the shop in which they were sold. If you were a doctor you could provide a portrait of yourself to inspire confidence in your healing powers. Christopher Pinchbeck also found his picture helpful in selling the articles of zinc and copper named after him.

The trades and occupations have an astonishing range, from the BOW and arrow maker to the Skeleton Seller, from the Italian Warehouseman (who has not yet quite disappeared) to the Rocking Horse Maker, from the Aquarellist (one of whom was Paul Sandby), the Attorney-at-Law and the Dancing Master to the Ratcatcher and Sow Gelder (how does one geld a sow?) and the Shampooing Surgeon; there are even cards for the engravers of cards, one of whom was William Hogarth—later, as we have seen, himself enshrined as Hogarth's Head on cards of print and map sellers.

218

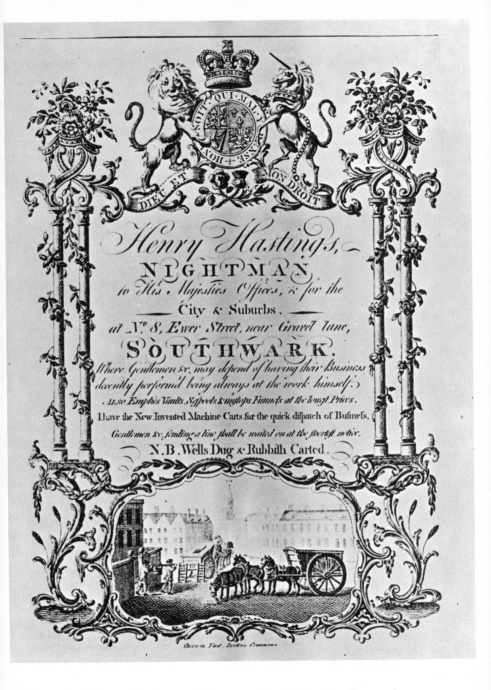

Trade card of Henry Hastings, nightman to his Majesty's offices, who 'empties vaults, cesspits and unstops funnels'. Mid-eighteenth century.

Sir Ambrose Heal [RL 256], that doyen of collectors in this field, has argued persuasively that Tradesmen's Cards as a term is to be preferred to the possible alternatives Trade Cards, Tradesmen's Bills or Shopkeeper's Bills, although they were not usually made of pasteboard but were generally sheets of paper ranging in size from quite tiny pieces to folio. They were sometimes used as bills or for estimates, as is often testified by the interesting entries on some of them, but this does not seem to be their primary function: they would presumably have been too expensive for anything but the sweet uses of advertisement.

Dating tradesmen's cards is not always easy. Few can be traced with confidence to the seventeenth century, and those of the first two decades of the eighteenth century are exceedingly rare. 'Primitives'—in style if not in date—are the crude woodcuts; the most sophisticated and elegant, as one might expect, seem to date from the middle and later years of the eighteenth century. A common feature was the sign of the shop itself, at first shown plainly and simply, then set in elaborate 'Chippendale' borders (which later shaded off into Adam, as did everything else in the way of decoration); and later still accompanied by fine drawings (Drawing Masters) of the wares offered or the trappings surrounding them, for example, a chemist's furnace and general paraphernalia. With the Adam styles comes the numbering of houses—signs were abolished in London in 1762. Royal Arms are also a help in dating British cards for they differed in design in each reign; so also are the records of trade guilds, insurance companies, well-known or Royal Personages.

The new collector should also, if he is near a good library, consult that omnivorous and insatiable putter-away of PRINTED EPHEMERA and of pretty well everything else, Mr. Hodgkin [RL 254].

TROMPE L'OEIL   Or 'cheat the eye'. Artists and craftsmen have for centuries adored to fool their audiences into thinking that a painted or carved object is real and actual—and audiences equally have adored to be fooled in this way.

There is a sense, of course, in which any realistic painting or carving can give some illusion of reality—for example, water drops on glass and dewdrops on flowers in some of the Dutch masters. There is also extraordinarily delicate carving like that in the cravat shown here, by Grinling Gibbons. Made in simulation of crochet work, it seems capable of movement, of falling into new folds. A well-known master in this craft was the Frenchman Demontreuil, who had the patronage of Louis XVI and Marie Antoinette, and who made the remarkable *L'Oiseau Surprenant* in Dr. Margaret Vivian's collection. This is indeed a 'surprising' bird; the dead canary hangs from a nail by a string against a panel, and all is carved out of the one piece of wood—which in any case makes it a wonderful piece of virtuosity in wood carving.

There is also another kind of realistic painting—like that of Raphaelle Peal in America, of Tristram Hillier and Edward Wadsworth in England, where the realism gives quite ordinary things—a coil of rope, footprints in the snow—a special significance and life. But there is no trick or illusion here.

True *trompe l'oeil* goes further than this. A stereoscopic, or 3-D effect is given by playing around with the spatial relationships in the picture: for example, shadows may be thrown *back* on to the plane of the picture, so that the object which makes the shadow seems to be coming forward into the room. Another device is to paint a shelf or a niche and throw a shadow upon it. Frames are painted on, and objects rest across them; in one case cracked and broken glass is painted over an engraving.

One favourite subject is the 'bag' of game hanging from a nail, as though on the wall in a hunting lodge or a farm kitchen. Another is a casual and untidy assembly of books and papers with perhaps a letter rack and a skull or two.

That the game has been going on for a very long time now is shown in a story told by Pliny of how one exponent of *trompe l'oeil* neatly tricked another. Zeuxis, the painter, had done a picture of a bunch of grapes so realistically that birds flew down and pecked at them: whereupon Parrhasios, a rival, invited Zeuxis to his studio to see some of his own work. Zeuxis was so eager to find if it was better than his that he

221

Cravat carved in wood in imitation crochet work, believed to be the work of Grinling Gibbons.

impatiently put a hand forward to lift the curtain hanging before the panel—and found that the curtain was only a painting on the wall. The point was that whereas Zeuxis had fooled only birds, Parrhasios had triumphed over a man, moreover a professional artist.

Like many practitioners of this art Parrhasios was also helping along his illusion by strong suggestion—Zeuxis had been anxious to look at the picture being shown him, and this distracted his attention from the curtain. Similarly, we expect (or aren't especially surprised) to find the glass of a framed picture cracked. I have also seen a card-table top in scagliola work—a kind of mosaic of coloured stones—with what seem to be real cards lying on it: the point is that that is exactly where you would expect to find real cards.

Trompe l'oeil has been used with great effect architecturally, notably by the Italian *quadratisti* in the baroque churches of southern Germany and Austria, where interiors have on their walls vistas across imaginary countrysides and long colonnades stretching infinitely; the insides of domes are painted with skies, clouds and angels; there are even people leaning over balconies looking down at you.

William M. Harnett founded a school of *trompe l'oeil* painters in the United States, and both Martin Battersby and Roy Hobdell have done some remarkable work in England. But many painters have tried their hands at the job merely as a *jeu d'esprit,* so the supply is never likely to dry up.

WALKING STICKS We do not use (or wear?) walking sticks today, presumably because we no longer walk. Henry VIII, who in 1536 possessed six 'walking staves'—one of which was fitted with a pouncet box, a DIAL and compass, a knife and file, and a whetstone—would today take a Comet of the King's Flight: at the other end of the time-scale, Bertie Wooster would no longer swing his smart malacca cane, but climb into his Aston Martin or his Alfa Romeo.

Lord Boyd is perhaps today's most renowned collector of walking sticks; but he was by no means the first, as was established when, a generation ago, the tomb of the boy

223

Pharoah Tutankhamen was found to contain among its many fabulous treasures a modest but well-chosen collection of walking sticks.

When Columbus was seeking out the New World, there were sticks of ebony and cane: mahogany came in, as it did for furniture, about 1740. Not only were they longer then, but they were sported by women also down to the beginning of the nineteenth century—as we are reminded when La Tosca arrives in the chapel and finds her Cavaradossi tactlessly painting a picture of a Virgin for which she herself had not posed.

Later sticks may be found in many different materials; and perhaps this is as good a collecting motif as any. Among woods, apart from ebony and mahogany, there are maple, ash, beech, teak, ironwood, snakewood, blackthorn, sapling oak, myrtle, kingwood, logwood, cinnamon, vine stems, and, of course, bamboo and rattan. They can also be of horn, either from the narwhal, or simply animals' HORNS —not used for music or for POWDER FLASKS but drawn out into a stick. They can be covered with leather, rhinocerous hide, silver, tortoise-shell, split whalebone, silver wire.

Wonderful variety is to be found in their heads. Pinchbeck and fine brass give the appearance of the gold used by wealthier folk: tin and pewter are burnished up to look like silver. Wood is carved with the heads of the same Turks, Moors and Negroes we meet on TOBACCO JARS .

Of other materials, Derbyshire Spar, or Bluejohn, is called in, so is 'Bristol stone'. The porcelain factories of Meissen, Chantilly, Berlin, also Bow and Chelsea, made knobs some-

224

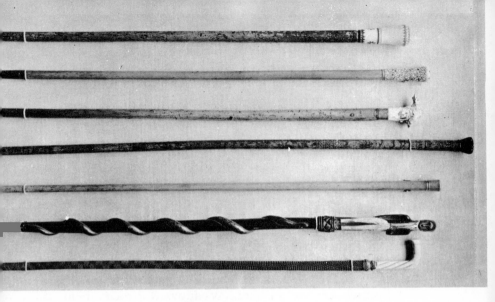

times decorated with figures or heraldic arms: the china makers of Victorian times offered them at the Great Exhibition of 1851. In Lord Boyd's collection there is a gathering of sticks made entirely of glass, not made for walking out, but to hang on the walls of cottage and villa displaying the charms of Nailsea and other coloured glass. There are longer ones which appear to have been made for carrying in glassmakers' processions.

Some walking sticks are disguised WEAPONS, as we have noticed under SWORDS: but there are also short clubs of the mid-eighteenth century with which dandies (and ladies on their own) protected themselves from molestation.

The *shooting stick* seems to have evolved from a kind of three-legged chair with a circular cane seat, perhaps originally used by ladies practising the art of water-colour in late-Georgian parks. There is also the *pipe-stick*, with a briar which screws in and out of the shaft and has a sealing cap, and a grating for smoking in a gale. There are *writing-sticks* which contain pen, pencils and ink bottle, *drinking-sticks* with glass flask and beaker. The nosologist carried his *snuffbox-stick*, the coper his *horse-measure* stick; other items found in combination with sticks are fishing rods, spy glasses, woodworking tools, compasses and (very usefully for those engaged in 'dog and stick' farming) dog whistles.

225

WEDGWOOD JASPER MEDALLIONS   In the autumn
of the year 1776 Josiah Wedgwood, who had established his
model pottery and village Etruria, in Staffordshire, only a
few years before, announced that he had perfected 'a fine white
artificial jasper of exquisite beauty and delicacy'. A catalogue
published later offered several hundred of such items for sale,
claiming that this jasper 'was capable of receiving colours
throughout its whole surface, in a manner which no other
body, ancient or modern, has been known to do. This makes
it particularly fit for cameos, portraits, and all subjects in *bas
relief*: as the ground may be made of any colour throughout,
without paint or enamel, and the raised figures of a pure white'.

Unlike many of the items in this book, therefore, these
jasper-ware cameos and medallions actually began life as
collector's pieces. In fact, Wedgwood issued them as 'a
Biographic Catalogue of distinguished Characters, for the
Illustration of that pleasing and Instructive branch of History'.
As they came out in their paper wrappers (some of which
survive) or mounted and framed by jewellers and 'toy'
makers, they were eagerly snapped up and either hung on
walls or put away in display cabinets. 'Besides an extensive
mythological Cabinet' announced the catalogue, 'we can
furnish a suite of *Grecian* and *Roman* history, from the Time
of the *Trojan War* to the *Removal* of the Seat of the Roman
Empire to *Constantinople*' and 'the thread of history is continued by a set of the *Popes* near *compleat,* and all the Kings of
England and *France*; and the more present periods of History
are illustrated by a considerable number of *Poets, Painters* and
other famous persons, from *Chaucer* to the present time'.

By this, of course, he meant his own time: though portraits
of some of his early personages were very largely guesswork,
those he made of his contemporaries were painstaking and
very often modelled from the life or taken from paintings and
sculptures; many of them are the only surviving likenesses of
celebrities of the day.

Among the 'Illustrious Moderns' he included not only the
famous ones of his own country, such as Captain Cook, the
explorer, Warren Hastings, conqueror of India, David Garrick
and Sarah Siddons from the stage, Sir Joshua Reynolds and

A set of 36 blue and white jasper medallions of the sovereigns of England, from William the Conqueror to William IV, 1830–37.

Dr. Johnson representing art and literature, but royal and noble personages from all over the world. Among the Americans were Benjamin Franklin and Washington, Lafayette, Paul Jones and William Penn. Wedgwood also executed commissions from private persons, sometimes whole families.

The portraits are usually in profile, and while most are in white on a blue ground, there are some which are in green or black and (very rarely) lilac and yellow. Sometimes the border is a different colour from the ground. Manufacture went on long after the time of Josiah Wedgwood I, but it is, naturally enough, the early ones, with their fine undercutting which attract the modern collector. For identifying marks on these wares the reader is referred to the READING LIST [256].

227

Trade card of John Smith, London map and print seller, showing on left a Zograscope.

ZOGRASCOPES   Auctioneers are sometimes troubled to put a name to many of the strange objects which appear in their rooms. One such is the zograscope (not to be confused with the zoetrope, which was an early form of the kine- matograph), or, to give it the name used by Mr. Smith, the Cheapside map and print seller, on his TRADESMAN'S CARD (see page 217), where an illustration of it appears, the 'Diagonal Mirror'. By the time of the Great Exhibition of 1851 it was known as the 'Optical Diagonal Machine'.

Its purpose was to magnify and (like the stereoscope, though quite unlike it in principle) to give enhanced perspective or depth to a picture. It comprises, as will be seen from the engraving on the left of Mr. Smith's card, a stand holding a lens vertically, with a mirror swung out at an angle of 45 degrees to the rear. You place your picture flat on the table under the mirror, and look through the lens into the mirror. There are also double zograscopes, with two lenses.

The zograscope was much used by connoisseurs of PRINTS not only for the additional pleasure given, but as a help in noting technical points about the subject, for example, its state: it was also, no doubt, a great boon to those viewers who preferred not to wear spectacles in company.

It has another possibility: if you like to be able to see every tiny bristle when shaving, you have only to lower the mirror flush with the viewing glass and you can do so, horrifyingly.

FAKES AND FORGERIES

When a collecting item becomes sought after—and therefore in short supply, and therefore highly priced—you have the classic opening for the faker and the forger. What, if any, is the difference between them? Mr. Savage, whose learned work [RL 256] on the subject should be on every collector's shelf—it makes absorbing reading too—maintains that a forgery is a work of art made for fraudulent purposes, whereas a fake is a genuine work which has been altered or added to in some way to give it greater value. This distinction seems to be supported by the Oxford English Dictionary, which notes that even in Middle English the word forgery was used of something made or devised to be passed off as something genuine; while the word fake seems to come from a later thieves' usage meaning to 'do up', to tamper with for the purpose of deception—for example 'a horse faked up for sale'.

Can we not say, then, that a copy of a picture deliberately intended to be passed off as the work of another man is a forgery, so is a bogus autograph; but a piece of porcelain which has had decoration added to increase its value, or has had the mark of a modern manufacturer removed from its base so that it may be taken for an older type, is a fake.

It should be remembered, however, that there are reproductions or replicas of genuine things made with no intention to deceive. Painters, of course, learn their craft by copying the works of the masters: it is only if they add the signature of a master, or otherwise 'utter' it as if it were that master's original work, that the forgery occurs. In the same way a Chinese porcelain vase of, say, the eighteenth century may bear marks used by potters of earlier times, not with intent to deceive, but as an act of homage and admiration for the work of the earlier men: it is at least a genuine work of the period in which it was made. But if a bogus mark has been added in a later age, then that is an act of faking.

There are, however, actual collectors of fakes and forgeries, among them, as it happens, some of our most learned museums.

A few years ago the British Museum put on a show of what it called 'Forgeries and Deceptive Copies'. Some of them had been 'collected' by that venerable institution inadvertently—and indeed what museum can truly claim not to have done so? Others had been acquired deliberately 'for the purpose of study in their own right'—in other words to give the museum opportunity to become familiar with the tricks of the deceivers. It may interest readers of the present book if we look over some of the items mentioned in it and see what the counterfeiter and the copier has to offer us.

ANCESTOR FIGURES, as noted under that head, have, like much of **ETHNOGRAPHICA**, been forged a great deal ever since they caught the fancy of the general art collector—rather than the student—in the early years of this century. They are also among the many items which have been made, as already noted, by genuine native artists in homage or as a pastiche; Mr. Savage warns his readers to be wary of what he calls 'Airport' or 'Christian Mission School' art. Style, feeling, the difference in spirit between the work which has been created from some deep religious or superstitious impulse and that which has been offered merely to please, should offer one criterion; another is the practical consideration that since the old craftsmen, as part of their training as artist-sculptors, made their own tools, the characteristic marks of modern imported ones should at least set up warning signals.

ANIMALIER BRONZES have not yet, like bronzes of ancient and Renaissance times, reached the value required by the forger or faker, though they may well soon do so: in which case the collector of them will also have to study matters of style, workmanship and the patina given by age and long years of loving care. **ARMOUR** has long been the happy hunting ground of the reproducer, ever since the novels of Sir Walter Scott and the Gothic writers set us all off on our romantic medievalising in the early years of the nineteenth century. Some of the items made then in the way of interior decoration have had attention given them by the faker sufficiently long ago in time to deceive modern collectors not informed on the methods of the old craftsmen and the idioms in which they were likely to have worked.

231

With ASSOCIATION ITEMS the forger and the faker really come into their own, as has been mentioned in that place. An article offered may be a perfectly genuine thing of its age and type; and when this is so all else must usually rest upon an act of faith. With autographs, on the other hand, the collector who knows his subject may know a great deal more than does the forger: for example over questions of fact about a person's life or habits, or the changes in handwriting which occur over a lifetime; it is also useful to have a knowledge of the kinds of paper, pens and inks used at the time. The collector will, for example, be on his guard against the improbable—for example such items as signed letters from Plato and Mary Magdalene written in modern French, which nevertheless sold well in Paris in their nineteenth-century day.

Collectors of APOTHECARIES' JARS will need to acquaint themselves with genuine examples of HISPANO-MORESQUE WARE, so that they can learn to suspect the stronger ground colours and the over-bright copper lustres of modern imitations. The same applies to the many more jars in Italian maiolica which were not only made in immense quantities in the nineteenth century by well-known firms, but received awards at international exhibitions for their faithfulness to the original wares, at that time much admired. Fakers have had no compunction in removing from the bottoms of these jars the marks which the potters put there in pride at having produced something which was as good as, if not better than, the pieces they were imitating.

The collector of BELLARMINES will be haunted all his life by nineteenth-century reproductions of the various types of Rhenish SALTGLAZED STONEWARE, made from exactly the same clay as the originals, probably even by descendants of the original potters. This was again due to the revival of interest in such wares at that time, and again they are usually accused by signs of the removal of marks. It will pay the collector here especially, not only to go to the authorities [RL 254], but to venture into the as yet inadequately charted seas of these latter-day wares.

Among the Staffordshire sections of the family, the famous 'pew groups' have been copied: Mr. Savage quotes an example where the forger set aficionados alight with frantic curiosity by impressing a 'pew group' of Adam and Eve with the mark **WEDGWOOD**: he was either foolishly over-ambitious or had a deep sense of humour. There is also later enamelling on the Staffordshire wares, some of it done in Holland, but usually perceptible to those who have studied the native woodnotes wild of the pre-industrial Staffordshire artist-craftsman.

BILLIES AND CHARLIES are forgeries which exist only as such, and alongside these may be placed unlikelinesses of natural history such as those exhibited in the British Museum exhibition referred to above—for example a mummified mermaid made out of a monkey and the tail of a fish and a unicorn's horn which was once a narwhal's tusk, to say nothing of such items as sea bishops made from skates and a whole group of fossils which were planted by some helpful students so that they would be discovered by their beloved but tedious professor.

BOTTLES AND FLASKS call for the usual precautions required of the collector of pottery and glass. In the latter case, one needs familiarity with the quality, colour and 'feel' of old glass, together with the presence or otherwise of air bubbles, dark spots and other signs of impurities in the old metal which are difficult (though not impossible) to simulate. The iridescence of ancient glass occasioned by long burial in the earth or exposure to certain atmospheres can also be provided by the industrious faker, using flakes from broken pieces and cementing them on to a surface, by painting with metallic oxides, or merely by long burial in a cesspit.

With drinking glasses especially the reproducer has remedied the shortage of supply—particularly in the department of the most generally desired types of all, the colour twists—with spurious versions, many from Holland. These should, however, be perceptible to collectors by the quite different quality of the metal, also subtle variations in the handling and colour of the enamel twists. On plain glasses one looks not only at the metal but at signs of the myriad scratches which the bottom of a glass acquires: on engraved ones, especially the Jacobites, one also watches for the inevitable signs of wear from caressing fingers on the engraved parts: for glass, though it appears to be solid, would like to become

233

a liquid again, and scratches on it can be removed by warmth and friction.

COMMEMORATIVE MEDALS, like any other kind of Renaissance metalwork, have been extensively reproduced almost from their inception. Where they were cast the multiplier had only to use the medal itself to make a mould from which he could cast as many copies as he liked, all sharing the imperfections, wear and tear of the original. They can usually only be detected by a less sharp relief than the original: but so long has the process gone on that your copy itself may be an antique of some value. COMMEMORATIVE POTTERY, of course, can be genuine pottery of the day whose value has been enhanced by an added inscription, otherwise it must be tested by the standards and criteria of its kind and period, for which there are many authorities [RL 254].

Some of the kinds of CURRENCY CURIOSA mentioned in that place are obviously as easy to imitate as many other kinds of ETHNOGRAPHICA—reproductions of West African manillas have been particularly noted. DAHOMEY BRASSES, I was told in the Marché aux Puces in Paris, are more plentiful than ever they were, though these latter-day ones are coarse in conception and workmanship. A warning has already been given of the differences between HORSE BRASSES which were actually made for a horse to wear and those which quite skilfully imitate them; also that much larger branch of the family which were frankly made for the tourist trade—though not always as frankly offered to it.

ICONS can be faked, like any other PICTURE: according to Mr. Arnau no fewer than seventeen of these hanging in museums and accepted as typical masterpieces from the early days of the art have been traced to a single forger in Paris, who was working as recently as 1957. The recent widening of interest in this art will probably lead to an extension of such shenanigans, but these latter-day imitations will doubtless be all the more easily spottable by the serious collector.

The buyer of old MAPS will, even in his elementary stages, learn to recognise printed reproductions torn out of books; as will the collector of PRINTS. With the latter, however, one moves into what has been a happy hunting ground for forgers

234

and fakers ever since the earliest days of the craft, when Marcantonio Raimondo cheerfully passed off as his own work the woodcuts of his great contemporary Dürer, signature and all. Some reproductions have been put out privately by societies of connoisseurs; there are also modern pulls from old blocks and plates which have perhaps been worked over again. Genuine prints which have fallen on evil times, as many of them have, with stains, tears, holes and even the burrowing channels of weevils and other beasties, can be brought back to pristine condition by the careful hand and the chemical bottle of the restorer. Margins can be enlarged where time has diminished them; contemporary paper, authentically water-marked, can be acquired from the end-papers of books and brought into use. Naturally such work has not been lavished on prints which are not of value, and the tyro still in the foot-hills will probably not be unduly troubled. By the time he reaches the higher slopes he should have learnt his way around: if not he should limit his buying to the wares offered by well-known and reputable dealers and auctioneers.

PEWTER TANKARDS have long been good sport for malefac-tions of the type we have been discussing, a great deal of it dating from the days, late in the last century and early in this one, when this ware was more avidly and expensively collected than at present. The delightful flat-lidded Stuart pots are favourites with the forger, and the faker has been active in adding commemorative dates and inscriptions to genuine wares of their period. Remodelled pieces are given a very fair imitation of the patina acquired by oxidation or the 'tinpest' disease, which can only be detected by the experienced eye: but there are pieces which have been so ruthlessly cleaned that other criteria must be used—metal, style, workmanship.

Even **MECHANICAL BANKS**, a field one would have thought it possible to bank on completely, have both forgers and fakers. Mr. Griffith [RL 253] lists 29 models which are 'wrong' in one way or another. They include 'Banks That Have Been Made Completely To Fool Collectors', examples of ordinary toys which have been made into banks, toy parts which have been assembled to make a mechanical bank and also genuine banks which have been mechanised.

235

The forger and faker of PAINTINGS, of course, are legion, and so are their methods; and deep is the knowledge needed to cope with them. Here, then, is perhaps the moment to turn aside and ask some general questions. How may, in fact, the collector in general arm himself against the restorer, the fixer-up, the downright forger or faker?

It will be obvious by now from what has already been said that he must familiarise himself not only with the subject matter or style of his quarry but also with the methods and the techniques of the artists and craftsmen involved. He will have to teach himself to discern not only whether a piece *could* have been made at such a time and place or by such a person, but whether it *would* have been. Twelve spurious 'Van Gogh's' produced by a German forger named Otto Wacker, and attested by many experts, were found to be spurious only after it had been shown under X-ray analysis that the thick impasto had been built up in a way quite impossible to Van Gogh's.

In the case of the Van Meegeren forgeries of Vermeer, where, by using contemporary materials and Vermeer's actual technique, enormous pains were taken to circumvent scientific analysis, the forger betrayed himself by the actual content, or iconography, of his pictures. Only in the hysteria of the times —the aftermath of the last war—and the blind obstinacy of certain experts could it ever have been supposed that the portraits of Christ and his disciples shown in these forgeries were the work of a seventeenth-century Dutchman of extra-ordinarily refined intellect and imagination rather than that of a modern painter of mediocre talent. Van Meegeren even went wrong on quite minor things. He had gone to a great deal of trouble to go round antique shops buying articles of Vermeer's time to stand as models; but the ceramically-trained eye of Mr. Savage has observed that there is at least one faience jug shown in the pictures which was late eighteenth century.

The moral is, therefore, the age-old one of *caveat emptor*: unless he is prepared to teach himself everything he must rely on the man with long experience, a high reputation, a willingness to back his opinions with a guarantee, and above all a love for the business which makes it quite impossible for him to want to deceive anyone about it.

CURRENT PRICES

Value is a difficult subject. Some will say that the true monetary value of a thing is the sum which anyone is prepared to pay for it. But 'anyone' is a wide term. If a man is desperate for the single specimen which will complete his collection of, say, 'signer' autographs, or—which often happens—if two equally determined citizens both want that one object, is the resultant sale price the true value of the piece?

In a professional journal recently a chartered auctioneer, disagreeing with this definition of value, pointed out that there was a legal basis for variations in value. Valuation for probate, for example, was the price which the object would bring if offered for sale on the market between a willing buyer and a willing seller—in fact auction room price. Valuation for insurance, however, was the cost of replacing that article as nearly as possible, which presupposed that a dealer's profit had been added.

The first of these definitions, of course, does not overcome our difficulty about the fanatic bidder: but the second seems to be reasonable enough. Perhaps the nearest one can get to the current value of an item is the price at which you can buy it from a reputable and informed dealer who is prepared to give a guarantee as to its authenticity and condition. A great deal of collecting money can be wasted by trying to get 'bargains' in the general market instead of paying the true value to a specialist who, if he knows his job, has bought at the 'right' buying price and therefore knows how much he can charge a collector. There are, however, other considerations, such as sentiment, as Mr. Peter Philp suggested in the journal already quoted: for example what would be the value to a millionaire of an authentic but rather bad portrait of his mother?

Collectors will often find themselves buying from general dealers who have put only a general asking price on a piece, which may be less than its real value—but which also may be much more. They will also find themselves bidding alongside professionals at auction, where they may find wide variations in the prices made—depending for example on whether many, few, or no informed buyers were present, or, if they were, did not particularly want to buy that piece at that moment.

Nevertheless, the general run of auction prices do provide some sort of standard; and since it would clearly be impossible to offer detailed prices of all the variety of things mentioned in the book, I have culled some specimen prices from auctions at famous salerooms like Sotheby & Co., and Knight, Frank & Rutley, of London; Wallis & Wallis of Lewes, Sussex, Malletts of Bourdon House and others. I have also sprinkled in a few of the 'asking' prices of dealers who make known their wares in the profession's journal already quoted (the *Antique Finder,* obtainable at 39b Harrington Road, London, S.W.7); from the price reviews given from time to time in that journal; and also from personal observation through the windows, sometimes highly polished, sometimes murky, of antique and junk shops.

A word, however, to those who wish to sell rather than buy. The least troublesome method of selling, of course, is to send your piece to an auction sale and wait for the cheque. Those who take this course must not be surprised if they find the result disappointing. There may have been no serious buyers present, or if there were they may be members of a 'knock-out' ring, whereby they have arranged among themselves to limit their bidding, afterwards sharing out the margin which would otherwise have gone to the unfortunate seller. If you sell by auction therefore, be sure to place a reserve upon your piece: the auctioneer should be able to advise you about this. If it is a really important piece, you may feel it worth while commissioning a valuation from a reputable valuer, agreeing the terms beforehand.

Another method of selling is to invite in a local dealer, wave your arm round the room and ask him to give you a price for the lot and take it away as soon as possible: for obvious reasons very high prices are unlikely to be realised in this way. A much better method is to get to know the value either from your own experience or from a valuation in the way already suggested, then offer the piece to specialist buyers until you get the price you want. There will be variations in the value *they* place upon it, of course, according to the price they think or know that they can make of it. One can also advertise it to other collectors—or answer their advertisements—in the collectors' journals, or in those which specialise in buying, selling and exchanging. Remember, however, that the price you may have paid for an object is not necessarily its value in the open market. You may have paid too much for it: if you bought it from a dealer you will have paid his necessary overheads and profit, which if he has held it in stock a long while, may be high.

And now for the prices—with fair warning that in most cases they are steadily rising, that many of them given here were paid by dealers for resale at a profit, and that condition can mean everything in valuing a piece. There are obvious gaps—such subjects as Pictures or Paintings, where you can pay anything from £30 for a landscape of the 'Dutch school' to £20,000 for a Constable and a six-figure sum for a Picasso, would need at least a dozen pages.

ANCESTOR FIGURES: Dogon wood ancestor figure of tall slender form, £30; Basonge standing wood male fetish figure, navel hollowed for magic material, £8; small Yoruba wood standing female figure with skirt, £40; Bayaka carved wood fetish figure with high crested headdress, square cavity below breasts for magic material, £15.

ANIMALIER BRONZES: Average group, £70/£80 (exceptionally fine casting, £100). Group of two greyhounds, after Gott, $4\frac{3}{4}$ in. on

238

marble base, £10; stag at the kill, on oval bronze base, by E. Delabrierre, 15 in., £4; pair bronze bulls, 22 in. long, Rosa Bonheur, £260.

APOTHECARIES' JARS: Pair of Lambeth delftware apothecaries' jars, painted with cherubs' heads with wings, £80; Deruta albarello and Venetian wet drug jar, painted with coat of arms, £65. Hispano-Moresque albarello, 15/16c. diaper patterns in copper lustre, £60; pair Caffaggiolo albarelli, with rope-twist handles, £320.

ARMOUR: Full suit of 19c. repro. armour Maximilian style, £200; $\frac{3}{4}$ suit of late 16c. Pisan armour, £165; a lot comprising 17c. *Gorget*, elbow piece with fluting, plume holder from 16c. close helmet, 16c. tilting lance, circular vamplate, two shoulder pieces, two joined plates from a 16c. suit, £17 the lot; $\frac{3}{4}$ suit mid-16c. black and white Landsknecht armour embossed with fleur-de-lys, £100; Milanese visored sallet, reinforcing breastplate and burgonet by Matthew Frauenpreis the Elder, Augsberg, formerly part of a field armour made for the Emperor Maximilian II in 1550, £2,400; German early 16c. chamfron, bright steel, nose with radially fluted ornament, £130; mail shirt, 16c., links rivetted with double cramp rivets, £48; pair russet steel greaves and sabatons, c. 1620, with radially fluted toe-plates, £220; pair Milanese 15c. Gothic sabatons with unidentified mark 'A.D.', £90; articulated gauntlet fluted and roped border, c. 1500, £70; set Indo-Persian armour—spiked helmet Kula Khud with camail, circular shield Dhal and armguard, and all-steel axe, all finely decorated, £85.

ASSOCIATION ITEMS: .500 Springfield model 1863 military rifle with socket bayonet, used in Buffalo Bill's Wild West Show, £30; small strip of red and white bunting in Vol. II of Southey's 'Life of Nelson', being a fragment of the flag which covered Nelson's coffin, £16. 10.; Marshall Hall murder items, (p. 30) £140.

AUTOGRAPH letters (8) from the Hungarian patriot Kossuth, £120; 9 A.l.s. from Einstein, £220; Benjamin Franklin, £55; Lafayette (in English), £15; complete set autographs of every President of the U.S. from George Washington to Harry S. Truman, £650; Letters Thomas Jefferson, £15; 5 A.l.s. from Karl Marx, £2,000; Nelson A.l.s. written 12 days before Trafalgar, £220; Letter book, 1771–1833, of 'Signer' Charles Carroll of Carrolltown, £350.

AUTOMATA: German 19c. musical automaton with three monkeys playing a harp, violin and cello seated in a flowery bower, £210; rope dancer with six Turkish instrumentalists in giltwood pavilion, £200; French 19c. musical a. of a monkey as an 18c. violinist in painted and papered 18c. room, by Valéry. Paris, £210; Victorian gilt metal bird cage with three singing birds, £75; 19c. gilt metal singing bird box, £70.

239

THE COLLECTING MAN

BICYCLES: original Hillman geared pennyfarthing, £100; boneshaker of 1865, £100; pennyfarthing by Albert Co. 'Timberlake's Patent', £34.

BOOK BINDINGS: Kelmscott Press edition of Caxton's 'History of Reynard the Fox', 1892, with elaborately tooled and inlaid binding by Riviere, £150; Bible (1690) and Book of Common Prayer (1730) in gilt tooled red morocco with silver mounts, £50; Officium B. Mariae Virg. Antwerp 1655 in Italian black leather with pierced silver scrollwork mounts, £38; a binding for 'Les Roses',˙by P. J. Redouté, 3 vols bound as two by Duplanil Frères, £6,200 the two.

BOWS AND SLINGS: hand crossbow, 12 in. with quarrel, £23. 10.; 18c. crossbow, 33 in. span (p. 57), £31; stonebow or prodd, 31 in. span, £30; four 18c. Persian bows and a collection of arrows, £22; Indian throwing weapon with five hinged double-edged blades and heavy balls at ends, £21; ten 16c. quarrels, facetted steel heads, oak shafts, leather flights, in pouch, £42; Flemish target crossbow, windlass mechanism, broad bow with stirrup, £110; German late 15c. crossbow, tiller striped in panels of bone and ebony, and German 16c. all-steel cranequin with ratchet system, £250 the two.

BUTTONS: as shown on p. 60 (a) 7 for £32; (b) 5 for £42; (c) 8 for £42. 200 modern Colonial, Commonwealth, and foreign Customs, air force, naval, etc., mounted, £2; 50 regimental cap badges and 300 regimental shoulder titles, £7.

CANNON: Bronze 17c. signal cannon with stylised dolphin carrying rings, and Burmese 18c. bronze cannon, with muzzle in form of a rose, £30 the two; pair Naval brass carronades, late 18c. (p. 62), £210; sundial gun (p. 63), £120; Malayan bronze Lantaka, £30; pair cannon from yacht by T. English, 1775, original brass furniture and oak carriage, £210; late 15c. bronze hand gun with rest lug, £300; Chinese bombard, 14c., £44.

CHESSMEN: Chinese stone set, £12; Canton Ivory in red and white, emperor and empress, mandarins, soldiers, etc., £12.

COMMEMORATIVE MEDALS: Charles I Coronation, N. Briot, £28; David Livingstone, £48; set of 16 Thomasons 'Holy Scriptures', £65; 5 English Historicals (including Oliver Cromwell, £32; 70 French celebrities, Dassier, £90; Louisiana Purchase, 1904, Philadelphia Exhibition, 1876, Hudson River Discovery, League of Mercy, £7 the lot; lead cast from Milanese medal of Mary Tudor by Jacopo da Trezzo, £10; Papal medal Paul II, medal after Matteo de Pasti of Isotta degli Atti, another papal medal, gilt medal of Prince Nicolo Contarini dated 1631 and a cast from a medal of Cardinal Mazarin, £10 the lot.

COMMEMORATIVE POTTERY: Liverpool Cream ware bowl, printed with American flag, £70; Staffordshire pottery jug, printed with 'Bonaparte's Last Shift', £30; Creamware teabowl and saucer with a portrait of George Washington and 'Washington his country's father', £45; Coalport china plate commem. Dr. W. G. Grace's century of centuries, 1895, £32; Coalport china plate commem. Boer War, with portrait of Lord Roberts, £30.

CURRENCY CURIOSA: block of Russian tea money, impressed with crest of Nicolas I, £13.

DAGGERS: Indian kard, £21; kukri, £27; Cossack kindjal, £38; (all shown on p. 81); Landsknecht, £42; mid-17c. gunner's stiletto, £35; Scottish dirk with companion knife and fork, £38; Burmese dha, £26, Balkan yataghan, £46; New Guinea cassowary leg-bone dagger, stylised human head terminal, £15; Indian jambiya, 9 in. blade, chiselled with elephants and bullocks fighting, £4; Burmese dha, large folding clasp knife, small African dagger and miniature German hunting sword, £7; katar, 14 in. silver overlaid hilt, £7; Indian knuckle duster dagger, £10.

DAHOMEY BRASSES: woman and child, £2. 10.; hunter and dog, £1. 10. (both p. 84/5).

DEATH MASKS, bronze Red Indian, £4.

DIALS AND NOCTURNALS: Items on pages 88/9: Italian ivory pillar dial, metal gnomen within column, 17c., £125; pedestal block dial by D. Beringer, Nuremberg, late 18c., £38; German tablet dial by Leonhard Muller, of unusual octagonal form, early 17c., £50; Dieppe dial, C. Bloud, £46; signed Augsberg diptych, 1582, £275; Butterfield silver pocket dial, £110; signed wooden cubical dial, £190; crucifix dial, £320; universal equatorial dial Leonhard Muller, Augsberg, £22; octagonal brass garden dial Elias Allen with declination, £300.

DOMESTIC MACHINERY: old-style Continental table telephone with dial base, £10. 10.; sewing machine, Willcox and Gibbs, 1860/70, £2: see also prices p. 91.

DRINKING GLASSES: airtwist Jacobean wine with rose, £45; ale flute 'Wilkes and Liberty', £55; baluster airtwist, £85; King's Lynn wine, £50: 18c. cordial, oversewn foot, £6.

ETHNOGRAPHICA: New Guinea painted bark helmet mask, £2; Ashanti carved wooden fertility doll, £27; Maori chieftain's staff Hani, £5. 10.; Benin carved ivory mask, £6,200; Benin bronze head, £2,000; tomahawk pipe engraved coat of arms dated 1760, perhaps German

241

for American market, £80; Red Indian eagle feather war bonnet, £18; Peruvian honey-coloured hardstone figure of a reclining jaguar, 4 in. £70; small Aztec white stone head of a condor, Mexico, 1367–1521 A.D., £25: Mixtec mottled greenstone figure of Tlaloo God of Rain, 4¼ in., Central Mexico, 1200–1521, £60; Chimu gold beaker, repoussé decoration of warriors and birds, Peru, 1300–1470, £600; Eskimo moose ivory tobacco pipe carved with scenes from Eskimo life, £250; North West American Indian squaw's cloth cap with multi-coloured beads, £5; beaded cloth bag as worn by Ojibwa and other Great Lakes and Mid-west tribes, £8; Pacific Northwest Coast knife sheath, small leather pouch, headband and fragments of cloth with beadwork flowers, all showing French influence, £10; basketry hat woven from spruce root, Haida Indians, Queen Charlotte Islands, £55; Polynesian circular wooden food bowl on four feet, £35; Trobriand Islands wooden ceremonial drum, £38; Solomon Islands head modelled over a skull. £250; Cameroons ivory tusk carved in relief with silver mounts for taking weight off the King's feet during ceremonies, £200.

FORE-EDGE PAINTING: Byron's 'Childe Harold's Pilgrimage', 1816, with fore-edge painting of scene from Battle of Waterloo, £13; Thomas Campbell's Poetical Works, 2 vols, 1833, contemporary green morocco gilt, with f–e's of Ravenscraig and Bamborough Castles, £14; 'Letters of Lord Lyttelton', 2 vols, painted with views, £65; Dante Aligheri 'La Divina Commedia', 3 vols, 1830, each vol with views in Florence, Venice and Rome respectively, £220; Longfellow's Poems contemporary mauve morocco gilt. f–e painting of mountain and river scenery (Charles River, U.S.A.?), 1854, £9; Martin Tupper's Proverbial Philosophy, similar binding, with f–e painting of Northumberland on the Susquehanna River, £5.

FIREARMS CURIOSA: Items on p. 99 from top, £100; £45: £85: £55: also walking stick shotgun, £6. .30 Unwin and Rodgers, Knife pistol, marked Crown VR, with bullet mould, £23.

GONGS AND BELLS: bronze church bell, 16½ in. high on wooden cradle, £17; Flemish bronze hand bell cast with annunciation and mark of Peter II van den Gheyn, Mailnes 1571, £75; another by Jan van der Ende, 1547, £92.

GORGETS: (p. 104) pouches, £21 (top) and £7; gorgets (left). £22; £13. Gorget, handwrought in deep relief with battle scene, £44.

GRANGERISING: John Forster's 'Life of Charles Dickens, 3 vols. 1872, extra-illustrated with 220 engraved portraits, views and other plates, and also A.l's from personalities of the day, £150; T. W. Walker, 'The History, Antiquities and Topography of the County of Sussex', 1835, 2 vols. extra ill. with upwards of 330 engraved portraits, views, etc., £105.

242

GUNS AND RIFLES: Persian matchlock gun 55, in chis., dam., carved and inlaid butt, £43; flintlock trade gun Sargant Bros., £22; wheel-lock comb. petronel and fowling piece from Cabinet d'Armes of Louis XIII, Jean Bourgeois, c. 1612, £2,600; Baker rifle signed Nock, £95; Louis XV garniture of fowling piece and companion pistols, J. Laurent, £900; 7 barrel flk volley rifle, Nock, £600; .577 Snider carbine, £21; .75 Brown Bess, £81; late 18c. flk blunderbuss, £82; on p. 110 (from top) £81, £20, £76; Suite Caucasian weapons—flk pistols, ramrod. flk gun and sabre, mounts and fullstocks, hilt and scabbard completely fashioned in heavy silver gilt, embossed niello, £500.

HELMETS (see also **MILITARIA**): Curassiers close helmet (pp. 118/9), £46; comb morion, £40; Dutch pikeman's pot, mid 17c., £30; peaked burgonet, £105; 14c. bascinet from Barry Coll., £9,000; Cromwellian lobster tail, £30; chapelle-de-fer (kettle hat), £125; Indo-Persian spiked helmet Kulah Khud and camail, £14; German early 16c. decorative tilting helmet, £110; English close helmet, c. 1570, £220; Italian armet-à-rondelle, c. 1490, probably Giovanni di Salimbeni, £2,800; highly important bascinet, c. 1380, said to have been looted from the Arsenal at Zurich by one of Napoleon's medical advisers, £9,000; North Italian 16c. 'Spanish' morion etched with elements of armour, £220; Italian visored sallet with unidentified Milanese marks, £4,000; late 16c. morion, Nuremberg Town guard type, £80.

HISPANO-MORESQUE WARE: Armorial dish with the arms of Gentili of Florence, 16 in. second half 15c., £3,300 (1961); armorial dish with arms perhaps of Aguilar, Valencia, 18 in. last quarter 15c., £3,100 (1961); charger, 15 in. diameter, painted in copper lustre and with moulded blue birds on the rims, £40; 15c. dish with raised centre boss, deep buff glaze, decorated with copper lustre, and two later dishes, £70.

HORNS: Old huntsman's horn, £4; copper coaching horn, of 1886, 38 in., £13, Tibetan ceremonial horn made from human thighbone, £10. 10.; German hunting horn of crescent shape, Nuremberg 1606, inscribed MACHT ANTONI SCHNITZER A.M., CCCC DCVI, £90

HORSE BRASSES: six old horse brasses (Elephant, wheatsheaf, Victoria etc.), £6 the lot.

ICONS: four small Russian brass icons one with blue and white enamel, £15; small Russian icon of Christ Pantocrator, dated Moscow, 1890, £32; early Georgian gold repoussé icon of St. George and the Dragon, $2\frac{3}{4}$ by $2\frac{1}{2}$ in., £500; Russian triptych of travelling type on gold background, late 17/18c., £180; Greek icon of St. George in colours on gold, c. 1600, £650.

243

JAPANESE SWORDS AND FITTINGS: Signed iron tsubas, £5, £8 upwards, tachi, with 27½ in. blade signed Sukesada, scabbard ishime lacquer, £14; katana, 23⅞ in. blade, signed Sukesada, Goto style mounts, £52; wazikashi 17¾ in. blade signed Nio Kiyotada, £20; fuchikashira in shibuichi by early Nara and Hamano masters, six for £20; silver ishime, four for £7; tanto, 11½ in. blade, by Koto Midzuta, (16c.) Higo work mounts, £50; aikuchi, 10 in. blade with black ishime lacquer scabbard, £42.

KNIVES: 'American Bowie knife' by W. Edward Barnes (p. 134), £54; Indian knife, £68; bowie by T. Read, Lambert St., etched 'We ask for nothing etc.', £26; Malay ripping knife. curved blade 3½ in., £5.

LOCKS AND KEYS: 17c. French key bow pierced with foliage, £14; 4 English steel keys, c. 1700, £20; 4 French and Italian keys, £30; French key with elaborate lantern bow, 17c., £100; Viking bronze key, 9c., £75.

MAPS: early Saxon, £40; Speed, £30; Mitchell's 'Map of the British Colonies in North America', £290; Blaeu's 'Atlas Major', 7 vols., £2,300; Camden's 'Britannia', £120; Richard Blome's 'The Present State of His Majesty's Isles and Territories in America', seven folding engraved maps, etc. H. Clark for D. Newman, 1687, £130: John Speed's 'Prospect of the Most Famous Parts of the World', 12-double-page engraved maps, J. Dawson for G. Humble, 1627; and 'Theatre of the Empire of Great Britain', 67 engraved double-paged country maps, £850; Thomas Jeffreys, 'The American Atlas: or a Geographical Description of the whole Continent of America', 29 engraved maps, R. A. Sayer and J. Bennett, 1775, £380; two engraved and coloured maps of Yorkshire with coats-of-arms, £22.

MECHANICAL BANKS: Tammany (p. 143), £6; Chief Bighorn, £15; Jolly Nigger, £8; Creedmore (soldier firing at target on tree), £18.

MILITARIA: 300 assorted Yeomanry badges (p. 144), £70; sabretache (p. 146), £20; model field gun, £21; helmets (p. 145), (a) £54, (b) £10, (c) £60 (inc. rest complete fulldress off. uniform 2nd Life Guards); Napoleonic shapka with crowned 'N', £380; cloth spiked military helmet, £15; Crimean Dragoon Guards Officer's helmet, £54; embroidered sabretache, £20; complete court and field dress uniforms Royal Company of Archers, King's Bodyguard for Scotland, £45; Hitler Youth leader's dagger, £56; Philip Wouverman's painting of soldiers plundering, £3,800; equestrian portrait Van de Meulen, £90; unidentified but good battle painting, £150; Pair English trooper's riding boots, 17th cent., £22; set military surgeon's instruments, Allen and Hanbury, £20.

244

MUSICAL AUTOMATA: Hurdy gurdy (p. 153), £550; singing bird cage in ormolu, *c.* 1820, £920; coin in the slot electric automaton 'The Execution' from Hastings Pier, £42.

PEWTER TANKARDS: Quart, three one pint and two half-pint 'tulip shaped' lidless tankards; a quart and a pint type with deep reeding at drum and base, early 18c., £24 the lot.

PISTOLS AND REVOLVERS: on p. 165 (top to bottom) £330, £60, £52, £38. Also, pair 12 bore perc duelling pistols by Tow, £200; Pair flk. duelling pistols signed Joseph Manton, London, £300; cased pair flintlock pistols by Richards (once owned by 'Bligh of the Bounty'), £370; cased ·44 'Colt' Army model 1860 perc rev. with spares, £1,600: on page 166 double-bore o. & u. Remington Derringer, £20; ·41 Colt No. 1 Derringer, £22; 7 shot Reid's patent 'My Friend' knuckleduster pepper-box, £25; 10 shot ·22 Cf Protector palm pistol, £31; double-bore ·28 Woodward's pat. Turnover Derringer, by McNaughton, £12. Pair Italian snaphance pistols finely engraved *c.* 1700, £395; flk. boxlk., side action pocket pistol Williamson, Hull, £6; cannon-bore flk. boxlk. pocket pistol 1770, £31; double-bore wheel-lock, Dresden, *c.* 1610, £5,000 (world record).

POWDER FLASKS: (on p. 170) (a) £7; (b) £11; (c) £7; (d) £9; (e) £12; (f) £8; cowhorn with scrinshaw (p. 169), £20.

PRAYER WHEELS: Tibetan copper and brass hand pw., paste jewels, complete with printed prayer inside drum, £5.

PRINTED EPHEMERA: 70 assorted watch papers, 12 on fabric, £75.

PRINTS George Morland, £25; Hans Holbein the Younger, £50 up; German 'Little Masters', £20 up; Goya, £20 up; Rembrandt £30 up; Durer, £15 up; lithograph of Yvette Guilbert by Toulouse Lautrec, £60; Audubon birds, £50; Japanese masters, £25 up; Wheatley's 'Cries of London' (L. Schiavanetti) £25/£35 each; Augustus John etching of 'Young Woman Musing' second state, £10; Walter Sickert etching 'The Old Bedford', £32; set of four coloured aquatints by C. Hunt after Henry Alken, £25; eight coloured engravings with views in Australia after S. Prout and J. C. Armytage, £10; coloured lithograph of Quebec by Day and Haghe after Capt. B. Beaufoy, £35; mezzotint of Hadleigh Castle by David Lucas after John Constable, £6; set of four aquatints 'The Battle of the Nile, 1798', by and after R. Dodd, £130; pair coloured aquatints by Smart and Hunt, £28.

SAND-GLASSES: Hour glass with brass ends, div for half hours, £13.

SHOP AND STORE SIGNS: Highlander holding snuff mull (p. 190), £37.

SILVER SNUFF BOXES: large presentation box, 1827, £110; German, c. 1740, lid enamelled *en grisaille* with a duelling scene, £24.

SNUFF MULLS AND RASPS: Regimental Scottish curled ramshorn table snuff mull, £8. 10.

SPURS AND GOADS: Italian 18c. spurs with rowel in form of fleur de lys, £28; Chilean spurs inlaid silver, spiked rowels, £18; English 15c. rowel spurs with right-angular heel plates, £20.

STAFF WEAPONS: Bill, 16c. engraved with castle, lion, three human heads, modern haft, £130; poleaxe, 15c. engraved and brass inlaid, £260; pair of tilting lances with deeply fluted shafts, £14; German 16c. boar spear, armourers' mark, £55; battleaxe 17c. armourers' mark, £100: early 16c. bright steel mace, six broad flanges, £120; German 16c. war hammer, £150; Imperial Russian sponton, mid-18c., £28; glaive, bill, mace pike, bow and arrows, £220; late 16c. halberd, armourers' marks of orb and cross, £30; Italian 16c. partizan, £20; bamboo cavalry lance, 1st Dragoon Guards, £3; 17c. Venetian pole-axe etched with winged lion, £34; 50 European and Oriental lances, halberds, forks and spears, £170.

SWORDS: German headsman's sword, 17c., £95; 17c. Spanish cup-hilted rapier, signed, £60; 16c. Swiss broadsword, £150; smallsword, c. 1790, £35; 17c. swept-hilted rapier, £75; court sword, £29; Caucasian silver kindjal, £60; Turkish yataghan, £25; Russian sabre shashka, £150; English 16c. hunting sword with encrusted silver dec., £30; German or Austrian 16c. hand-and-a-half sword with crossbow maker's mark, £65; German 16c. tuck with hand-and-a-half grip, £300; German 16c. Landsknecht sword, £50; German boar-sword, c. 1510, £280; German 15c. two-handed sword, £95; medieval sword, c. 1350–1380, hand-and-a-half grip, tapering diamond section blade, found in Lake Constance, £550; Georgian naval dirk, 12 in. blade, no sheath, £5; 1834 pattern cavalry officer's sword, etched Royal cypher, £9; Borneo head hunter's sword, $21\frac{1}{2}$ in., carved bone hilt, silver mounted, with companion knife, £12; Persian sabre shamshir, 31 in. curved blade, £10; Landsknecht, sword, blade $20\frac{1}{2}$ in. by $2\frac{1}{2}$ in. with straight tip bearing Nuremburg town mark, £90; Turkish Yataghan, 24 in. blade, silver and gold dam, hilt embossed and filigree silver, £42; U.S. cavalry sabre, 28 in. Holloway and Bullock, no scabbard, £8. 10.

246

READING LIST

GENERAL COLLECTING
Bogner, L. A. and H. Batterson. *The Dictionary of Antiques and the Decorative Arts*. New York, 1957.
Enciclopedia dell'Antiquariato. Firenze, 1966.

Connoisseur, The. London. *Concise Encyclopedia of American Antiques.*
Concise Encyclopedia of Antiques.

Drepperd, Carl W. *Handbook of Tomorrow's Antiques*. New York.

Fosca, François and François Daulte. *Le Manuel du Collectioneur*. Fribourg, 1952.

Keysers *Kunst-und Antiqutätenbuch*. Heidelberg-München, 1957.

Mebane, John. *New Horizons in Collecting*. South Brunswick, N.J. and London, 1966.

Rigby, Douglas and Elizabeth. *Lock, Stock and Barrel: The Story of Collecting*. Philadelphia, New York and London, 1944.

Savage, George. *The Antique Collector's Handbook*. London, 1959.

ANCESTOR FIGURES
See Ethnographica.

ANIMALIER BRONZES
Mallelt at Bourdon House Ltd. *The Animaliers: French Animal Sculpture of the 19th Century* (Catalogue of Exhibition, Nov. 14, 1962).

APOTHECARIES' JARS
Dorveaux, P. *Les Pots de Pharmacie: Leurs Inscriptions Presentées sous Forme de Dictionnaire*. Paris, 1908.

Howard, G. E. *Early English Drug Jars*. London, 1931.

Pedrazzini, C. *La Farmacea Storica ed Artistica Italiana*. Milan, 1954.

Squibb, E. R. *The Squibb Ancient Pharmacy*. New York, 1940.
See also Saltglazed Stoneware.

ARMOUR

Bashford, Dean. *Catalogue of Loan Exhibition at Metropolitan Museum of Art*. New York, 1911.
Helmets and Body Armour in Modern Warfare. Yale, 1920.

Beard, C. R. Miniature Armour, *The Connoisseur*, December, 1928.

Blackmore, Howard L. *Arms and Armour*. London, 1965.

Blair, Claude. *European Armour 1066–1700*. London, 1958.

Howard, J. F. *Armour* (Victoria and Albert Museum Handbooks). London, 1951.

Mann, Sir James. *European Arms and Armour* (Wallace Collection Catalogues). London, 1962.

Peterson, Harold L. *Arms and Armour in Colonial America 1526–1783*. Pennsylvania, 1956.

Stone, George Cameron. *A Glossary of the Construction, Decoration and Use of Arms and Armour in All Countries and at All Times*. New York. 1934.

AUTOGRAPHS

Benjamin, Mary A. *Autographs: A Key to Collecting*. New York, 1946.

Broadley, A. M. *Chats on Autographs*. London, 1910.

Charnwood, Lady. *An Autograph Collection*. London, 1930.

Munby, A. N. L. *The Cult of the Autograph Letter in England*. London, 1962.

BELLARMINES

Falke, O. von. *Das Rheinische Steinzeug*. Berlin, 1908.

BICYCLES AND TRICYCLES

Caunter, C. F. *The History and Development of Cycles*. Part I, Historical Survey; Part II, Descriptive Catalogue for the Science Museum. London, 1958.

BOOK BINDING

Carter, John. *Taste and Technique in Book Collecting*. Cambridge, 1949.

248

Hartham, J. P. *Bookbindings* (Victoria and Albert Museum). H.M.S.O., 1950.

Hobson, G. D. *English Bindings in the Library of J. R. Abbey*. 1940.

McLean, Ruari. *Victorian Book Design and Colour Printing*. London, 1963.

Nixon, H. M. *Broxbourne Library, Styles and Designs of Bookbindings*. 1956.

Sadleir, Sir Michael. *The Evolution of Publishers' Bindings Styles*. London, 1930.

BOTTLES AND FLASKS
Bedford, John. *Bristol and Other Coloured Glass*. London, 1964.

McKearin, George S. and Helen. *American Glass*. New York, 1942.

Ruggles-Brise, Sheelah. *Sealed Bottles*. London and New York, 1949.

BOWS AND SLINGS
Payne-Gallwey, Sir R. *The Crossbow, Mediaeval and Modern*. London, 1903.
See also Armour, Guns and Rifles.

BUTTONS
Albert, L. S. and K. Kent. *The Complete Button Book*. 1949.

CANNON
Cipolla, Carlo M. *Guns and Sails in the Early Phase of European Expansion. 1400–1700*.
See also Armour, Bows and Slings, Guns and Rifles.

CHESSMEN
Hammond, Alex. *The Book of Chessmen*. London, 1950.

COMMEMORATIVE MEDALS
Hill G. F. *Medals of the Renaissance*. Oxford, 1920.
British Museum Catalogues of Medals.

Panofsky, Erwin. *Studies in Iconology*. New York, 1962.

Seznec, Jean. *The Survival of the Pagan Gods*. New York, 1961.

COMMEMORATIVE POTTERY
Haggar, Reginald G. *English Country Pottery*. London, 1950.
Staffordsnire Chimney Ornaments. London, 1955.

Moore, N. Hudson. *The Collector's Manual*. New York, 1906.

CURRENCY CURIOSA
Einzig, P. *Primitive Money*. London, 1951.

Quiggin, A. H. *Survey of Primitive Money*.

DAGGERS
See Firearms Curiosa, Knives.

DAHOMEY BRASSES
Herskovits, M. J. *Dahomey*. New York, 1938.
    See also Ethnographica.

DEATH MASKS
Benkard, Ernst. *Undying Faces* (trs. of *Das Ewige Anlitz*. Berlin, 1927).
    New York, 1929.

Hutton, Laurence. *Portraits in Plaster*. New York, 1894.

DIALS AND NOCTURNALS
Museum of the History of Science, Oxford. *A Catalogue of Scientific
    Instruments from the Collection of J. A. Billmeir, Esq.* Oxford, 1954.
    Supplement, 1957.

Ward, F. A. B. *Time Measurement* (Science Museum Handbook).
    H.M.S.O. London, 1955.

DOMESTIC MACHINERY
Casson, Herbert N. *The History of the Telephone*. Chicago.

Museo Nazionale della Scienza e delle Tecnica, Milan. *La Macchina per
    Cucire* (The Sewing Machine). Milan, 1962.

Science Museum, London. *The History and Development of the Typewriter*.
    London, 1964.

Scott, Amoret and Christopher. *Collecting Bygones*. London, 1961.

DRINKING GLASSES
Barrington Haynes, E. *Glass Through the Ages*. London, 1948.

250

Hughes, G. Bernard. *English, Scottish and Irish Table Glass.* London, 1956.

Bedford, John. *English Crystal Glass.* London, 1966.

ETHNOGRAPHICA
Adam, Leonhard. *Arts of the Primitive Peoples* (Pelican History of Art). Forthcoming.
Primitive Art. London, 1954.

Fagg, William. *Tribes and Forms in African Art.* London, 1965.

Wingert, Paul A. *Primitive Art, its Traditions and Styles.* New York, 1965.
Sculpture of Negro Africa. New York, 1950.
See also Ancestor Figures, Dahomey Brasses.

FIREARMS CURIOSA
Hayward, J. F. *European Firearms* (Victoria and Albert Museum Handbooks). London, 1955.

Winant, Lewis, *Firearms Curiosa.* New York, 1955.

GONGS AND BELLS
Bushell, Stephen W. *Chinese Art* (Victoria and Albert Museum). London, 1921.

Ingram, Tom. *Bells in England.* London, 1954.

Morris, Ernest. *Bells of All Nations.* London, 1951.
Tintinnabula. London, 1959.

GORGETS
See Armour.

GUNS AND RIFLES
Blackmore, Howard L. *British Military Firearms.* London, 1964.

Cipolla, Carlo M. *Guns and Sails in the Early Phase of European Expansion 1400–1700.* London, 1965.

Ffoulkes, C. H. *The Gunfounders of England.* Cambridge, 1937.

Hayward, J. F. *European Firearms* (Victoria and Albert Museum Handbooks). London, 1955.
The Art of the Gunmaker. Vol. 1, 1500–1660; Vol. 2, 1660–1830. London, 1962/3.

HELMETS
See Armour.

HORNS
Baines, Antony (Ed.). *Musical Instruments throughout the Ages*. London, 1966.

Scholes, Percy A. *The Oxford Companion to Music*. London, New York and Toronto, 1955.

HORSE BRASSES
Hartfield, George. *Horse Brasses*. London, New York and Toronto, 1965.

Sturt, George. *The Wheelwright's Shop*. Cambridge, 1963.

ICONS
Gombrich, E. H. *Art and Illusion*. London, 1962.

Talbot Rice, Tamara. *Russian Icons*. London, 1949.

JAPANESE SWORDS AND FITTINGS
Hakusiu, Inama. *Nippon-to* (The Japanese Sword). In English. Tokio, 1948.

Koop and Inada. *Japanese Names and How to Read Them*. London, 1923.

Robinson, B. W. *The Arts of the Japanese Sword*. London, 1961.

Turk, Frank A. *Japanese Objets d'Art*. London, 1962.

KNIVES
Himsworth, J. B. *The Story of Cutlery*. London, 1953.

LOCKS AND KEYS
Epings, C. A. Collecting Locks and Keys, *The Connoisseur,* September, 1940.

Eras, Vincent M. *Locks and Keys Throughout the Ages*. 1957.

MAPS
Brown, B. J. W. *Astronomical Atlases, Maps and Charts*. London, 1932.

Fite, Emerson D. and A. Freeman. *Book of Old Maps*. New York, 1965.

Goodman, Marie C. *Map Collections in U.S. and Canada* (Special Libraries Association). 1954.

Lee, R. J. *English County Maps*. 1953.

Lister, Raymond. *How to Identify Old Maps and Globes*. London, 1966.

Radford, P. J. *Antique Maps*. Denmead, Portsmouth, England, 1965.

Tooley, R. V. *Maps and Map Makers*. London, 1952.

MECHANICAL BANKS
Griffith, F. H. *Mechanical Banks*. P.O. Box 10644, Pittsburgh, Pa.

MILITARIA AND NAVALIA
Carman, W. Y. *British Military Uniforms*. London, 1962.

Stephens, F. J. *Nazi Daggers, Swords and Bayonets*. Wallis and Wallis, Lewes.
See also Armour, Bows and Slings, Cannon, Daggers, Firearms Curiosa, Gorgets, Guns and Rifles, Helmets, Japanese Swords and Fittings, Pistols and Revolvers, Staff Weapons, Swords.

MODEL SOLDIERS
Garratt, John G. *Model Soldiers: A Collector's Guide*. London, 1959.

Harris, Henry. *Model Soldiers*. London, 1962.

MUSICAL AUTOMATA
Chapuis, A. and E. Droz. *Automata,* 1960.

NEFS
Oman, Charles. *Medieval Silver Nefs* (Victoria and Albert Museum). London, 1936.

PAINTINGS
Alston, R. W. *Painter's Idiom*. London, 1954.

Doerner, Max. *Materials of the Artist and their Use in Painting*. London, 1949.

Grosser, Maurice. *The Painter's Eye*. New York, 1955.

Venturi, Lionello. *Painting and Painters*. New York and London, 1950.

PEWTER TANKARDS
Bedford, John. *Pewter*. London, 1965.

Cotterell, Howard H. *Old Pewter and How to Collect It*. London, 1913.

253

PIPE CASES

Pinto, Edward H. *Wooden Bygones of Smoking and Snuff Taking.*
London and Massachusetts.
See also Snuff Mulls and Rasps.

PISTOLS AND REVOLVERS

Ricketts, Howard. *Firearms.* London, 1962.
See also Armour, Firearms Curiosa.

POSTCARDS

Staff, Frank. *The Picture Postcard and its Origins.* London, 1966.

POWDER FLASKS

See Armour.

PRINTED EPHEMERA

Hindley, Charles. *Life and Times of James Catnach.* 1878.
The History of the Catnach Press. 1886.
Curiosities of Street Literature. 1871.

Hodgkin, J. E. *Rariora.*

Lewis, John. *Printed Ephemera.* Ipswich, 1962.

Winslow, O. E. *American Broadside Verse.* Yale, 1930.

PRINTS

Hayden, Arthur. *Chats on Old Prints.* London, 1900.

Hayter, S. W. *About Prints.* London, 1962.

Hind, A. M. *A History of Engraving and Etching.* London and New York, 1963.

Linssen, E. F. *The Appreciation of Old Engravings and Etchings.* London. 1951.

SALTGLAZED STONEWARE

Hannover, Emil. *Pottery and Porcelain.* London, 1925.

Honey, W. B. *European Ceramic Art.* London, 1952.

SHIPS IN BOTTLES

Monk, C. *How to Make a Ship in a Bottle.* London, 1948.

SHOP AND STORE SIGNS

Christensen, Erwin O. *Popular Art in the United States.* London, 1948.

Lambert, M. and E. Marx. *English Popular Art*. London, 1951.

Larwood and Hotten. *History of Signboards*. London, 1966.

Little, Nina Fletcher. *The Abbey Aldrich Rockefeller Folk Art Collection*. Colonial Williamsburg, 1957.

Norman, Philip. *London Signs and Inscriptions*.

SILVER SNUFF AND TOBACCO BOXES
Bradbury, Frederick. *Guide to Marks of Origin of British and Irish Silver Plate from the Mid 16th Century to the Year 1954*. Sheffield, 1955.

Curtis, M. M. *The Book of Snuff Boxes*. 1935.

Delieb Antiques, Ltd. *Quarterly Bulletin*. London.

Jones, E. A. *Old Silver of Europe and America*. 1928.

SNUFF MULLS AND RASPS
Scott, Christopher and Amoret. *Tobacco and the Collector*. London, 1966.

SPURS AND GOADS
James, James. *The Book of Spurs (Journal of the British Architectural Ass*. 1858.

Lacy, Charles. *The History of the Spur*. London, 1911.

STAFF WEAPONS
Cowper, H. S. *The Art of Attack*. Ulverston, 1906.

Demmin, Auguste. *Weapons of War*. London, 1870.

Fuller, J. F. C. *Armament and History*. New York, 1945.

Oakeshott, R. Ewart. *The Archeology of Weapons*. London, 1960.

Weller, Jas. *Weapons and Tactics: Hastings to Berlin*. London, 1966. See also Armour, Cannon, Firearms Curiosa, Guns and Rifles, Japanese Swords and Fittings, Knives, Militaria and Navalia, Pistols and Revolvers, Spurs and Goads.

SWORDS
See Armour, Firearms Curiosa, Weapons.

TIN BOXES
Can Manufacturers' Institute. *The Pictorial History of the Metal Can. The Metal Can: Its Past and Future*. Washington D.C.

255

Davis, Alec. 'History Printed on Tin', *Country Life,* Dec. 7, 1961.

TOBACCO BOXES AND JARS
See Pipe Cases, Snuff Mulls and Rasps.

TOKENS
British Museum. *Catalogue of the Montague Guest Collection of Badges Tokens and Passes.* London, 1930.

Mathias, Peter. *English Trade Tokens.* London, 1962.

TOBY JUGS
Bedford, John. *Toby Jugs.* London, 1968.
Looking in Junk Shops. London, 1961.

TRADESMEN'S CARDS
Heal, Sir Ambrose. *London Tradesmen's Cards of the 18th Century.* London, 1925.

Landauer, Bella C. *Early American Tradecards from the Collection of Bella C. Landauer.* New York, 1927.

WEDGWOOD JASPER MEDALLIONS
Bedford, John. *Wedgwood Jasper Ware.* London, 1964.

Mankowitz, Wolf. *Wedgwood.* London, 1953.

FAKES AND FORGERIES
Arnau, Frank. *Three Thousand Years of Deception in Art and Antiques* (trs. from the German by J. Maxwell Brownjohn). London, 1961.

British Museum. *Catalogue of an Exhibition of Forgeries and Deceptive Copies.* London, 1961.

Farrer, J. A. *Literary Forgeries.* 1907.

Savage, George. *Fakes, Forgeries and Reproductions.* London, 1963.

CURRENT PRICES
Reitlinger, Gerald. *The Economics of Taste.* Vol. I (Pictures), London, 1961; Vol. II (Objets d'art), London, 1963.

Sotheby and Co. *Catalogues.* London.

Wallis and Wallis. *Catalogues.* Lewes, Sussex.